Male Trouble:
A Crisis in Representation

Male Trouble:
A Crisis in Representation

Abigail Solomon-Godeau

With 119 illustrations, 8 in color Thames and Hudson

Designed by Liz Rudderham

First published in the United States of America in 1997 by
Thames and Hudson Inc., 500 Fifth Avenue, New York,
New York 10110

Library of Congress Catalog Card Number 96-61191
ISBN 0-500-01765-4

Printed and bound in Slovenia

Contents

A famous art historian, it was reported to me, once told a graduate student that one could learn more from a great artist than from a lesser one. This might have, perhaps should have, prompted the rejoinder, "Learn what?" since it is obvious that there are many different questions to be posed, as it were, to works of art. What one learns is largely a consequence of what one asks, and if art historians can now pose previously unasked questions it may well be that wittingly or not, they are either exiting the "proper" frame of art-historical inquiry, or changing its very shape, nudging it towards merger with more expansive fields such as visual studies or cultural studies. Furthermore, if the questions newly posed are feminist questions, and thus bound to the investigation of gender ideologies, subjectivity, and visual forms of embodiment, we are perhaps already somewhat "outside" the disciplinary constraints of art history. This is because feminist inquiry presupposes a critical rather than appreciative stance, and, in keeping with such an approach, the impulse behind *Male Trouble: A Crisis in Representation* has not been celebratory. Which is not to say that the motivation has been primarily that of the *démolisseur*, or more properly, *démolisseuse*. Rather, one of my intentions has been to denaturalize, to make strange, to make visible for analysis what generations of art historians have found by no means remarkable in itself. I refer, as my title announces, to the nature of the representation of ideal manhood within (mostly French) Neoclassicism, a form of embodiment that in either its mature or adolescent incarnations can be seen as bizarrely excessive, whether in respect of its overemphatic virility or, alternatively, in its exaggerated effeminacy or androgyny.

Specifically, the book is an attempt to recover certain meanings, both manifest and latent, in the imagery of masculinity in the decades before and immediately after the French Revolution. The "crisis" of the book's title is the historical turning-point during which the beautiful male body ceded its dominant position in elite visual culture to the degree that the category "nude" became routinely associated with femininity. It also refers to the transition from earlier courtly models

1 CHARLES MEYNIER Adolescent Eros Weeping over the Portrait of the Lost Psyche (detail), 1792

of masculinity to recognizably modern, bourgeois ones, a transition fostered by the expulsion of femininity (and women) from increasingly masculinized cultural and political domains. The "trouble" refers to the attendant and copious production of images of androgynous, unconscious, menaced, expiring, dead, or otherwise disempowered male protagonists who thereafter also largely disappear from French painting. The extremism of both versions of ideal manhood can thus be seen to register, however obliquely, the process of metamorphosis in the ideology of masculinity as it evolves from an aristocratic model to the modern order of gender to which we are still heir.

Neither an iconographic study in the traditional art-historical sense, nor a stylistic examination of the representational vicissitudes of the male body within Neoclassicism, *Male Trouble* fits less comfortably into the disciplinary category of art history than it does into the newer and more interdisciplinary study of visual culture. A fundamental characteristic of this approach lies in what could be called its de-aestheticizing assumptions and methods. In contrast to mainstream art-historical scholarship, the paintings or sculptures, prints or photographs, clothing or decorative arts that are examined as visual culture are judged worthy of investigation by other than aesthetic criteria. Which is to say that visual culture is by definition an arena that encompasses all aspects of visual representation: mass and popular forms as well as elite production, the work of hacks and the works of masters. Insofar as one is asking different sorts of questions of images and objects, determinations of quality, originality, and stylistic evolution are not of central importance. Instead, one examines the complex relations of cultural artifacts to ideology, reception, and to political, cultural and psychosexual formations. Visual culture, one could say, presents us with the traces, the evidence, of these discursive and psychological processes, and it is the historian's task to make sense of them. Disrespectful of hierarchies, including conventional aesthetic ones, scholars in visual studies have generally tended to concentrate more on popular than elite forms of culture. Consequently, although the works of art treated in this book are, in fact, elite cultural productions (primarily history painting, the most elevated of the academically defined genres), and although at least one of the central artists in this study (Jacques-Louis David) is a major figure in art history, in keeping with the more ecumenical method of visual studies, I make few if any qualitative distinctions between the undisputed quality of his art compared to the lesser accomplishments of his predecessors, contemporaries, or descendants. However, in jettisoning a vertical hierarchical construction of art history (one that logically requires a ranked place-ment of artists, styles and tendencies) the historian of visual culture is presented with the possibility of creating a horizontal, that is to say, a synchronic field. Because I am concerned, among other things, with the question of why Neoclassical art is so preoccupied with certain kinds of male bodies and heroes and relatively uninterested in female ones, I use a vocabulary detached from aesthetic criteria. As a feminist scholar, my questions are inevitably political ones, focusing on the manner in which visual culture both reflects and produces ideologies of gender, affirming the hierarchies of sexual difference and thereby naturalizing male dominance and female subordination. Such an admission of intent must confirm the worst fears of cultural conservatives who suspect, not without reason, that feminists have different stakes (and different agendas) when they venture into the territory of art history.

Considered in relation to mechanisms of power as they inform cultural production, the theoretical formulation that visual culture is not only gendered, but actively productive of gender ideology has long provided the impetus for feminist revisionism within art history. For the most part, however, and in the twenty-odd years in which feminist art history has developed, feminist art historians have concentrated, vari-ously, on the excavation of neglected women artists or the terms of women artists' exclusion; on the visual construction of femininity; or on unpacking the masculinist ideologies of art history itself and its familiar totems, the genius, the canon, the masterpiece, et alia. All of which is well and good, but to date, few studies have focused on the construction of masculinity in elite visual culture and even fewer on the dynamics of the male gaze in relation to male bodies. In part, this is due to the way feminist theory has tended to concentrate on the psycho-sexual and political implications of a male subject's active gaze on a female object. Hence, the rhetorical question asked by the film theorist E. Ann Kaplan, "Is the gaze male?" has the unintended consequences of implying that the gendered dynamics of looking are reducible to the relations of empowered male subjects and disempowered female ones. Alternatively, Male Trouble explores the representation of male bodies at a particular historical juncture in order to understand what gave rise to a particular visual economy in which passive, disempowered or feminized male bodies were produced for male spectators. Such an inquiry takes as its starting point the assumption that the image of ideal manhood is as much a product of fantasy, and certainly of ideology, as the more familiar icons of eroticized femininity. Moreover, the currency of new postmodern incarnations of eroticized or indeed, feminized masculinity makes us conscious of the absence of such representations in the nineteenth and most of the twentieth century. In much the same way that feminist theory and criticism have revealed femininity to be a historically variable and fully social construction, so too can we now examine the shifting forms of masculinity, acknowledging its role in shaping subjectivity, and its registration of changing historical circumstance. Hence, the recent appearance of mass cultural imagery featuring spectacular male bodies in elaborate display, a chorus of voices identifying and diagnosing a crisis in contemporary manhood, and, within the study of visual culture, a new attentiveness to the mechanisms of gender and ideology within representational systems, have collectively operated to render visible what was once altogether taken for granted. Our ability to recognize the singularity, indeed, the symptomatic qualities of ideal masculinity within French Neoclassicism is, as I argue in the first chapter of this book, a direct consequence of the new visibility of *contemporary* masculinity. In this respect, the first chapter is intended as a methodological overview of the book, whose project could further be described as an attempt to examine art-historical objects with the critical perspectives and methods associated with feminist and psychoanalytical theory, gender studies, and ideology critique.

Certainly one of the most striking characteristics of the Neoclassical art that emerged in Rome in the 1770s, and which subsequently became the official style of French painting (indeed of the revolution itself), is its presentation of two opposing, but equally idealized, paradigms of masculine beauty, both of which eclipse and replace the rose and ivory *féminités* of the preceding Rococo style. Drawing on classical prototypes, Neoclassical artists produced their *beaux idéals* in conformity with two venerable models: an active and virile warrior type whose most well-known example is undoubtedly David's *Oath of the Horatii* (fig. 4), or alternatively (and far more prevalently), the graceful and more or less feminized ephebe, exemplified also by David in his rendering of the boy martyr, Joseph Bara (fig. 61). The currency of both types, and the concomitant marginality of women in Neoclassical art, is, as I argue in the second chapter, "The Body Politics of Homosociality," best understood by recourse to the notion of homosocial desire. This is a formulation developed by the literary and gay studies theorist Eve Kosofsky Sedgwick, who employed it to examine the psychosexual dynamics between men in a number of English-language literary texts. For my purposes, it is an extremely useful framework for understanding what the art historian Thomas Crow has justly described as the intensifying "masculinization" of both political and cultural spheres in late eighteenth- and early nineteenth-century France. The second chapter is thus a consideration of the ways in which male artists in largely all-male environments, and irrespective of what would now be termed individual sexual orientation, circumvented, repressed, or elided the "problem" of sexual difference. Simultaneously, they fashioned an imagery of masculinity that, while repudiating the eroticized feminine iconography of the *ancien régime*, also covertly incorporated it. To a certain extent, it appears that the very process of forming what the German political theorist Jürgen Habermas termed the bourgeois public sphere–importantly preceded by the "republic of letters"–depended on the consolidation of masculine bonds between putatively equal, sovereign subjects. Unlike the hierarchical relations of the absolutist state, these relations between men of letters, *philosophes*, artists, dilettanti, and the like were fraternal, professional, vocational, or intellectual, accompanied by a strong ethos of male friendship. Like freemasonry, these new alliances between men (the theme of so many Neoclassical paintings of oath-taking) effectively *require* the exclusion of women. As feminist historians of the revolution have argued, it is as though the public sphere was in part constituted through the exclusion of women, and there are many reasons to connect the dominant iconographic role of masculinity with parallel political and social developments.

The implications of the flight from difference, or its inscription within a single-sex model of the masculine ideal is the subject of the third chapter, whose title, "Ephebic Masculinity: The Difference Within" signals my belief that ideologies of masculinity regularly provide evidence of an internal division, providing the possibility of both a "masculinized" and a "feminized" masculinity. What is of particular interest here is the clear implication that the imagery of masculine impotence and debility appears not to contradict an official language of gender that condemns if not excoriates effeminacy and is further concerned to secure rigid distinctions in gender. Nevertheless an imagery of disempowered and androgynous masculinity proliferated even as republican discourse limned its own ideal of masculinity in phallic, martial and stoic terms. It is as though in violently "expelling" the frivolity, decadence, and corruption of the *ancien régime* and its courtly culture, and linking these to a malign femininity (or a perverse and depraved masculinity), republican culture required a stand-in for an eroticized femininity deemed inimical to republican and civic values. The ubiquity of the ephebic body and the erotic investments to which it testifies suggest its escapist, even utopian facets. Given the nature of class and gender conflicts in the revolutionary period, there is reason to think that the beautiful ephebe is a kind of imaginary resolution of intractable contradictions, its pathos and grace a respite from the cataclysms of revolutionary change, its corporeal ambivalence and sensual appeal an escape from the misogyny (and homophobia) of republican discourse. As an idealized male figure, it is charged with all the exalted and "public" values traditionally incarnated in the image of masculine beauty, yet its androgyny or effeminacy permits it to function as a surrogate for sexual difference, indeed, for desirability itself. This is not to deny that the image or sculpture of a beautiful youth could serve straightforwardly as an object of desire for a desiring gay subject, as it evidently did for the German scholar Johann-Joachim Winckelmann. Nevertheless, the more complicated question is how and why such imagery appealed to male spectators, irrespective of personal sexual proclivity. For however we may wish to reconstitute "gayness" in history, and how far we are justified in speaking of a "homosexualization" of Neoclassical culture, the prestige and appeal of the male body seems on the evidence to extend beyond identifiably gay artists or audiences. As surrogate of difference, the Neoclassical ephebe marks the vacated space of a discredited femininity associated with pleasure and eroticism. Many currents converged in the revolution's need to expel what could be called a voluptuary and carnal femininity while it strove to re-contain and domesticate republican women, legally defined as "passive" rather than "active" citizens, and designated positively only as wives, mothers, daughters, and sisters.

As a signifier of beauty, pathos, and timeless "classical" values, the androgynous or otherwise feminized ephebe thus represents the historic swan song of an erotically invested masculinity. In this sense, it looks back to earlier models for ideal manhood that sanctioned male narcissism and bodily display, as well as echoing previous cultural themes such as the mid-eighteenth century cult of *sensibilité*, which Neoclassicism refigures under the sign of pathos. At the same time, an analysis of painting and sculpture featuring the ephebic body suggests that it presages the visual syntax of the nineteenth-century female nude, a body designed for display and delectation, a "legitimized" sensuality that henceforth the male body must nominally abjure.

The final chapter, "The Political Economy of the Male Nude" has a wider chronological scope, examining the terms by which classical art styles, from their inauguration in fifth-century Greece to French Neoclassicism provide a visual language for (and of) male supremacy. While this is doubtless to state the obvious, a closer look at the symbolic labor performed by the ideal male body in classical art and theory suggests that homosocial (and arguably homoerotic) desire here too is at stake, securing social and political solidarity between men while implicitly rationalizing, or naturalizing, women's exclusion from the body politic. The visual language of the ideal male body, including its modestly scaled genitalia, can thus be analyzed functionally, even as (in the post-classical period) it maneuvers within the procrustean constraints of homosexual proscription and homosocial desire. Perhaps even more fundamentally, in establishing maleness as the emblem of (ideal) humanity, and relegating femaleness to the realms of alterity, difference, and corporeality (the body itself), classical art styles promote a dichotomy that affirms the equivalence of "Man" with "human" and all that that implies. Significantly, the male nude has been privileged in periods traditionally viewed as fostering new freedoms and possibilities (fifth-century Greece, the Renaissance, the French Revolution, for example), which have not necessarily extended to women. Hence, there is ample justification for studying the role of the masculine ideal within this framework of "uneven development." Hence too, the imaginative identification with classical antiquity that figures so prominently in Neoclassical and revolutionary culture, producing its characteristic expressions of ideal manhood, requires consideration of what "Other" has been repressed in the celebration of the radiant One.

Whatever its flaws and weaknesses, which are, of course, entirely my own, *Male Trouble* is rooted in the work of feminist and gay scholars active within a diverse array of academic fields. Among art historians I would acknowledge especially the work of two: Carol Duncan, whose pioneering essay on "Happy Mothers" so deftly historicized a bourgeois invention as it was popularized and purveyed by elite and mass culture. Even more important for this book, her 1973 "Fallen Fathers" provided a way to "think" the iconography of masculinity in relation to the unconscious and to concrete political, historical formations. More recently, Alex Potts's reading of the work of Winckelmann has demonstrated the complex networks of masculine identifications, projections, and denials that underpin the Neoclassical passion for an imaginary and highly sanitized antiquity. With respect to my historical framework for the revolutionary period, the feminist revisionary interpretations of Carol Blum, Carole Pateman, Joan Landes, Dorinda Outram, and especially, Lynn Hunt have been crucial, indeed defining of my project. Lynn Hunt's psychosocial recasting of the French Revolution as "the family romance" has made new sense of cultural artifacts even as it has persuasively demonstrated how psychological and historical forces converge in revolutionary discourse. If, however, this book is concerned with questions that rarely, if ever, arise in or art history or history proper, it must be said that the impulse to ask them comes from further afield. If, as a reputable scholar I am permitted to ask why ideal male nudes have small genitalia, and female ideals have none, it is because classicists such as David Halperin and John Winkler whose work has been informed by new theoretical discourses (such as queer theory) have provided conceptual frameworks within which to formulate these issues. While not everyone would agree that these are questions worth asking, their relevance for feminist analyses is obvious. Moreover, the need for more histories of the body-in-representation extends beyond the boundaries of art history, and it is within this wider compass of historical inquiry that this book should be situated.

My personal, institutional, and intellectual debts accrued in the writing of this book are extensive. A postdoctoral fellowship from the J. Paul Getty Grant Program coupled with a University of California President's Fellowship in the Humanities permitted a year of academic leave in 1994-95, without which the book could not have been completed. Grants from the Interdisciplinary Humanities Council and the Academic Senate of the University of California, Santa Barbara, expedited research in 1992 and 1993. Colleagues and students at a number of colleges and universities where I presented material from this book asked difficult and probing questions and greatly enriched my thinking. Among these, the students and faculty of Northwestern University, at Mount Holyoke College where I was invited to give the Amy M. Sackler lectures, at the Clark Institute where I gave the William Sterling Clark Lecture, and faculty and students at the Whitney Independent Study Program, deserve special thanks. Scholarly friends and friendly scholars have over the years made more contributions than I or they possibly even recognize. Among them, I am greatly beholden to many conversations with Whitney Davis, Stephen Eisenman, Tamar Garb, Ewa Lajer-Burcharth, Linda Nochlin, Alex Potts, Robert Simon, and Margaret Waller, as well as to Catherine Nesci, Ann Adams, Tania Modleski, and Robert Williams, the last three of whom read and commented on the first chapter. But one of my greatest debts is to Mechthild Fend, whose work on the androgyne in French art has provided me over the past five years with countless conversations, debates, information, formulations, and reformulations of the issues that engage us both. Her great generosity as a scholar and a friend is deeply appreciated. Last, and hardly least, I must thank Nikos Stangos for his friendship, patience, his confidence in me, and his exemplary editorial stewardship of this project.

1789 The French Revolution
27 Aug Declaration of the Rights of Man
and the Citizen
1791 5 Oct Women's march on Versailles
Sept Olympe de Gouges writes *Declaration
of the Rights of Woman*
1792 20 April War declared on Austria (France
was to be at war 1792–1802, 1803–1815)
10 Aug Storming of the Tuileries
Louis XVI takes refuge in the Assembly
Publication of Mary Wollstonecraft's
Vindication of the Rights of Woman

The Jacobin Republic: 1792–94
21 Sept Convention (legislative assembly)
abolishes the monarchy
Women granted right to witness public
documents and contracts
Divorce legalized
1793 21 Jan Execution of Louis XVI
25, 26 Feb Paris food riots led by women
Feb Counterrevolution in the Vendée
10 March Revolutionary Tribunal and
Committee of Public Safety set up
4 May Convention decrees the *maximum*
for grain prices
10 May Foundation of Society of
Revolutionary Republican Women
2 June Jacobin coup ousts Girondins
24 June Convention accepts new
constitution
13 July Corday assassinates Marat
18 Aug French Academy disbanded
23 Aug Conscription for single men 18–25
17 Sept Law of Suspects begins the Terror
10 Oct Proclamation of revolutionary
government until advent of peace
16 Oct Execution of Marie Antoinette
30 Oct Convention dissolves Society of
Revolutionary Republican Women and
declares all women's clubs illegal
3 Nov Execution of Olympe de Gouges

1793 24 Nov Calendar dated from Year I of
the Revolution (22 Sept 1792)
Women granted the right to share in
communal properties
1794 5 Feb Robespierre addresses Convention on
need for "Virtue and Terror"

The Thermidorian Republic: 1794–95
21 July/ 9 Thermidor Fall of Robespierre
and Committee of Public Safety
1795 March, April, May (Germinal and Prairial)
Riots in Paris, led by women calling for
"bread and the constitution of 1793"
Women banned from Convention galleries
31 May Revolutionary Tribunal suppressed

The Directory 1795–99
23 Sept Proclamation of Constitution of
Year III (the Directory)
1796 Principle of marital equality struck from
third proposal of Civil Code

The Consulate 1799–1804
1799 9–10 Nov/18–19 Brumaire Napoleon
Bonaparte's coup d'état
1804 21 March Promulgation of the Civil Code.
Principle of paternal authority affirmed
Husbands to be guardians of wives
Divorce restricted to three categories
(adultery, "excess," and grievous insult)

The Empire: 1804–14
18 May Napoleon hereditary emperor

The Restoration of the Monarchy: 1814–30
1814 Louis XVIII
1824 Charles X
1830 July Revolution against Charles X
(The Three Glorious Days)

The July Monarchy 1830–48
31 July Louis Philippe king of the French

History is the subject of a structure whose site is not homogeneous, empty time, but time filled by the presence of the now.

WALTER BENJAMIN "Theses on the Philosophy of History"[1]

In 1988 the R. J. Reynolds Tobacco Company, manufacturer of Camel cigarettes, adopted "Joe" as their emblem, a cartoon character whose leering camel head resembles nothing so much as an amalgam of penis and testicles. Depicted in an array of stereotypically virile roles, loca tions, and poses, Joe Camel rapidly became—and still remains—an inescapable presence on American billboards, kiosks, building walls, matchbooks, and the printed page. Accustomed as we are to many other advertising icons of stylized machismo (the Marlboro cowboys are perhaps the most familiar example), the Camel emblem provoked public controversy only when it was discovered that little boys were among its most avid devotees, and thus presumed to be at risk of smoking Camels. While it is scarcely necessary to undertake any sustained analysis of the Camel advertisements' semiotic structure or rhetorical address, it may be useful to recall that the advent of Joe was contemporary with the emergence of the so-called "men's movement," a populist manifestation of male backlash against the gains of feminism that demonstrated a corresponding anxiety about men's roles at a time of economic and social uncertainty.

Equally suggestive, Joe Camel's debut was accompanied by the appearance of another, more surprising avatar of masculinity, namely, that of the passive, beautiful and seductive youth presented and posed in ways commonly associated with the display of desirable female bodies. Principally deployed for the merchandising of men's clothing, toiletries and perfumes (these latter having become significant growth markets in the 1980s), such contemporary variations of ephebic desirability might seem to occupy the opposite pole of ideal manhood from the exaggerated phallicism of Joe Camel and the Marlboro man. One could, of course, account for these new mass cultural icons with purely empirical explanations. These would include the development of new products (such as toiletries and cosmetics for men) and recently targeted groups of consumers (gay men, for instance) as well as the revamping of their products' images by advertising agencies themselves.[2] Nevertheless, it seems equally clear that these new, what I will provisionally call "feminized" iconographies of masculinity in the mass media may also presage or reflect tidal shifts in the articulation and, by implication, the lived subjectivity of contemporary men. What is presaged or reflected is another matter altogether: advertising imagery, like any other complex cultural expression, is not reducible to a single meaning and is subject to multiple determinations and indeed, diverse receptions. Accordingly, the current spate of images of exhibitionistic or narcissistic adolescence or apparently gender-bent manhood need not in itself be cause for feminist celebration.

Whatever else it might signal, the recent discursive visibility of masculinity attests to the growing perception that there is nothing whatsoever "natural" about masculinity and nothing preordained about the forms it might take. Cut loose, as it were, from a presumed isomorphism with biological sex, the concept of masculinity has ceded its taken-for-granted status, its previous transparency. It is this loss of transparency that is indicated by the term "discursive visibility," signaling the ways that masculinity can now be approached as a subject for literary or artistic investigation, a disciplinary object within feminist theory, gender studies, cultural studies, and—most recent arrival on the academic scene—men's studies. Accompanying this discursive visibility, we are confronted with newly minted representations of masculinity that seem particularly feminized in that the male body is presented as an object for erotic contemplation. This I believe to be of significant historical importance insofar as it was historically the *withdrawal* of the unclothed male body from dominant representational systems, and the concomitant hypervisibility of the female body that has characterized and secured the visual economy of bourgeois culture. In this respect, and harking back to Laura Mulvey's much-cited distinction between men as bearers of the gaze and women as objects of it, it was masculinity's foreclosure as a site of desirous looking and femininity's progressive monopoly of this position that constitutes one of the distinctive aspects of gender ideology within the culture of modernity.[3] If this once-secure division seems currently in flux, there are many reasons to question what this instability portends. What does it mean for masculinity to have so recently become an object of spectacle and erotic display?

At this point I should specify that I am employing the term masculinity in much the same way as the term femininity is addressed within feminist theory; that is, as a concept that at least some feminists would claim bears only an adventitious relation to biological sex and whose various manifestations collectively constitute the cultural, social, and psychosexual expression of gender. Biological sex, in this sense, is thus fundamentally distinguished from gender, which is conceived as a contingent, variable, and inescapably social ensemble of values, beliefs and behaviors projected and imposed upon the physical givens of sexual difference. Masculinity and femininity are accordingly conceived as ideological formations and therefore inevitably historical, culture-specific, and perpetually in process. Both terms, however, are produced within the overarching framework of patriarchy which is itself subject to historical mutation and adjustment: fifth-century Athens, revolutionary France and contemporary America do not manifest the same kinds of patriarchal organization. Consequently, patriarchy, which can be generally characterized as a type of social organization in which greater power accrues to men, thus fostering forms of male domination and female subordination, produces in turn ideologies of gender that are reciprocally and relationally defined (for instance, woman is to nature as man is to culture) but always within a hierarchical structure in which greater power is possessed by men.[4]

Considered in relation to these overweening determinations of power and subordination, the theoretical formulation that visual culture is not only gendered, but actively productive of gender ideology, has provided the impetus for feminist revisionism within art history. Within contemporary visual culture, a marked change in the representation of masculinity, the emergence of its seemingly new incarnations, and masculinity's new status as an object of academic study, invite some kind of analysis and explanation. Clearly, there are numerous factors that converge in these related phenomena. Supplementing the analyses generated by a quarter century of feminism, the aggregate effects of the gay liberation movement, the investigation of homosexuality, the interrogation of sex/gender systems undertaken in fields from anthropology to philosophy, have all operated to render visible what was until recently taken as the invisible ground of being. Doubtless, it is this loss of transparency that contributes in some measure to the now-frequent invocations of a "crisis" in masculinity, the subject of at least one book with that as its title.[5] And to the degree that masculinity and its representations are currently conceived by many to be as much a socially and sexually constructed object as is femininity and its representations, it is not surprising that such a formulation has sparked an explosion of scholarly investigation, including, of course, my own. Accompanying, or perhaps capping, the men's movement in America, there now exists a duly constituted Men's Studies Association, and in addition to the recent appearance of dozens of books and hundreds of articles, both popular and scholarly, a new journal entitled *Masculinities* has just been launched.

However, even before this eruption of scholarly interest, there were abundant signs that the unmarked status of masculinity was in some kind of transition. When in 1983 the *New York Times Magazine* inaugurated a guest feature column entitled, with disarming simplicity, "About Men," my initial response was somewhat incredulous; after all, most of what appeared in the *New York Times* could be said to be about men. What did it mean that the *Times* felt it necessary to devote column inches to men as men, or at least men as bourgeois white men? Retrospectively considered, the invention of "About Men" signaled a new self-consciousness in the making, the "about" suggesting that despite abundant evidence that masculine concerns received their due, there yet existed a range of issues and problems related to manhood that required specific address and analysis.

But as I've suggested, while the discovery of masculinity as such, in academic journals or the daily newspapers, is clearly related to the influence of feminist theory and to the women's movement overall, this does not mean that it qualifies as a symmetrical counterpart either to feminism's critique of patriarchy (a word rarely encountered in the new men's studies) much less a fraternal embrace of the political claims (or gains) of women. Similarly, the appearance of images of strong naked men cuddling babies (fig. 3) or ironing their designer trousers does not necessarily prove that a kinder, gentler masculinity has replaced more oppressive models once and for all. Nevertheless, and however we may attempt to account for it, the fact remains that masculinity was for the most part not an identifiable issue twenty years ago and is very much one now; that images of unclothed male bodies were scarcely then to be encountered outside gay venues and publications, and few, if any, invoked the notion of a crisis in masculinity or its representations.

In recognizing the coexistence of radically different, and equally widespread, expressions of idealized masculinity in mass culture today—for shorthand, the opposing types represented by the languorous

3 DAVID SANDISON Father and Baby, 1996

Versace boy and the penis-headed Joe Camel—and acknowledging that these are equally "successful" icons of manhood, it remains to question what these icons should be taken to signify. Furthermore, to the extent that we accept the notion that masculinity is indeed currently experiencing some kind of crisis, we must ask whether it is the caricatured priapism of Joe Camel or the supine ephebe—or their cohabitation in the pages of the same magazines—that should be read as symptoms of crisis, crisis here understood in the dictionary sense of "turning-point for better or worse"?

Referring to the invention of Joe Camel as an advertising emblem, or to the frequent presence of superb male bodies on display might seem a frivolous way to introduce a scholarly study of the iconography of ideal masculinities in French Neoclassical art and the circumstances of their disappearance. My general argument, however, depends on the claim that crises in masculinity are neither unprecedented nor exceptional, and, accordingly, that contemporary representations of masculinity, either in elite or mass cultural forms, reveal significant correspondences to older visual paradigms of ideal masculinity. In this respect, I take my cue from Walter Benjamin's crucial insight that the cultural production of past epochs (he was referring to literary texts, but the argument holds for visual culture) becomes available, meaningful, *reactivated* in the critical act that forges connections between present and past, "blasting open the continuum of history." That it is now possible to consider French history painting of the late eighteenth and early nineteenth century in terms of its images of masculinity is a consequence of the current academic investigation of masculinity. No longer invisible and no longer transparent, contemporary masculinity is now an entity to be investigated from different scholarly and theoretical perspectives, and conversely, the exploration of masculinity's latent as well as manifest meanings in the visual culture of the past may yield crucial insights for its current incarnations.

Changing places: The Gender of the Nude

The historical point of departure for such an inquiry begins with the observation that the ideal male nude for centuries occupied the place that we currently assume belonged by rights to the female body. The visual evidence of Western art history, beginning with the Greek invention of the nude as an aesthetic category, seems to justify the view that the dominance of the female body in nineteenth- and most of twentieth-century iconography was a historically specific mutation, one tied to the particular determinations of modernity, and to the emergence and consolidation of bourgeois ideologies of gender. In fact, the overwhelming preponderance of imagery of eroticized femininity was relatively unprecedented. Since classical antiquity it has been the male body more often than not that constituted the aesthetic category of the nude and the male rather than the female body that formed the core of classical art theory, pedagogy and practical training. "In order to begin with the masterpiece of nature's productions which is man," wrote Charles-Antoine Jombert in his influential treatise of 1755, "the young painter must instruct himself in anatomy and proportion, because these two elements are the fundamentals of design."[6] Even in periods such as the Italian Renaissance or the first half of the eighteenth century that did produce significant numbers of female nudes, the aesthetic or philosophical justification for the nude was premised on the male body—the universal man as universal human. I will discuss this point at greater length in Chapter Four, but here it is worth noting that these splendid male bodies, so abundantly produced in pre-nineteenth-century art as vehicles for the most exalted and "public" meanings, have now returned—after an absence of nearly two centuries—as compelling presences in postmodernity. Morphologically restyled and culturally re-encoded, conscripted to the service of commodity culture instead of ecclesiastical, royal or civil authority, our current array of ideal masculinities attest, if nothing else, to an iconographic return of the repressed. Put somewhat differently, it seems that we are witnessing something that could be thought of as a desublimation of masculinity in the visual field whereby the masculine body is again permitted to be an object of desirous looking.[7] Although there have long existed circumstances and contexts in which the male body has obviously been on display (for example, in sports, in rock concerts, in movies), it is nonetheless fair to say that the unclothed and conspicuously "developed" body on visual offer in so much contemporary mass media constitutes a quantum leap in the recent history of masculine self-display. Consequently, the art-historical imagery that I explore in this study is refracted in the light of contemporary culture's new figurations of masculinity which have provoked both my fascination with and my recognition of the erotics of masculine display in the history painting of the French revolutionary and post-revolutionary periods.

It is a no less important part of my general argument that the two polar types of masculinity repeat, at least in structural terms, a binarism—an internal gendering, as it were—that is recognizable in the elite and revolutionary culture of Neoclassical France as well as in the art of classical antiquity. Ideal masculinity may thus internalize sexual difference, expressed alternatively as a "masculinized" masculine as in the Horatii of Jacques-Louis David (1784–1825) in fig. 4, or a "feminized" masculine as in the Eros and Orpheus of Pierre-Narcisse Guérin (1774–1883) in figs. 6 and 7, and the anonymous Orpheus in fig. 5. In this respect, the aggressive phallicism of Joe Camel may be seen as a pop cultural descendant of the Farnese Hercules (fig. 8); the languid Versace boy an incarnation of the Capitoline Faun (fig. 9). Which is not to say, however, that the existence of these two alternative (but equally ideal-ized) models of masculinity are identifiable uniquely or especially in these two historical moments. On the contrary, it seems as though this division of ideal masculinities into "hard" or "soft," phallic or feminized incarnations are consistent features within the larger cultural context of bourgeois and pre-bourgeois ideologies of gender. This does not by any means imply that both models are at any point equally sanctioned, or equally popular, or even equally manifest within dominant cultural

4 JACQUES-LOUIS DAVID The Oath of the Horatii, 1785

formations. Nor does the possibility (or availability) of a comparatively androgynous model of masculinity necessarily signal any relaxation of what the poet Adrienne Rich famously described as the coercive injunction to "compulsory heterosexuality." Still less does the visual presence of perfected male bodies elaborately displayed imply any abrogation of the institutionalized and individually internalized homophobia that accompanies this injunction. On the contrary, masculinity, considered as an ideology of gender as it is both culturally represented and subjectively lived by biological men has itself been theorized as *a priori* internally divided and split. While this is a theoretical model of subjectivity generally associated with psychoanalytic models, one can readily identify the expression of this split in the art of classical antiquity, or, as I will argue, in the art of late eighteenth- and early

5 ANONYMOUS Orpheus in the Underworld, c. 1800

6 PIERRE-NARCISSE GUÉRIN Eros Goading a Tortoise

7 PIERRE-NARCISSE GUÉRIN Orpheus at the Tomb of Eurydice

nineteenth-century France. In both periods culturally sanctioned representations of ideal masculinity allow for two generic archetypes: a heroic, virile, and purposeful manhood understood as active and dominating, and a typically younger model—adolescent or ephebic—whose sensual and erotic appeal derives at least in part from its relative passivity. And while the specifically *sexual* implications of either type may be publicly acknowledged and accepted, as in fifth-century Athens, or implicit and largely disavowed as in late eighteenth-century France, the point to be made is that the opposing types exemplified by Joe Camel and the Versace boy have venerable lineages and numerous precedents. The question to be asked, therefore, is why at any given point one model of masculinity may be privileged over the other, or, alternatively, how the coexistence of both models conforms, or fails to conform to society's official prescriptions (and proscriptions) for its masculine norm.

How then does something called "homosexuality" fit into this equation? Granted that there exists an iconographic tradition in which images of St. Sebastian, Bacchus, Ganymede, Hyacinthus and so forth have been variously coded (or received) as homoerotic figures, given too the actual historical existence of gay artists, gay patrons, gay sub-cultures and so forth, is there not justification for parsing out, so to speak, those types from the representational continuum of masculinity as such?

To this deceptively obvious question there are a number of compli-cated answers, the gist of which is that our current concept of homo-sexuality, or the homosexual, maps ill upon premodern visual culture. On the most fundamental level, however, there exists the central prob-lem of the term "homosexual" itself. No one disputes the recent vintage of the word, and what it designates. The word "homo-sexuality" entered the Oxford English Dictionary only in 1892; the German cognate terms for homosexual and homosexuality were coined in 1869.[8] That the terms "heterosexual" and "heterosexuality" were coined even later (1900) suggests that what is at stake in this particular naming process is a distinctively modern epistemology not only of "deviance," but of "normalcy." And as the classicist David Halperin remarks, "Although a blandly descriptive, rigorously clinical term like 'homosexuality' would appear to be unobjectionable as a taxonomic device, it carries with it a heavy complement of ideological baggage and has proved a significant obstacle to understanding the distinctive features of sexual life in non-Western and pre-modern cultures."[9] But in replacing earlier terminologies for same-sex desire, predilections, or activities

8 Farnese Hercules, early 3rd-century AD copy

9 The Marble Faun, 2nd-century AD copy

("inversion"—also a nineteenth-century term—or, for most of Western history, sodomy or "pederasty") these new locutions shifted the meaning of this area of sexuality from a category of acts to a characterization of persons. In Michel Foucault's famous formulation:

> We must not forget that the psychological, psychiatric, medical category of homosexuality was constituted from the moment it was characterized...less by a type of sexual relations than by a certain quality of sexual sensibility, a certain way of inverting the masculine and the feminine in oneself. Homosexuality appeared as one of the forms of sexuality when it was transposed from the practice of sodomy on to a kind of interior androgyny, a hermaphroditism of the soul. The sodomite had been a temporary aberration; the homosexual was now a species.[10]

It is in this sense that recent scholarship speaks quite literally of the invention of homosexuality. Hence, the use of terms such as homosexual or homosexuality as historical descriptions of persons or acts is not only anachronistic, but something like an epistemological impropriety. For those espousing these views—collectively labeled social constructivist—sexual identity and behavior, far from being innate or essential to the human subject, are on the contrary actively produced within culture and society which variously operate to construct the sexuality of the subject. In this materialist approach to sexuality, sexual behavior, orientation, or indeed sexual norms are inseparable from the concept of *praxis*. As Robert A. Padgug has cogently described such an approach:

> When we look more directly at the social world itself, it becomes apparent that the general distinguishing mark of human sexuality, as of all social reality, is the unique role played in its construction by language, consciousness, symbolism, and labor, which, taken together—as they must be—are *praxis*, the production and reproduction of material life...The content of sexuality is ultimately provided by human social relations, human productive activities, and human consciousness. The history of sexuality is therefore the history of a subject whose meaning and contents are in a continual process of change. It is the history of social relations.[11]

Needless to say, not all cultures—in fact, very few—have ever thought to define human beings in terms of either sexual orientation or sexual behavior. This is precisely Foucault's point of departure in his unfinished *History of Sexuality*, as it is for virtually all social constructivists.[12] On the other hand, historians of sexuality, social historians and historians *tout court* have amply demonstrated the existence of behaviors, subcultures, and indeed identities that do seem to accord with our modern-day notions of gay identity and subjectivity. The arguments made for the historical, and in this instance premodern, existence of gay people and gay relationships are exemplified in John Boswell's landmark study of 1980, *Christianity, Social Tolerance and Homosexuality: Gay People in Western Europe From the Beginning of the Christian Era to the Fourteenth Century*.[13]

Nevertheless, and especially in the case of the interpretation of cultural artifacts, a certain caution in deploying the concept of homosexuality is necessary, and in this book I tend for the most part to avoid speculation about the lived sexuality of the artists whose work I am addressing. Instead, I employ the concept of homosociality, which describes networks of relationships between men that involve both power and desire and which may be expressed in cultural production.[14]

Homosociality may include homosexual acts or meanings within its purchase, but is in no way limited to them. The more nuanced, flexible and inclusive meanings of homosociality are, moreover, of greater descriptive utility in discussing works of arts made, historically speaking, before homosexuality. While there may be justification in identifying what would be now called a gay subject, or gay subtext within a historical work, there exists the risk of retroactively imposing upon it a modern meaning, or missing altogether its contemporary one. For example, an iconographic type such as Ganymede, the beautiful mortal boy abducted by Zeus, which one might take to be a straight-forwardly homoerotic subject, could be employed by artists meta-phorically to signify things quite apart from homoerotic desire—could even be represented parodically, as in Rembrandt's version of the subject.[15] It would thus constitute a gross oversimplification to assume that the representation of a figure like Ganymede is inevitably cast in homoerotic terms; it may well have been fashioned to represent symbolically, for example, the soul's spiritual aspirations. On the other hand, an image of political martyrdom, such as David's 1794 *Death of Joseph Bara* (fig. 61), which was nominally intended to convey edifying patriotic and civic meaning demands, nevertheless, to be read in terms of its sensual address and homoerotic appeal.

Because works of art are characterized by their multiplicity of meanings and associations—manifest and latent, conscious and unconscious—interpretation therefore needs to extend beyond mere iconographic deciphering or biographical reference. Indeed, it is what semiotics designates as the polysemic or multi-signifying aspect of imagery, especially in the complex and highly wrought forms of elite painting, that makes any given work of art productive of meanings greatly in excess of simple denotation. The meanings of a work are thus never reducible to its contents, its subject, its style and mode of execution, but are equally bound to its context and its reception which may or may not be available to historical reconstruction. Which is to say that once we venture into considerations of the sexual politics inherent in representations of masculinity, we must still take a broad range of contextual factors into account, acknowledging also such elements as authorial intention even as we accept—*pace* the lessons of post-structuralism—the problematic aspects of such a formulation. In other words, the task at hand is to navigate between the Scylla of a concept of unconstrained authorial freedom (the artist knowingly intending and orchestrating all of a painting's meanings) and the Charybdis of a concept of cultural and psychic overdetermination.

A second justification for avoiding the use of the term homosexuality derives from the material circumstances in which a genre such as history painting was actually produced. In many instances, the subject of history paintings was not selected by the artist, but by the institution or the patron. Furthermore, even if we grant (and can empirically establish) an operative gay sensibility at work in a particular historical period, during which a gay artist figures a gay iconographic subject that will be recognized as such by a gay spectator, the artist nevertheless employs a visual idiom that is already more or less given in advance, irrespective of the particular inflection imposed upon it. Whether the artist or milieu is to be now considered as gay, straight, or bisexual, (or not usefully to be considered within any of these modern terms) the visual language is itself drawn from a spectrum of available masculinities. Although art history tends to privilege artistic originality, innovation, and formal invention, most European painting and sculpture is characterized by its conventionality of forms—including bodily forms—as well as meanings. The observance of prior models, types, and schemata is thus far more the rule than the exception. Hence, whether the image of Ganymede is intended to signify same-sex desire, or the soul's aspirations, artists could only choose between the existing conventions for the representation of masculinity (a child's body or an adolescent one; a plump and rounded form, or a graceful, lissome one); they could not, in any case, invent a type out of whole cloth.

Sexuality, Mentalities and Visual Culture

In bracketing the concept of homosexuality or the homosexual from an examination of masculine representation, this does not mean we can, or should, dispense with the no less modern category of the sexual itself. Any consideration of the meanings generated in the depiction of the human body that exceed the purely formal, stylistic, or iconographic, must reckon with the fact that the image of the body, over and beyond its public meanings, is also a locus of unconscious identification and projection, both for the artist and for the spectator. And while these exist on the level of individual subjectivity, they are no less operative in the culture at large. It is in this sense that scholars have come to examine forms of cultural production employing such concepts as "libidinal politics," or a sexual politics of representation. With specific reference to the French revolutionary period, historians such as Lynn Hunt, drawing upon interpretative models from psychoanalytical theory, have virtually remapped the field, demonstrating in the process how fantasy, sexuality, and sexual politics are actively at work within the terrain of the political. For example, Hunt's *The Family Romance of the French Revolution* uses a number of core concepts derived from Freud's writing, including those of castration, totemism, and the family romance in order to explore the unconscious dynamics of revolution, regicide, and the post-revolutionary reconstruction of civil and family law. Similarly, Neil Hertz has examined the political implications of male fantasies of castration as they are mobilized in revolutionary moments, such as those of 1848 and the Paris Commune of 1871.[16]

These do not, of course, replace other forms of historical explanation, any more than my own reading of the sexual politics at work in French history painting replaces more traditional art-historical models of analysis or interpretation. They do, however, provide a set of concepts, a language, an explanatory model to address cultural phenomena that purely empirical approaches cannot adequately address or even apprehend. What considerations of sexual politics and unconscious investments and displacements do accomplish is itself analogous to the processes and functions of cultural production. For even as art, visual or literary, enacts, elaborates, and gives nuances and palpable form to official ideals and values, including those that govern the terms of gender, so too do they give expression to otherwise unspoken—or unspeakable—social and psychosexual relations and formations, fantasies, fears and desires. Like human subjects, cultural texts may manifest symptoms—internal contradictions, fissures in meaning, incoherences—

that bear witness to unconscious pressures and processes. An attentive reading of cultural texts that takes account of unconscious meanings therefore enables the investigator to grasp that part of social reality that rarely announces itself as such. This is the domain of what French historians have termed *mentalités*, a concept broader than that of ideology as it has been developed in Marxist thought. Visual culture provides a particularly rich lode for exploration precisely because cultural creation engages unconscious processes, both in production and in reception.[17] As the French historian Michelle Vovelle has commented:

> Moving from social structures to collective attitudes and representations involves the whole problem of complex mediators between real human life and images, or even the fantastic representations, which people construct and which are a basic part of the history of mentalities. The history of mentalities can be defined as the study of the mediations and of the dialectical relationship between the objective conditions of human life and the ways in which people narrate it, and even live it. At this level the contradictions between the two notional systems...—ideology and mentality—fade away. The exploration of mentalities, far from being a mystifying process, can ultimately lead to an essential widening of the field of research, not as a venture into foreign, exotic territory, but as the natural extension and cutting edge of all social history.[18]

In keeping with Vovelle's formulations, the history of masculinity and its representations belongs squarely in the discursive realm of mentalities. And equally in keeping with his formulations, we need to consider the dialectic between "objective conditions"—the familiar "real" of historical, or art-historical inquiry—and the "narrative" strategies by which human beings represent themselves and make sense of their lives. This collectively encompasses the mediations of culture, which more or less constitutes a culture's story about itself. If, to take a specific example from this study, Jacobin discourse held the corruption of the *ancien régime* to derive in large part from the "unnatural" and malignant power of women within it, this should hardly be taken as objective political analysis. Instead, we need to question what it was within the nascent discourses of parliamentarian and representative democracy and the formation of the bourgeois civil sphere that required the demonization, and indeed, the expulsion of women from the emerging modern polity.[19] Similarly, the devotion to the ethical ideal that the French revolutionaries routinely (and apparently redundantly) characterized as *la vertu mâle* requires sustained analysis. In this respect, the constant evocation of the menace of "effeminacy" in republican discourse suggests the presence of a pervasive anxiety attached to masculinity that may be one of the clearest indices of crisis. Accordingly, if one strand of my argument concerns itself with the powerful determinations of patriarchy in the formation of the cultural Imaginary,[20] another deals with the specific attributes of revolutionary or post-Thermidorian culture which shaped and inflected its representations of desirable masculinity. Thus, instead of viewing the characteristic productions of post-revolutionary artists like Guérin and his followers (figs. 2, 5, 6, and 7) simply as indices of cultural and political accommodation if not reaction, I consider them in relation to the mobile field of homosocial desire and gender ideology.

From such a perspective, the progression from David's bristling Horatii of 1785 (fig. 4) to Girodet Trioson's swooning Endymion of 1791 (fig. 20) to Flandrin's mummified Theseus of 1832 (fig. 109) irresistibly suggests something like "stations" in the masculine Imaginary, from the heady moment of Jacobin self-fashioning to the relative constraints of bourgeois manhood. These constraints operated both to contain male eroticism (evident, for example, in the gradual disappearance of form-fitting clothing like breeches, or in strictures against too effusive or too demonstrative romantic friendship) and to de-corporealize masculinity, thereby delegitimizing male nudity as the form of ideal beauty. Historically, this period marks the transition from the culture of the *ancien régime* (a court culture of spectacle, specularity, and the privileging of masculine display) to the fully bourgeois culture of the July Monarchy and with it, the visual disappearance of ideal masculinity from most elite visual culture.

To the degree that Western culture regularly provides us with numerous examples of feminized masculinities and masculinized femininities and Freud provides us with a model of gender that stresses both its abstraction and precariousness, we do well, therefore, to emphasize its historical, contingent, and indeed performative nature.[21] But with specific respect to masculinity, anthropologists and ethnographers of almost all stripes concur in their observations that it appears in most cultures as something to be acquired, achieved, initiated into—often involving painful if not mutilating rites and rituals. Furthermore, the weight of anthropological evidence suggests that while most cultures assume that a girl becomes a woman through inevitable biological process (although many cultures have rituals to mark this passage), becoming a man seems to require far more by way of cultural intervention. The attention given to this rite of passage suggests the possibility that there is a greater difficulty, if not uncertainty, attending accession to manhood. Lastly, considering Freud's own work on the tortuous and always ambivalent circuits by which male human beings may become appropriately masculine, appropriately heterosexual, appropriately "Oedipalized" subjects, there is abundant evidence to suggest that there never is, and never was, an unproblematic, a natural, or a crisis-free variant.

For this reason, I take respectful issue with arguments such as those proposed by Kaja Silverman in her important study Male *Subjectivity at the Margins.*[22] Working with and expanding upon theoretical models derived from Freudian and post-Freudian analytic theory—principally those of Jacques Lacan—Silverman here examines a number of modern and postmodern films and texts in order to excavate models of masculine subjectivity which refuse or subvert what she terms "the dominant fiction" of normative, heterosexual, Oedipalized masculinity, that provides the foundation for the symbolic order. These "alternative" models of masculine subjectivity are those "which not only acknowledge but embrace castration, alterity, and specularity and refuse, in various ways, the active, dominant, and masterful position that is the masculine prerogative."[23] Although the specific texts and films that she discusses—the fiction of Henry James, T. E. Lawrence's memoirs, a group of post-World War II Hollywood films and a number of films by Rainer Werner Fassbinder—span a period from the 1880s through the 1970s, she anchors her interpretation of various "perverse" or masochistic masculinities to a crisis in masculinity that she locates in the nineteenth century *fin de siècle.*[24] For Silverman, this is the historical juncture during which the non-equivalence of phallus and penis became evident—a crisis in masculinity *par excellence.* Succeeding this decisive rupture, she considers instances of particularized historical traumas, such as World War II, "which brings a large group of male subjects into such an intimate relation with lack that they are at least for the moment unable to sustain an imaginary relation with the phallus, and so withdraw their belief from the dominant fiction."[25] Silverman's use of the term "dominant fiction" is somewhat more specific than a comparable term, such as dominant ideology, meaning the presiding ensemble of beliefs that at any given time defines what reality is thought to be. It is closest in meaning to Lacan's concept of the symbolic order; that is, the aggregate field of language and indeed all forms of representation founded on the law of the father and the differential relation of male and female human beings to the phallus. The symbolic order thus encompasses the ways that human beings are placed in the world as duly sexed subjects, and their different relations to the phallus, the "transcendental signifier." Insofar as Lacan argued that male subjects do not possess the phallus (which is, in any case, symbolic) but are charged with the task of representing it, a disinvestment, or breakdown in the imaginary equivalence of phallus and penis, or the ability of male subjects to represent it, operates to put in crisis all other givens in the symbolic sphere.

My own research in the fields of eighteenth- and nineteenth-century visual culture convinces me, on the contrary, that the existence of cultural forms of masculinity which "not only acknowledge but embrace castration, alterity, and specularity" is a recurring theme in Western art (and presumably in other cultural forms as well). If I am correct in this recognition, it remains an open question as to whether the cultural expression of such "alternative" variants of masculinity can be directly linked to larger cultural and historical crises, or whether they merely represent the flip side of more familiar versions, and whose emergence is facilitated, or favored, by particular historical and cultural conditions. In either case, and judging from the range of periods that scholars and theorists have proposed for their particular masculine crises, it would seem that these crises and their attendant representations are closer to the rule than to the exception and are, in fact, recurring psychosocial phenomena.

However one wishes to place them chronologically, the task of interpreting any identifiable crisis in masculinity requires a distinction between psychological and historical tributaries even as one acknowledges the indivisibility of these factors. Where psychoanalytical theories are deployed, one operates with an interpsychic model of subjectivity, premised on such "ahistorical" notions as the unconscious, the Oedipus and castration complexes, fetishism, sublimation and so forth. A historical investigation, however, depends on the analysis of the material components of the crisis, those contingent (and thus mutating) circumstances in which human subjectivity is equally forged. An exploration of the characteristic forms in which ideal manhood is expressed at a given historical moment, in crisis or not, requires recourse to both modes of analysis which can be said to exist in a dialectical relationship to one another. Hence, despite the charge of ahistoricism routinely launched against psychoanalytical theory, empirical forms of historical inquiry cannot and do not provide an adequate explanatory framework for understanding the formation of sexual identity, the constitution of masculine and feminine norms, much less explain such pervasive phenomena as misogyny and homophobia. Neither can they account for the characteristic forms in which Western culture has figured its visions of an ideal human being. To take one obvious example, for nearly two thousand years the classic female nude, virtually by definition, could be depicted neither with pubic hair nor with genitalia, a convention invented by the Greeks and observed until well into the nineteenth century. Without recourse to the Freudian concept of fetishism, it is difficult, if not impossible to explain the persistence, not to say the perversity of this convention. In a similar way, the symbolic prestige of the phallus, and its apparently universal currency as a signifier of power and privilege, clearly goes beyond the significance of the anatomical organ. Here too, it is psychoanalytical theory that provides a way of thinking about its symbolic status.

Lacan's categorical distinction between the phallus and the penis, and the merely provisional ability of the latter to represent the former, provides a useful point of departure for the consideration of the representation of masculinity. Although the elaboration of this distinction belongs to Lacan, the differentiation of symbol and organ is at least implicit in Freud, insofar as concepts of, for example, the phallic mother, are to be understood not as the woman endowed in fantasy with an actual penis, but as the all-powerful mother of the dependent human infant who does not yet perceive the mother's actual status, that is, lacking, "castrated," subordinated within the hierarchical structures of patriarchy. One need not, however, subscribe to Lacanian models to perceive the gulf that separates the individual male human being in his frailty and mortality from the abstract and largely unrealizable ideal that culture and society designates as its masculine norm. And where it is a question of the mimetic and figurative depiction of an idealized masculinity in visual terms, there exists always a disjunction between the ideology of gender in the abstract and in actual corporeal reality. In this respect, I would suggest that an implicit recognition of the distinction of phallus and penis, far from being an "event" of the turn of the century, as Silverman asserts, is in fact the locus from which representations of ideal masculinity are routinely generated. The diminutive scale of the genitalia on the male nude in its classical, Renaissance or post-Renaissance incarnations announces this non-equivalence, as does the frequent counterpoint of large swords, bulky scabbards, and bunched masses of drapery. I will return to this issue in Chapter 4, but for now it is sufficient to note that the prevalence of these pictorial devices suggests that the phallus/penis distinction has a lengthy visual history. Similarly, the graceful contours of Ingres's Patroclus in *Achilles*

Receiving the Ambassadors of Agamemnon (fig. 10), the muscle-bound excess of the Farnese Hercules (fig. 8), the straining sinews of David's Horatii (fig. 4), or the armored torsos of today's male models are collective testimonial to a compensatory fetishization of the body itself evoking the gap between its symbolic labor in the service of patriarchal ideologies and its actual, mortal status.

Obviously, the nature of the symbolic labor performed by the Farnese Hercules is not the same as that performed by the model for Calvin Klein underpants. For this reason, an interrogation of the meanings of masculinity within visual culture or its putative crises needs to take strict account of the wider historical field and its particular determinations that inform, and indeed shape its articulations. Silverman's identification of a *fin-de-siècle* crisis in masculinity (why then?) is consequently too vague to have much explanatory force. Furthermore, rather than privileging a certain articulation of male masochism, as Silverman appears to do, it seems equally possible to consider images of non-phallic masculinity as still operating within the framework of narcissistic identification and homosocial desire. And from a specifically feminist perspective, the identification and description of forms of male subjectivity variously feminized—non-phallic, "castrated," and so forth—need not signal any breach in the actual workings of male power. On the contrary, and as the feminist scholar Tania Modleski has argued, "…however much male subjectivity may currently be 'in crisis,' as certain optimistic feminists are now declaring, we need to consider the extent to which male power is actually consolidated through cycles of crisis and resolution, whereby men ultimately deal with the threat of female power by incorporating it."[26]

In this respect, it is one of my contentions that the widespread production of manifestly androgynous or otherwise feminized masculinities in the 1790s and after are instances of this incorporation of femininity and should be understood, in Modleski's terms, as in some measure a response to the threat of female power. Such an approach considers the mythical figures (fig. 2) of artists such as Charles Landon (1760–1826) to be as redolent of patriarchal power as the virile warriors imagined by David.

The female power that seemed to threaten was a power manifest on the popular level, as in women's participation in the revolutionary *journées*, within the feminist discourses of activists such as Etta Palm van Aelders and Olympe de Gouges, and finally, by women's political participation within Jacobin and *sans-culottes* clubs and societies, both in Paris and in the provinces. The suppression of women's political speech and activities after 1793 has been termed "the world historical defeat of women,"[27] but what primarily concerns me here are the ways in which women's political agency may have influenced the terms of masculine subjectivity. The fear and loathing provoked *especially* by working-class women's militancy is apparent in all kinds of official, archival, literary, and other textual sources. The Goncourts' description may be taken as a *locus classicus* of the anxiety such women inspired:

> They [the women fishmongers] gave the revolution weapons and tongues. They were the revolution, the terrible vestals, drunken bacchantes of the new god Liber. They hurled themselves into riots, they dragged the men along with them, they made the national militias march, they put themselves between the royal troops and the patriotic hordes, they launched the attack, they paralyzed the defense. The men killed; the women massacred.[28]

Crossing the Channel, the terrifying specter of rioting women attending the imprisonment of Louis XVI and Marie-Antoinette was described by Edmund Burke in blatantly hysterical language: "amidst the horrid yells, and shrilling screams, and frantic dances, and infamous contumelies, and all the unutterable abominations of the furies of hell, in the abused shape of the vilest of women."[29] Male responses to the power (real or imagined) of women are not, however, to be understood by recourse to a crude cause-and-effect model by which cultural forms simply reflect the alarming fact of women's agency or political demands, much less to be understood as simply reducible to a response to those demands. On the contrary, the nature of the imagery of masculinity in elite and revolutionary visual culture is shaped by other factors as well, some with roots in the *ancien régime*—for example, the immense influence of the writings of Johann-Joachim Winckelmann (1717–68), and the continuing prestige of antiquity in either its Roman Republican or Grecian "Anacreontic" guises—some more immediate—the fulcrum of the revolutionary experience itself, its violences, its reversals, its trauma. For if indeed an argument is to be made for a crisis in masculinity in the revolutionary period, the objective facts of historical trauma are inescapable factors to reckon with. The approximately forty-year period on which this study focuses is thus one imprinted by historical cataclysm (the revolution itself) as well as the less visible alchemy of encompassing economic, social and cultural transition (the tidal shift from aristocratic to bourgeois culture)—the *longue durée* of historical change. In this regard, once we acknowledge that gender is historical, and thus in process, it is evident that it manifests the same "uneven development" identifiable in other social and economic formations. Similarly, what Raymond Williams described as "residual" and "emergent" forms of cultural development are equally in play.[30] The grace and *mollesse* of androgynous bodies celebrated in Salon criticism has roots in the cult of *sensibilité* of the mid-eighteenth century; the boneless androgynes of Meynier and Prud'hon look forward to new paradigms for the representation of desirable femininity. At the time of their making, however, they may also be seen as stand-ins—substitutions—for a femininity pervasively denigrated and deemed inimical to a republic grounded in manly values.

What needs, however, to be stressed is that whether we are considering masculinity in the French Revolution or in the present, both phallic and non-phallic versions of masculinity are generated within psychic and cultural arenas fissured by intense contradictions. Central among them is the aesthetic celebration of male beauty that is at the same time obliged to disavow any libidinal investment in this beauty. Which is another way of saying that the production and consumption of images of desirable masculinity in patriarchal culture takes place within historically mobile social and cultural contexts that can, however, rarely afford to acknowledge fully their own erotic economies, either on the register of the individual artists or that of the culture. A more local contradiction, operative in the context of Neoclassical art production, is the fascination with the sensual ephebe or the androgyne coexisting with public discourses the misogyny *and* homophobia of which are signaled by their obsessive invocation of the threat of effeminacy and emasculation.

Continually in Crisis

Exploring the representations of masculinity in the crucible of the French Revolution and its aftermath, or considering its various manifestations in contemporary mass culture in the wake of the epochal challenge of feminism and the women's movement consequently suggests that a stable masculinity outside crisis is something of a chimera. There is, in fact, every reason to think that like capitalism, masculinity is always in crisis, but like the phoenix—an appropriately phallic simile—it continually rises again, retooled and reconstructed for its next historical turn. This, it seems to me, is the crux of the issue; rather than prematurely assuming that the symptoms of crisis herald a radical destabilization of masculine power, we do better to proceed cautiously in assessing the degree to which the changing appearance of gender heralds any substantial change in power relations. What Silverman describes as the "dominant fiction" of male supremacy—that is, the collective beliefs, values, and identifications that are sustained through the cultural fixing of meaning, the denial of difference, and the neutralization of contradiction—can well survive an expansion, or even a transgression of normative models. Without overemphasizing the similarities between our own cultural fantasies revealed in the contemporary imagery of masculinity and those produced at the threshold of modernity, the fact remains that the dissemination of idealized but non-phallic masculinities can readily thrive in a context of misogyny and patriarchal reassertion. We should not forget that our seductive ephebes in alluring undress, or our sensitive musclemen cradling babies or ironing their own trousers, exist simultaneously with a backlash against women's rights, and an ominous ascendancy of right wing politics and its attendant ideologies. If indeed the imagery of nude, eroticized, musclebound or passive male models can be shown to appeal to female consumers (for such imagery is in the first instance a lure for consumption), this does not automatically attest to female empowerment, any more than the vogue for male stripteasers could be said to reverse the norms for feminine objectification. Accordingly, the visual history of "male trouble" suggests that the cultural expression of "soft" masculinities need not necessarily dismantle the worldly prerogatives of privilege and power which is what, after all, the word "patriarchy" denotes. Hence, the emergence in the past decade of a men's movement concerned to excavate male fears, anxieties and desires, or the celebration of forms of gay male sexuality that relinquish a position of mastery and control, or the theoretical revision of male masochism, do not in themselves dislodge the determining power of patriarchy. This dismantling is the historical task of feminism, and while it seems unlikely that there exists an Archimedean point outside ideologies of gender, and equally unlikely that there exists an authentic and un-alienated masculinity—or femininity—there is nevertheless much to be learned from their historical investigation. If the exploration of male trouble teaches us anything, it must surely be that the imagery of feminized and vulnerable manhood is as much an index of the resilience of patriarchy as it is a sign of its fragility.

La grâce, dans les ouvrages de l'art, regarde principalement la figure de l'homme.

J.-J. WINCKELMANN "De la grâce dans les ouvrages de l'art"[1]

In the course of the four decades between the French Revolution of 1789 and the establishment of the July Monarchy in 1830, the heroic male nude, alpha and omega of history painting, gradually lost its privileged position *in practice*, to be increasingly eclipsed, and ultimately supplanted, by the female nude. I emphasize this qualification because one of the many interesting contradictions attending this historical shift was the fact that throughout this period, the male nude retained its *theoretical* priority in pedagogy and art theory and its literal primacy in certain highly specific arenas, such as the yearly Prix de Rome competition at the École des Beaux-Arts.[2]

Apart from such institutional preserves, however, and as the century progressed, the male nude came to symbolize the obsolescence of academic precepts and values. Indeed, the long drawn out death throes of history painting in the nineteenth century is integrally linked to the waning fortunes of the ideal male nude, which classical art theory considered as its foundation stone.

A survey of the titles of paintings in the Salon *livrets* at various intervals beginning with the Salon of 1781 and concluding with the Salon of 1831 is sufficient to indicate that even as the total number of works displayed increased enormously, paintings featuring the male nude, or male figures lightly and "classically" draped, consistently diminished while their female equivalents figured ever more prominently.[3] Even more suggestively, whereas male nudes had traditionally been embedded in narratives, their nudity itself a signifier of their ideal and heroic status, the female nude gradually became a genre in itself, detached from narrative, myth, or allegory.

11 MERRY-JOSEPH BLONDEL Aeneas Carrying his Father Anchises (detail), 1803

Unlike the male nudes of the previous century, female nudity came increasingly to be supplied with a "realist" rather than mythological or Biblical justification. Although bathing, dressing and undressing, preparation for the toilette, and so forth—staple motifs in the depiction of the female nude going back to the Renaissance—can also be considered as a form of narrative, this should be distinguished from the "heroic" nudity of religious or classical myth and history where nudity functions as a signifier for elevated and edifying values. Therefore, what the art historian Beatrice Farwell has aptly called the female "display nude" of the nineteenth century, was a body shorn of its loftiest connotations, demoted, as it were, to the plane of purely visual beauty and delectation.[4]

So thoroughly was the male nude supplanted by the female nude in the course of the nineteenth century and so deeply rooted the ideological shift that both attended, enabled, and naturalized this transformation that even those contemporary scholars concerned with the significance of the nude tend automatically to assume that the referent for the aesthetic category "nude" is self-evidently the female body.[5] In fact, the female nude, whose classical lineage is considerably less venerable than the male's, has historically occupied a far more equivocal and unstable position, one, moreover, that was rarely the object of critical and theoretical commentary until its final and definitive hegemony in mid-nineteenth-century French visual culture.[6]

In seeking to account for the eclipse of the male nude and the ascendancy of the female nude it would be absurd to pretend that a transformation of this kind is ultimately to be explained by reference to internal developments in the history of art, be they stylistic, institutional, or discursive. On the contrary, it is one of my working assumptions that the image of the body is itself a historical matrix, marked and molded in a crucible of social, cultural, and psychosexual circumstance. Furthermore, the image of the nude—a discrete aesthetic category if not, strictly speaking, a genre—is itself a palimpsest of aesthetics and sexuality, locus and producer of cultural and psychological meanings that are themselves inseparable from ideologies of gender.[7] And while the individual artist's imaginative and formal work of representing is obviously crucial to the appearance of any given image, it must also be acknowledged that artists operate within what the literary theorist Hans-Robert Jauss described as a "horizon of expectations."[8] As such, the appearance, meaning, codes, connotations and significance of visual imagery at any given historical moment are jointly produced and received against a background of shared assumptions and conventions with determined boundaries and parameters. In this regard, the forty-year period in which the male nude was displaced by the female is one in which this horizon was gradually, perhaps imperceptibly, altered, but as it altered it cast forth images that testify to a profound reorganization of sexuality and desire in visual representation.[9]

These include the appearance of distinctive avatars of masculinity, some of them well known, some of them not, and it is these artifacts that I want to consider as symptomatic of "male trouble"–a crisis in and of representation, precipitated in the wake of revolution and large scale political, social and cultural transformation.[10] In this reading, the production of imagery featuring iconographies of masculine passivity, debility and disempowerment, frequently embodied by androgynous or otherwise "feminized" male bodies, is by no means to be considered as a purely aesthetic or stylistic phenomenon. Similarly, the iconography of hypervirile, martial masculinity may also be considered symptomatically. Graceful ephebe, or sinewy warrior, it is the excessive qualities of both types that alert us to the existence of meanings beyond, or behind their nominal identities or narrative roles. Which is to say that the crisis of the male nude is itself inseparable from a wider phenomenon, namely, a post-revolutionary crisis of masculinity, even if one assumes it to have been circumscribed by factors of age and class. As Carol Duncan and more recently, Lynn Hunt have persuasively demonstrated, high cultural representations of masculinity may well be implicated in larger political struggles.[11] As such, these representations bear witness to the ways in which the image of the body may furnish a field upon which historical conflicts and transformations are registered and inscribed. And while it has been an assumption of feminist art history that the Western easel painting tradition thematizes the sovereign male subject's gaze of possession and mastery (often directed at a female object) there have been relatively few discussions of the dynamics of the male gaze as it falls on beautiful male bodies.[12]

In focusing attention, therefore, on the iconographic swan song of ideal masculinity, we must ask what spectator is being addressed (and produced) in these images, and what kind of gaze is being solicited? How is masculinity being discursively constructed and visually represented? What forces are at work, what psychological investments are at stake in the production of these two contrasting images of ideal masculinity? It is with these questions in mind that I intend to examine the history painting of the revolutionary and post-revolutionary decades. Furthermore, because one of the characteristic features of the Neoclassical period in France was an intensifying "masculinization" not only of visual, but of political culture, it raises questions about the place of femininity within it, as well as larger questions about the representation of sexual difference. In the pages that follow, therefore, I am concerned to recover the web of meanings clinging to images of ideal masculinity; meanings, moreover, that spanned the public realm of the speakable and equally, the private, psychological realm of the *non dit*, the unspeakable.

The Studio Fraternity

Beauty is a certain vital and spiritual grace, which is infused first into the Angel by the divine ray, then into the spirits of men, and following these, into corporeal forms; and this grace by means of reason and sight moves and delights our spirit; and in delighting, enraptures, and in enrapturing, inspires ardent love.
(From Marsilio Ficino's *Commentary on the Symposium of Plato*, 1491)[13]

One of the most curious passages in E. J. Delécluze's classic memoir *Louis David: son école et son temps*[14] occurs when "Etienne," Delécluze's youthful *alter ego*, then a student of David, admires the pretty white neck of Mme de Noailles, an aristocratic woman of fashion who has recently entered David's studio as a student. Observing her as she works, he wonders how David, "ancien ami de Robespierre," has now become "nouveau protecteur des émigrés."

Pensively, he kept his gaze mechanically fixed on Mme de Noailles, whom he saw only from behind. Her dark chestnut hair, gathered up in red bands in the antique style, brought out the whiteness of her neck, which was slender and very beautiful. The red and this white neck suddenly struck Etienne's imagination, which was already stimulated by the reflections that David's visit had suggested to him, and he imagined seeing the pretty head of this young woman cut off. It was only by making a great effort that he succeeded in mastering the interior agitation that so tested him at that moment.[15]

He then immediately goes on to recall a day in 1793 (29 Germinal, Year II of the Republic) when as a very young child, he and his mother were caught in the route of a convoy to the scaffold, obstructed by the crowd of spectators pressed between them and the Pont-Neuf. Among the twenty-five or thirty condemned persons in the wagons, he sees "for the first and the last time" M. de Laborde, banker to the court, and father of Mme de Noailles.

The train of associations produced in Etienne's contemplation of Mme de Noailles is as suggestive psychologically as it is historically. While the latter element leaves open the question of the nature of David's transformation from Jacobin radical and regicide to protector of emigrés and imperial court propagandist, the recollection of the Terror points to the political dimension of David's activities that the text will only explore much later. But the implications of the train of thought that starts with the dark brown hair of Mme de Noailles, and moves from the red ribbons binding her hair and her snowy neck to the decapitation of her father are perhaps of even greater interest, not merely in the textual contiguity of femininity and death, or, for that matter, sexuality and castration, but in the fact that Mme de Noailles then disappears from the text, only to be briefly resurrected more than a hundred pages later.

In this respect, the abrupt disappearance of Mme de Noailles as artist, or even as amateur, is consistent with Delécluze's treatment of virtually all the other women artists in David's studio; effectively conjured away, banished from historical memory, and for the most part, banished from modern art history as well.[16]

The erasing of women is by no means an idiosyncratic foible of the elderly Delécluze, looking back on his period as art student from a distance of half a century. Paintings and graphics illustrating David's studio from the revolutionary or post-revolutionary years—Jean-Henri Cless's *The Studio of David*, c. 1804, and the 1814 *Studio of the Students of David at the Collège des Quatre Nations*, by Léon-Mathieu Cochereau (1793–1817), for example (figs. 12 and 13)—typically show no women in the studio, neither Constance-Marie Charpentier (1767–1849); nor Marie-Guilhelmine de Laville, later the Comtesse Benoist (1768–1826); Césarine Davin, née Mirvault (1733–1844); Angélique Mongez, née Lavol (1775–1855); Aimée Duvivier; nor Nanine Vallain.

Whatever the reasons for this obliteration of the feminine it has an equivalent in the silencing of women and their exclusion from the public sphere at the time, a process begun under the Jacobin dictatorship and legally formalized with the promulgation of the Napoleonic Code. I will explore the implications of this historical development throughout this book. However, in the context of Delécluze's memoir there is yet another line of inquiry prompted by the treatment of Mme de Noailles, namely, the mechanisms and determinations of homosociality both in the studio of David and in the contemporary artistic culture at large. For it will be one of my contentions that the iconography of post-revolutionary painting and the social relations of the artistic milieux that produced it are charged with a singular admixture of homosocial, if not what we would today call homosexual, eroticism accompanied by an anxiety that illustrates the "uneven development" of gender ideologies in historical transition.

The sense in which I will be employing the term "homosocial" or "homosocial desire" is taken from Eve Kosofsky Sedgwick's groundbreaking study *Between Men: English Literature and Male Homosocial Desire*.[17] As Sedgwick employs the terms, they are as much to be understood politically as sexually; indeed, their descriptive utility lies precisely in their integration of both elements. Although Sedgwick

12 JEAN-HENRI CLESS The Studio of David, c. 1804

13 LÉON-MATHIEU COCHERAU The Studio of the Students of David at the Collège des Quatre Nations, 1814

nowhere gives a hard and fast definition of homosociality, it is clear from her discussion that homosociality describes a network of relationships that are themselves a derivative of patriarchal social and sexual organization. Citing Heidi Hartmann's definition of patriarchy, "relations between men which have a material base, and which, though hierarchical, establish or create interdependence and solidarity among men that enable them to dominate women,"[18] Sedgwick elaborates some of the modalities and circuits by which male power is secured and perpetuated. Drawing upon the triangulated model of desire proposed by the literary theorist René Girard, in which the bond that links two rival men is seen to be more powerful than the link of either to the beloved woman, Sedgwick interrogates the ways in which the woman "between men" may operate as a kind of switching station—a conduit—between the trajectories of male desire. For Girard, as for Sedgwick, the rivalries that foster powerful bonds between men need not have anything to do with sexual desire: "…any relation of rivalry is structured by the same play of emulation and identification, whether the entities occupying the corners of the triangle be heroes, heroines, gods, books, or whatever."[19] In situations, sites, and relations where no women are present, relations between men are in a sense doubly charged, both along the vertical axis of hierarchy and the horizontal one of peer relations. Homosociality is thus distinguished from homosexuality not because of the absence of erotic relations between men—on the contrary, homosocial relations may be intensely eroticized—but primarily through the shaping agents of explicit homosexual proscription and the accompanying homophobia that functions to enforce it. Thus while certain historical forms of patriarchy, for example, that of classical Greece, may exhibit *both* homosocial *and* homosexual structures and relationships, societies that proscribe the latter do not on that account dilute or mitigate the powerful determinations of the former.

Returning to David's studio as it is recalled by Délécluze, and with Sedgwick's model of homosociality in mind, we may identify certain aspects of its social organization as conforming to Sedgwick's model. Most obviously, the retrospective disappearance of women from Délécluze's account (which probably reflects their actual marginality within the life of the studio as much as it suggests a wish-fulfilling fantasy on Délécluze's part), ensures that the various hierarchies, rivalries, factions, and friendships described are seen as exclusively masculine and variously articulated in relation to David himself, the charismatic master who structurally occupies the position of father/teacher and homosocial object of desire.[20] Moreover, the life of the studio revolved around the male body and artistic training was predicated on drawing from the male model—the male body was the single most important element in the history paintings that David and his students were producing. It is worth mentioning in this context the occasional practice of having the most attractive and well formed male students pose nude in lieu of the professional model. This may well have contributed its own erotic *frisson* to the atmosphere of the studio, however disavowed.[21] Studio practice was dominated by the male body, whether in the form of venerated classical statuary from which students endlessly drew, or from the living male model, from which they also endlessly drew, and this had important parallels in the world outside the studio. Revolutionary culture, by which term I include political language as well as cultural production, defined itself in terms that identified republicanism and civic virtue with masculinity, and the evils of the *ancien régime* with the "unnatural" power and influence of women. Art criticism, no less than political discourse was characterized by a persistent gendered binarism in which the the word "male," employed as an adjective, stood for all the positive attributes of a civic, moral, and ethical ideal in opposition to a cluster of terms negatively associated with the feminine. The rallying cry of the Davidians—"Van Loo, Rococo, Pompadour"—included Louis XV's mistress (who was, of course, an important patron of Rococo artists) as its final strophe, and should be understood as one of the ways revolutionary thought subsumed its "bad objects" under the sign of femininity. Thus, if *ancien régime* visual culture was associated with female patronage and female bodies, one of the ways the art of Neoclassicism announced its salutary difference was through the celebration of male virtue and male bodies.

The erasure of women from the studio and the more generalized tendency to erase women artists altogether from the artistic scene was fully institutionalized by the time of Delécluze's memoir, and has, as I have indicated, remained a feature in most subsequent art history. Despite the fact that one of the interesting features of the organization of David's studio was precisely its inclusion of women, as well as its relative democracy (for example, students drew lots for their positions before the model in contrast to the Academy's traditional system of ranked placement), Delécluze's reconstruction foregrounds the network of homosocial relations that run the gamut from awed hero worship (the youthful Etienne himself), Oedipal rejection (Girodet's description of his *Endymion*: "What has given me above all the greatest pleasure is that not a single voice has said that I resemble M. David in anything"[22]), to eager emulation (Drouais's almost uncanny reversal of Girodet's comment, in a letter to David: "What gives me the most pleasure is that the efforts that I've made weren't wasted since they gained honor for you, and that the things [I've done] which have pleased me are those which bear some resemblance to your work"[23]), to open aesthetic rebellion (the contentious faction of young "primitives" in David's studio called the Barbus because of the beards they sported, or the *penseurs*[24]). Relations *between* students were occasionally marked by strong rivalry in relation to David, as, for instance, the tensions between and among Anne-Louis Girodet-Trioson (1767–1824), Jean-Germain Drouais (1763–88), François-Xavier Fabre (1766–1837), and Louis Gauffier

(1761–1801). There were, as well, important political divisions between these men; Girodet was (briefly) an enthusiastic republican; Fabre and Gauffier were monarchists and remained in Italy throughout and after the revolution.

Although one must be cautious about projecting the atmosphere of David's studio on to other studios, there are enough echoes and resemblances in the memoirs and accounts of Hippolyte Flandrin (1809–64) and Eugène Amaury-Duval (1805–85) of the studio of Jean-Auguste-Dominique Ingres (1780–1867), or descriptions of the studios of Girodet, Guérin, Antoine-Jean Gros (1771–1835), Horace Vernet (1789–1863) or Théodore Géricault (1791–1824)–to suggest that the complex identifications, passionate romantic friendships and rivalries between students and masters, enacted in an overwhelmingly masculine environment, have some bearing on the nature of these studios' cultural production.[25]

In this respect, the retrospective disappearance of those women artists who did (in whatever measure) participate in the life of the studios and did receive instruction from the master artist may reflect not only their marginality, but their irrelevance to the fraught relationships between the young men and their prominent masters. Despite their admission to David's studio as pupils, and also to other artists' studios, such as those of Joseph-Marie Vien (1716–1809) and Jean-Baptiste Regnault (1754–1829), the women artists appear to have been excluded from various standard studio practices, such as drawing from the nude model. They also seem to have lived in far more supervised and constrained circumstances. Consequently, it seems fair to assume that women artists' training was largely separate, and hardly equal. Nevertheless, their presence in the studio, or their activity as artists, frequently appears as a textual locus of male anxiety, as in Delécluze's decapitation fantasy, or in their later consignment to oblivion, or, more empirically, in the opposition provoked by their attempts to achieve greater parity with male artists.[26]

In this last instance, women artists fared no better in the revolutionary years than they had in the *ancien régime*. For example, the statutes of the Académie Royale des Beaux-Arts had from 1753 onward permitted the admittance of a maximum of four women academicians to their ranks. In 1790, and in the context of reforming the Academy, Adélaïde Labille-Guiard (1749–1803) attempted to expand their number. For her pains, her proposals generated such responses as this, written by M. Renou, secretary of the Academy, to M. Huet de Froberville, deputy to the Legislative Assembly:

...at the head of these latter [those who want to be at the head of the Academy] is a "Joan of Arc." It won't be because of her that the Academy falls to the distaff line. She has sown the most dangerous divisions among us....Two cocks lived in peace: a hen dropped in, and *voilà*, war breaks out. This hen, through "weak complacency and without authorization of the law," sets herself in the midst of the cocks. It is for this abuse that we ask for her removal before the legislators whose predecessors excluded the women of the Regency. They say that talent has no sex, but those who possess [talent] have a sex, and when it is feminine, it needs to be placed far away from the masculine, because of its inevitable influence.[27]

Such a response was entirely in keeping with the more general hostility expressed towards women's political aspirations in Jacobin political culture. The art historian Vivian Cameron recounts the response of the Jacobin Club of the Section Quatres Nations to a woman's delegation who asked for the use of their meeting rooms: "...in the ensuing discussion one member said, 'If we permit the women citizens to meet here, thirty thousand women would assemble themselves and provoke in Paris a movement disastrous to liberty.'"[28] Eventually, the Academy decided to retain their limit of four women. Furthermore, and as Cameron also demonstrates, the radical successor organization to the disbanded Academy, the Commune des Arts, was even more hostile to women artists' participation:

In fact...those associated with the Commune des Arts were even more opposed to professional artistic careers for women than those on the right. Only after the fall of the Academy, on August 18, 1793, did the Commune alter its rules, perhaps under pressure from Robespierre and the Montagnards, who had established good relations with the Société des Citoyennes Républicaines Révolutionnaires. Following Madame Tardieu's successful entry on August 24, 1793, the Commune was inundated with female applicants all of whom were admitted to the association. Their inclusion, however, was temporary....Less than two months later, the Commune des Arts, debating the issue of women in their organization, decided, for political and personal reasons, to exclude them.[29]

In eighteenth-century art practice, women artists such as Labille-Guiard, Angelica Kauffman (1740–1807), and Elisabeth Vigée-Lebrun (1755–1842), could and did achieve considerable fame and success (although this was rare), and important studios usually contained some

14 HORACE VERNET The Studio of the Artist, 1821

women students within their ranks, (David's studio may have had more
than the average number), but by the post-revolutionary period, at least
some of the most prominent artists, for example, Girodet and Abel de
Pujol (1787–1861), were running separate art schools or separate art
classes for women.[30] This provides additional support for the perception
that there was, if anything, a trend toward the greater segregation and
isolation of women artists thereby contributing to a more exclusively
masculine environment in the principal studios. Further, when artists
received their Prix de Rome and their state-supported sojourns at the
Mancini palace (the home of the Academy in Rome), they were pro-
hibited if married from bringing their wives with them. Institutionally,
socially, and pedagogically, therefore, everything operated to promote
homosocial networks among male artists.

In this context, Horace Vernet's 1821 *Studio of the Artist* (fig. 14) is of more than anecdotal interest, depicting as it does a scene more reminiscent of a men's sporting club than the aesthetic and professional space of high culture. Surrounded by the accoutrements of "nature" (a horse, a dog, a doe) and Napoleonic military memorabilia, the assembled artists fence, box, smoke, read the newspaper and make art. Whatever the putative documentary value of the painting as a record of Vernet's studio, no less suggestive is its Boy's Life ambience, an environment rather like that of the fashionable, Anglicized men's clubs of the period.[31] The studio paintings of Louis-Léopold Boilly (1761–1845) too—particularly the 1798 *Studio of Isabey*—are consistent in depicting an exclusively male membership, characterized by a clubby, informal, but *mondaine* atmosphere (fig. 15). Nothing could be further from Henri Murger's July Monarchy evocation of the *bohème* of the artist's studio (as recalled in his *Scènes de la vie de Bohème*), with its (heterosexual) romantic entanglements and dramatis personae of *grisettes*, seamstresses, and working-class female models.

15 LOUIS-LÉOPOLD BOILLY The Studio of Isabey, 1798

I do not, however, mean to suggest that the homosocial structure of artists' studios constituted a particularly dramatic departure from previous or later incarnations. Rather, I am suggesting that the social organization and psychosexual economy of revolutionary and post-revolutionary culture (at least in the spaces of art and art production) manifest forms of homosociality inflected by an increasing segregation and exclusion of women–part of the ongoing masculinization of most social space outside the domestic sphere. This tendency to marginalize–even eliminate–femininity (from art), and women (from production) may in turn have operated to promote a recuperation of difference *within* the representation of masculinity, a phenomenon I will explore in the following chapter. Moreover, the emergence of a new political discourse of republicanism and popular sovereignty which defined itself–at least in part–through its denigration of femininity (although exalting maternity) played its own role in privileging male beauty and the male body. All three of these interpretative claims will be developed further, but at this juncture it is nonetheless relevant to emphasize the homosocial organization of the site of production. Thus, even if it proves difficult to reconstruct historically the psychosexual climate of the most prominent Parisian studios, there remains the visual evidence of the paintings that emerged from within them and the textual evidence of the period's memoirs and heroicizing biographies. Both attest to the heightened masculinization in the content of art and the social relations of the art world. And in the former respect, it is the specific iconography and the specific themes of the paintings of this period that support the interpretative utility of Sedgwick's concept of homosocial desire, bearing witness as they do to an intense erotic investment in the male body and in the relations between men as described within classical myth or classical history.

Such an investment may account for the iconographic popularity, evident from the 1760s on, of the Achilles/Patroclus couple (fig. 10), as well as for fraternal oath-taking subjects of which David's 1785 *Oath of the Horatii* (fig. 4) was neither the first nor the last.[32] While it is undoubtedly the case that the theme of men pledging themselves to act–even to die–in unison for a shared and noble cause expresses notions of a lateral, hence egalitarian fraternity between men (in implicit contrast to the hierarchical relations of absolutism), the motif is equally expressive of the dynamics of homosociality. Another popular motif in Neoclassical painting was that of Aeneas's flight from the burning city of Troy with his father and son, as in *Aeneas Carrying his Father Anchises* (figs. 11 and 16) by Merry-Joseph Blondel (1781–1853)

16 MERRY-JOSEPH BLONDEL Aeneas Carrying his Father Anchises, 1803

which won the Prix de Rome of 1803. Blondel here represents the three ages of ideal masculinity; the noble patriarch, the purposeful and virile warrior, and the delicate ephebe, physically linked in a pyramid as they are genetically linked by relations of blood and succession. Compositionally separated from her husband, son and father-in-law by Aeneas's sword, Creusa, the wife and mother, exits the picture (and the narrative) at the painting's left, indicating her redundancy to the history to come. As the art historian Carol Duncan justly observed of depictions of this incident from the *Aeneid*, what is at stake is the continuity of the cultural patrimony through three generations of male subjects, underscored by the narrative's expedient elimination of Creusa. Unlike the imagery of tension and conflict between patriarchs and sons so frequent in the pre-revolutionary years, Aeneas's escape with his father and son thematizes the supremacy of masculine and patriarchal bonds in securing both the cultural legacy of the past (represented by Anchises and the holy idols he saves from the flames) and the promise of the future, the Rome-to-be. As for Creusa, who has somehow drifted off in the initial flight and returns briefly as a shade, as Duncan remarks, "…having produced Aeneas' son, she is (as her ghost declares) no longer needed. The same is not true of Anchises, the father, who represents the cultural patrinomy."[33]

One need not look far to discover other popular classical themes and narratives in the period that variously confirm the masculinity of the polis, and the decisive determinations of male bonds, be they familial, political or affective. Nevertheless, it is worth mentioning at least one other example of the homosocial ethos, given its unrivaled prominence in the revolutionary years. I refer here to the history of the Roman Consul Lucius Junius Brutus, surely one of the most vividly imagined heroes of the republican imagination.[34] As Plutarch, Livy and Ovid recount the story, the events that propel Brutus and Collatinus to overthrow the last king of Rome, Tarquin the Proud, and establish the republic, begins with Tarquin's rape of Lucretia, the wife of Collatinus. Tarquin's rape, however, is prompted by Collatinus's boasting of Lucretia's beauty and virtue. After her violation, she summons her father and husband, who arrive with Brutus and another Roman, Publius Valerius. In their presence, she stabs herself to death. It is Brutus who withdraws the bloody knife from her breast and over which he swears to avenge the crime and expel the Tarquins. Husband, father, and Publius Valerius then swear the oath together and it is over the dead body of a woman that the fraternal bonds of the republic-to-be are founded. Moreover, Lucretia's suicide is determined by a violation understood as defiling her *as her husband's wife*. The rape is therefore as much, if not more of an insult to her kinsmen as to herself. As with other variants of homosocial relationships in which a living woman is desired by two competing men, the relations between men are in all senses more potent and more determining of the action than those between men and women because the woman's place is *a priori* defined by her relations (conjugal and familial) to men. Similarly, a later chapter in the life of Brutus—that chosen for David's 1789 *Lictors*

17 JACQUES-LOUIS DAVID The Lictors Returning to Brutus the Bodies of his Sons, 1789

Returning to Brutus the Bodies of his Sons (fig. 17)—has its own homosocial subtext, insofar as the drama resides in Brutus's sacrifice of his treasonous children to the higher cause of the republic. The execution of disobedient sons features too in the story of Manlius Torquatus, another popular theme in revolutionary history painting. Such narratives are obviously concerned to affirm the primacy of civic loyalty over personal ties, but because the republic is an exclusive ensemble of male citizens, it is to a social contract of other men that the ultimate fealty is offered. The awed response to David's *Brutus* by certain commentators hinged precisely on the convincing interweaving of its implacable patriotic values with its masculinity: "The style of this painting is male, severe, terrifying, and its oppositions are perfect."[35]

To a considerable extent, the production of works featuring male protagonists of a certain type (martial, stoic, patriotic, self-sacrificing) was prompted by the royal arts administration, and it was the administration that also encouraged the "return to the antique" as part of the larger project of encouraging history painting. Hence, "the elegant mythologies, the gracious genre, the 'petite manière'...began to pass out of fashion towards 1750....It was above all after 1760 that the 'return to the antique' manifested itself in a tangible fashion."[36] Such an institutional initiative had the result of further emphasizing the male rather than female body as the primary focus in painting and sculpture, but it was nevertheless the case that even before their official encouragement, depictions of male bodies occasionally manifested a realism, and a dramatic presence quite distinct from the highly stylized and conventional rendition of female ones.

Horaces and Brutuses notwithstanding, the Salon painting of the 1790s and after is striking for the greater frequency of representations of androgynous male youths dead, dying, or otherwise disempowered, visual evidence suggestive of important shifts in the symbolic figuration of masculinity occurring in the transition from the culture of the *ancien régime* to that of the early nineteenth century. The images of the republican heroes of the 1780s and '90s can be said to exemplify masculinist versions of homosociality, while the imagery of Endymion or other androgynous types can be read as their feminized Other. The explanatory force of the concept of homosociality therefore lies in the ways it provides a structural model for grasping the appeal of both versions. Taken altogether, the currency of themes and narratives of homosocial bonding, the centrality of the beautiful male body, the comparative rarity of its female analogue, and the prominence of the eroticized ephebe suggest an investment in masculinity that seeks to circumvent difference and (sexual) Otherness, and where masculinity takes precedence as the object of desire. But what, we may well ask, is the meaning of this male preoccupation with idealized masculinity, and what is the role of sexual difference within this insistently masculinized universe?

Leaving open for the moment the connections between the social relations of the studio, those of the culture at large, and the imaginary and symbolic components of the art itself, I want now to discuss a series of individual works that collectively establish some of the meanings and terms of what I have already designated as "male trouble"— the indications of a pervasive binarism in the imagery of masculinity in the decades before its later resolution under the sign of bourgeois and fully modern ideologies of gender. That this resolution takes the form of a *withdrawal* of the eroticized male body from visual culture, and its replacement by an eroticized female one can be traced in the careers of many of the period's artists, such as Jean-Baptiste Regnault as well as David's own students—notably J. A. D. Ingres, and it is to the youthful Ingres that I now turn.

Sexual Difference Without Women

Ingres's *Achilles Receiving the Ambassadors of Agamemnon* (figs. 10 and 18) won the 1801 Grand Prix de Rome, thereby officially launching him at twenty-one in his anticipated career as a history painter. The subject of the painting, determined, according to the competition's rules by a committee of École academicians, was by no means a particularly esoteric one; Homeric themes, particularly those drawn from the *Iliad*, were immensely popular at the end of the eighteenth century. They had been actively encouraged thirty years earlier under the revived state arts administration of the Count d'Angiviller and had featured decades earlier in the works of British artists like Gavin Hamilton (1723–98) and Benjamin West (1738–1820) who were among the first painters to develop a recognizably Neoclassical style, often employing Homeric subjects. Staples of history painting thereafter, the Homeric vogue intensified noticeably in the revolutionary and post-revolutionary periods.[37] Among the most favored Homeric heroes were Achilles, Patroclus, Hector, and Paris, all of whom figure in the subject of this painting, as do Odysseus, Ajax, and the elderly Phoenix, who stands between them in front of the two heralds. Achilles, holding his golden lyre (he has been singing and playing to Patroclus) rises to greet the messengers, emissaries who have come to beseech him to return to battle. The *Iliad*'s narrative begins shortly before this encounter, with Achilles' stormy departure from the field of combat after Agamemnon takes from him the woman Briseis—part of Achilles' booty—to console himself for the loss of *his* female booty Chryses. In the epic, Chryses has already been returned to her priest father, the Greeks having been struck by plague in punishment for their impiety in abducting her. Briseis, the object of exchange, who by narrative rights should not be present at all, has been depicted by Ingres as a kind of shadowy phantom; a dim and insubstantial presence in the dark recesses of the tent, witness to sets of relations that in every sense can be described as taking place between men. Like the dim figure of Creusa in Blondel's painting (fig. 16), femininity is here displaced to the margins of the visual and indeed the narrative field. As in the *Iliad* itself, the roles of

Briseis and Chryses are significant largely for how their abductions and exchanges determine the relations between male protagonists. In conformity with this homosocial economy, it is Achilles and Patroclus who are compositionally and narratively coupled, the messengers of Agamemnon with whom they interact, and the background group of four nude warriors observing the scene who constitute the active players, the agents in the narrative. Where Briseis is a cipher of femininity, of minimal interest either to the actors in the scene or, I would submit, to the spectators of it, the erotic interest, the libidinal economy of the picture, is entirely focused on the splendid bodies of the men.[38]

One reason why the painting was so well received by the academicians, and indeed by so many of Ingres's peers, was its assured demonstration of total mastery over the recognized codes of masculine beauty. At least three distinct body types are represented in the painting, as is Ingres's own erudition as to each type's significance. This was an erudition largely based on Winckelmann's writings, fostered in David's studio and adhered to by Ingres in dutiful obedience to Davidian practice and theory. The more muscular, mature and articulated bodies of Ajax and Odysseus are closer to Phidian or Polycleitian prototypes and Ajax himself is a more sinewy relative of David's Romulus in his *Intervention of the Sabine Women*, 1799 (fig. 96). The brooding Phoenix also conforms to classical precepts; in keeping with the principles of aesthetic decorum, his body is recognizably older than the others' but still quite presentable. (Obeying the dictates of this principle of decorum, an older body was, by definition, an *ideal* older body, devoid of wattles, paunches, or unsightly bulges.)

Achilles and Patroclus, however, are made of somewhat different stuff. Smoother, lissome, younger, graceful, less muscular and conspicuously whiter-skinned than the others, their pedigree is Praxitelean, and they are closer morphologically to the ephebe than to the mature warrior type as codified by Winckelmann. But it is Patroclus's strikingly exaggerated outflung hip—what is called in French its *déhanchement*—even more than skin color or body proportions, that signals one of the forms by which erotic differentiation could be incarnated in male bodies. Although far more pronounced than its classical prototypes (for example, the Apollo Sauroctonos, fig. 65), Patroclus's pose, the arch of hip and overall presentation of the body, alludes to its antique prototype, which always retained some trace of the androgynous eroticism with which it had been originally invested. Between men, in other words, there is itself an array of masculinities, ranging from what I have designated the feminized masculine to the masculinized mascu-

18 JEAN-AUGUSTE-DOMINIQUE INGRES Achilles Receiving the Ambassadors of
Agamemnon, 1801

line, a spectrum that a single artist, such as David or Ingres, could
confidently negotiate. It is in this sense that I will be speaking of the
way Neoclassical artists suggest an internal gendering of masculinity,
pa dimorphism which—especially in the case of the feminized ephebic
body—might be seen as the attempt to figure sexual difference in a
same-sex system—sexual difference without women.

The ethos, the aesthetics, the erotic sensibility of Ingres's Prix de
Rome winner is echoed in David's *Leonidas at Thermopylae* (fig. 19), a
colossal painting on which he and his students—Ingres included—
worked on periodically from 1800 to 1813. Where the story of the
messengers of Agamemnon inaugurates a second stage of the heroic
bloodbath of the Trojan War, the story of the doomed three hundred
Spartan soldiers under Leonidas's command that David chose to

commemorate is oriented less to martial exploits themselves than to the fatalistic acceptance of certain death in the service of one's country. Not surprisingly, and according to Delécluze, Napoleon, learning of this project from David during a visit to the studio in 1800, was unenthusiastic about the choice of subject: "...you will tire yourself out painting the defeated," he is said to have commented. However, as the historian Warren Roberts has noted, the Spartan defeat at the pass at Thermopylae had been a commonplace theme in the 1790s, the subject of a least two plays, and an epic poem by Louis de Fontane, which was read at meetings of the Third Class of the Institute of which David was a member.[39] The relevance of the story to French military realities in 1800 is obvious, but as Roberts also notes, "To identify literary sources that could have suggested the Leonidas story to David is not to explain how he approached it."[40]

Here, and in forms that mirror Ingres's display of ideal masculine types, the array of male bodies ranges from the rosy-cheeked but massive-chested Leonidas, whose musculature invokes that of the Belvedere torso (another talismanic work from antiquity, much admired by Winckelmann and his followers), to the graceful ephebe who fastens his sandal. As in *Achilles Receiving the Ambassadors of Agamemnon*, the masculine ideal is embodied in forms that are either athletically muscled and relatively mature (for example, the blind Spartan on the left, supported by his slave, and the warrior seated just to the right of Leonidas), or in more slender and youthful incarnations. Notwithstanding Delécluze's ingenuous assertion that the tenderly embracing couple to Leonidas's left represent "a father and son," we are clearly in a universe of homosocial and homosexual relations, one in which, as the art historian Alex Potts has described it, "the ideal male body takes over the whole panorama of ideal selfhood in a radically short-circuited economy of identity and desire. He needs no female supplement, or only one that exists quite apart from the heroic male subject's testing ground."[41] In fact, the painting depicts a romanticized panoply of various male bonds beginning, at the far left, with the blind warrior guided by his attentive slave, moving to the garland-throwing youths with their interlaced arms, to the warrior seated at Leonidas's feet, gazing at his leader with somber intensity, to the kiss exchanged by the ephebe and his older lover. What Potts further calls the "quasi-totalitarian monism" of this masculine universe has probably little, if anything, to do with David's or Ingres's sexual proclivities, even if they could be known. On the contrary, the ease with which Ingres progressed from male to female nudity in his career, or David's equal facility with icons of male or

19 JACQUES-LOUIS DAVID Leonidas at Thermopylae, 1814

female desirability suggest that an examination of Jauss's concept of a horizon of expectation will be more useful in this context than psychobiography. Accordingly, in the discussions that follow, I largely defer the question of individual psychology insofar as I am more concerned with the erotic sensibility of an epoch than of any given individual.

The expulsion of femininity accompanying a heightened emphasis on the erotics of masculinity is given even more extreme expression in the twenty-four-year-old Girodet-Trioson's *Sleep of Endymion* (fig. 20), painted in 1791 during Girodet's tenure at the Mancini palace and subsequently exhibited in the Salon of 1793. For Girodet, nineteen years younger than David and one of his most valued students, the choice of subject as his obligatory *envoi* from Rome was itself remarkable, conceived as it was on the stylistic crest of the uncompromisingly virile Neoclassicism of the revolutionary period and the height of his own

youthful republican enthusiasm. However, Girodet's desire to differentiate himself from Davidian precepts, if not from David himself, as
expressed in his letter to Dr. Trioson (see note 22) helps to account for
the choice of Endymion as his subject and its treatment. For in choosing
a mythological subject possessing neither any obvious moral/political
nor ethical exemplarity, and inverting the Davidian model of active and
public masculinity, Girodet, like such artists as Bénigne Gagneraux
(1756–95) and Pierre-Paul Prud'hon (1758–1823), was presaging a new
archetype of desirable masculinity that would subsequently compete
with, if not altogether replace, the previous one (figs. 22 and 23).
Furthermore, as we shall see, by the 1790s the androgynous ephebe was
by no means an uncommon presence in French art and also had a
considerable ancestry—and increasing currency—in European Neoclassicism, in sculpture even more than painting. Notwithstanding
the originality or singularity of Girodet's *treatment* of the ephebic
body, Girodet was working with an already established motif, not
inventing one.

However one wants to account for it, the *Sleep of Endymion*, exhibited two months after the fall of the Gironde on 2 June 1793, and just
prior to the decree of 5 September making terror official government
policy, was enthusiastically received and immediately established
Girodet's reputation, although his later career was subject to distinct
troughs and crests, relative dry spells, and periodic—perhaps neurotic—
illnesses. The critics were particularly taken with what they agreed was
the "originality" of Girodet's treatment, but significantly, the remarkably effeminate quality of Endymion and the erotic dynamics implied
between the Zephyr figure and the sleeping shepherd provoked no comment as such. Consistent with the nature of most Salon criticism of the
period, commentary is more general than specific, based on consensual
academic precepts governing composition, color, tonality, and "truth"—
that is to say, the mimetic persuasiveness of the representation. For
example, among the positive responses, one finds the following: "…the
painting is really original [both] for its happy and poetic inventiveness
and for its daring and lively effect. The composition is of great character, the brushwork generous and velvety; in general, a bluish tint reigns
over the painting which is not sufficiently truthful."[42] Among the negative responses is this example: "…the study [that is to say, direct
observation of nature] has been sacrificed to the subject; for, in order to
give a lunar color to his painting, one sees nowhere the local color of
the flesh, the tone is bluish everywhere, which is not sufficiently truthful, and in order to present the exceptional form of Diana's lover, the

20 ANNE-LOUIS GIRODET-TRIOSON, The Sleep of Endymion, 1791

21 HYACINTHE AUBRY-LECOMTE after GIRODET-TRIOSON Head of Endymion, 1822

22 After BÉNIGNE GAGNERAUX Love Taming Strength, 1792

painter represents none of the truths of the natural."[43] Literal readings of Salon criticism do not, for the most part, provide a great deal of insight into the more psychological dimensions of subjective response or pictorial affect and it goes without saying that most Salon critics were neither Diderots, nor for that matter, even Chaussards.[44] The use of standard academic formulas to discuss works that seem so intensely eroticized to contemporary eyes is, however, itself an index of the shift in ideologies of gender, such that the audacity of the *Endymion*, at least with respect to the treatment of the two male figures, appears far more remarkable now than it evidently did to its contemporary audience.

The painting seems to have occupied a talismanic place for Girodet, a fact noted by all Girodet's biographers. He refused to sell it even to foreign royalty, exhibited the work in almost every Salon, and even signed his name as "Endymion" in a youthful letter to François Gérard.[45]

23 PIERRE–PAUL PRUD'HON The Union of Love and Friendship, 1793

While the *Sleep of Endymion* is probably Girodet's best-known painting and is now widely perceived as an unambiguously homoerotic staging of the male body, we do well to note that like his teacher David, Girodet moved easily between the antinomies of stalwart, virile masculinity (as in his history painting of the following year, *Hippocrates Refusing the Gifts of Artaxerxes,* an *exemplum virtutis* entirely in keeping with official aesthetic programmes of the 1790s) and later to quite conventional depictions of "normative" gender roles, (as in his *Pygmalion and Galatea* of 1819 with its simpering female nude and fatuous Cupid). Other contemporary French artists, such as Jean-Baptiste Regnault, demonstrated a similar fluidity, producing (somewhat exceptionally for the period) icons of eroticized femininity, as in the 1812 *Judgment of Paris* (fig. 24), succeeding manly heroes, or even couples in which a doll-like and diminutive femininity is contrasted

24 JEAN–BAPTISTE REGNAULT The Judgment of Paris, 1812

with an exaggerated masculinity, as in his *Abduction of Alcestis* of 1799 (fig. 25).

Throughout his career, Girodet's work, qualitative variations notwithstanding, is, like that of so many of his contemporaries, sufficiently flexible with respect to the expression of the (visual) codes of gender as to frustrate any attempt to extrapolate a particular sexual identity from the evidence of his work. Although he never married, Girodet was nevertheless linked for many years in close friendship with a woman—Julie Simons-Candeille—although their extant correspondence gives no indication as to whether their intimacy was sexual or not. Early biographers, who were also personal friends, such as P. A. Coupin and E.-F. Miel, hint at some kind of "sentimental" disaffection or disability,

25 JEAN-BAPTISTE REGNAULT The Abduction of Alcestis, 1799

but, in keeping with my earlier arguments, it seems clear from his other correspondence that intense relationships with other men were at least of equal importance.

Such bonds between men were a commonplace of Neoclassical culture. No breath of scandal attached to David, for example, in his undisguised desolation over the death of his young student Drouais, nor in his construction of a private monument to Drouais, containing his letters, in the garden of his house. If, in the case of these artists, we accept the compelling relevance of the notion of homosociality as the determining framework for aesthetic production, the biographical fact of David's marriage and its issue of four children, or Girodet's liaison with Julie Candeille, does not by that token diminish these artists' intense relationships with other men or their manifest investment in the sensual appeal or eroticism of male bodies.[46]

Girodet's *Endymion* turned out to be as much a popular success as a critical one. In addition to the lithographs produced after the painting or based upon the individual figures and heads—a number of versions exist (fig. 21) by Girodet's students Hyacinthe Aubry-Lecomte (1787–1858) and Charles de Chatillon—the painting inspired numerous reprises in the following fifteen to twenty years. The *Endymion* by Antonio Canova (1757–1822), sculpted in 1814, was clearly inspired by Girodet's example (fig. 26). Even as late as 1822 there were two paintings of the subject in the Salon. The *Endymion* of Louis-Edouard Rioult (1790–1855) also appropriated the device of the moonlight as surrogate for the goddess's bodily presence (fig. 28). Although modestly draped, Rioult's version still plays with visual codes of eroticized masculine display. Compositionally reduced to the sleeping youth alone, with its elaborate sfumato effects and Correggio-like modelling, it borrows as

26 ANTONIO CANOVA Endymion, 1819–22

27 C. MÜLLER after JÉRÔME MARTIN LANGLOIS Diana and Endymion, c. 1815

28 LOUIS-EDOUARD RIOULT Endymion, 1822

much from Prud'hon as from Girodet. The interpretation of the subject by Jérome Martin Langlois (1779-1838) features both the goddess and the Zephyr figure (engraved version fig. 27). Although upright, the position of Endymion's head and arms is almost identical to Girodet's figure, but what is striking in Langlois's treatment is the Zephyr's gesture of unveiling, drawing back the youth's mantle better to display him for the goddess's admiration. These are pictorial tropes whose prototypes are traditionally found either in sacred subjects, especially the display of the child Christ, or conventionally used to reveal the eroticized female body, as in so much Rococo and Restoration erotica. Langlois thus makes explicit one of the pervasive traits of Neoclassical art, namely its presentation of the male body as a body fashioned for display, a site of desirous looking. As a student of David, and, moreover, one who worked under his teacher's supervision on the *Leonidas*, it would seem to be the case that Langlois, like Girodet and Ingres, considered the display of the beautiful male body as a central tenet of Davidian aesthetic practice. David had himself been one of the first French artists to add an element of pictorial drama to his *académies*

29 JACQUES–LOUIS DAVID Hector, 1778

30 JACQUES–LOUIS DAVID Patroclus, 1780

31 JEAN-GERMAIN DROUAIS The Dying Athlete, 1785

32 LOUIS LAFITTE The Dying Warrior, 1795

33 FRANÇOIS–XAVIER FABRE Roman Soldier at Rest, 1788

(nude studies) as in the so-called *Hector* of 1778 and *Patroclus* of 1780 (figs. 29 and 30) whose titles derive not from David, but from later commentators' projection of a heroic narrative that their theatricality provokes. Moreover, works such as Drouais's *Dying Athlete* (1785) and the *Dying Warrior* (1795) of Louis Lafitte (1770–1828) were not only provided with specific classical identities, they were also charged with an almost palpable aura of presence, far exceeding the expected terms of the obligatory *académie* (figs. 31 and 32). François-Xavier Fabre himself produced a *Roman Soldier at Rest* in 1788 during his first year in Rome, and this work too makes of the Academy's requirement something more serious, more emotionally resonant than was typical for standard studio productions (fig. 33). A seductive and meditative *Paris* (previously attributed to Drouais) gazing somberly at his fatal apple is another such type (fig. 34).[47] In all these works, and many more, the presentation of the male nude suggests that the male body functioned not only, or not merely, as the fleshy envelope of the ideal, nor a routine academic excercise, but as an intensely cathected and psychologically loaded representation whose successful embodiment was perceived as a serious artistic challenge.

This element of bodily display is clearly a central feature of the *Sleep of Endymion*, and is further emphasized by Girodet's disembodiment of the female presence—the goddess Diana or Selene; earlier treatments routinely included her in the narrative. Comparison with Rococo treatments of this and similar subjects, such as François Boucher's 1739 *Aurora and Cephalus* (fig. 37) are themselves instructive. Despite his milk-and-rose complexion and silken blond curls, Boucher's Cephalus, the young hunter held in Aurora's loving gaze, is given a body that is still closely related to the sort of the sinewy and muscular model who would have posed for the initial *académie*. Although asleep, he is depicted in a semi-upright position. In fact, I have located no eighteenth-century versions of such subjects where the youth is represented entirely supine, body open to the gaze as in Girodet's version. Typically, as in an engraving by the seventeenth-century printmaker who illustrated the myth for Michel de Marolles's 1655 *Tableau du temple des Muses* (fig. 35), Endymion's body is positioned in a manner closer to a sitting than a sleeping position and typically too, he is given some attribute of actual or potential agency; in this instance, the arrows he still grasps firmly in his hand. In a similar manner, in the version of 1768 by Louis Lagrenée (1724–1805) Endymion is in a semi-upright position, and also is depicted with a powerful, full-chested body and decorously covered groin (fig. 36). In contrast to Girodet's treatment of

34 ANONYMOUS The Shepherd Paris, 1786–87

35 ANONYMOUS Endymion, "Tableau
du temple des Muses," 1655

36 LOUIS LAGRENÉE Diana and
Endymion, 1768

37 FRANÇOIS BOUCHER Aurora and Cephalus, 1739

Endymion, when treating a subject in which conventional gender roles are reversed, these earlier eighteenth-century artists often seem to be attempting a kind of equivalence and balance, so that despite the narratively motivated passivity of the shepherd, his body is given some degree of autonomy and self-possession. Likewise, it is often the body of the goddess that is more emphatically displayed so that despite her greater sexual assertion there is an effective dissipation of her power.[48] Even more significantly, where the male figures often appear more anatomically realistic, closely derived from the male model used by the artist, the goddesses are far more conventionalized, stock images of Rococo pulchritude. Neoclassical paintings such as Girodet's reverse this general tendency, not in the greater realism of the female figures, but in the greater idealization of the male bodies. This too suggests a transformation of erotic investment from the female body to the male.

Girodet's most dramatic departure from earlier renditions of the subject, however, resides in his decision to eliminate the goddess altogether, and in fact, his use of moonlight to signify her presence was considered by the critics of the time to have been one of the painting's happiest and most original features.[49] The elision of the goddess in turn ensures that the erotics of looking, exposure and bodily display are exclusively enacted between the two male figures, Endymion and Zephyr, and the implied male spectator. Although different versions of the myth exist, and certain among them ascribe a more active role to the shepherd (in one version, he fathers fifty children with the goddess), Girodet chose quite deliberately to emphasize his passivity.[50] Depicted in a languorous swoon of sleep, Endymion, object of the goddess's desire, becomes in Girodet's version the principal object of the viewer's look. Narratively speaking, although Endymion should be positioned towards the striking moonlight which is the medium, as it were, of the goddess's desire, he is instead positioned towards the viewer (a familiar pictorial device for the presentation of the female body) thereby providing maximal visual access to his limp, marmoreal and attenuated body, a body whose *raison d'être* resides primarily in its corporeal but unworldly beauty.

The pose predates the final composition and was conceived and fixed before Girodet worked through his conception of the goddess's implied presence in the moonlight itself.[51] There are numerous possible sources for the Endymion figure, including the Borghese Endymion sarcophagus and even a Hellenistic marble statue of Endymion, restored and renovated in Italy by Gavin Hamilton in 1776, now in the British Museum (fig. 38). Whatever his sources, however, they did not supply

38 Endymion (detail), Hellenistic statue restored by Gavin Hamilton in 1776

him with those features of the finished work that push Endymion's anatomy to the very brink of the grotesque. The head, especially, is startlingly stylized; the swelling neck enlarged, the jawbone nearly imperceptible, the profile strangely compressed. Much attention has been lavished on the glossy mantle of curls, limned by the light and touched by a ribbon. Although there was no recorded comment on the figure's androgyny at its first public reception, in 1814, when the painting was again exhibited, the issue was raised only to be resolved:

> The Englishman: "Doesn't Endymion's head look too much like a woman's head? Isn't Zephyr too heavy, and given too mannered a pose?"
>
> The Frenchman: "I'm not of your opinion with respect to Endymion's head; it is beautiful and likely to charm a divinity, who, like our women, would be captivated more through her eyes than her heart: Girodet seems to me to have rendered the *beau idéal* as well as the best Greek artists of Pericles' time, and you admire in their works what you believe you have the right to criticize in this instance. Be consistent."[52]

While the painting's contemporary critics as well as the Academy's judges were most taken with the novelty of Girodet's treatment—the moonlight effect, the elision of the goddess—consideration of the painting within the context of homosociality requires that we attend to the relations between the two male figures. For despite the narrative frame—the desperate passion of the goddess for a beautiful youth—what we actually see is the figure of Eros/Zephyr, prepubescent and fully as eroticized as Endymion, gazing directly at the sleeping youth, a surrogate *both* for the invisible goddess and the unacknowledged spectator. That look, playful and knowing—even salacious—troubles those recent readings of this work, such as Thomas E. Crow's, that want to recover a political, indeed a Jacobin meaning for the image, but in so doing pass far too quickly over considerations of its insistent sexual dynamics.[53] Even if one wishes to argue, as does Crow, that Endymion is the symbolic representation of the ideal, tailored to the needs of Jacobin political discourse, it is still necessary to acknowledge that two eroticized male bodies inhabit the pictorial space, that both are displayed for an implied male spectator, and while the subject of the work is the love of the goddess for the shepherd, the manifest content of the work pivots on the male gaze at the male body. Moreover, the accentuated carnality of the winged boy invokes a lengthy art-historical lineage of seductive or licentious ephebes, Ganymedes, Amors, Zephyrs and angels garnered from classical, Renaissance and Mannerist prototypes, hardly in keeping with the exigencies of republican propaganda.

The oneiric atmosphere of sensual plenitude and the erotic self-sufficiency of the two male figures also trouble an earlier reading by Roland Barthes, who suggested that the painting's theme was the aporia of sexual difference, an anxious evocation of castration that made it the apt emblem for Balzac's castrato Zambinella.[54] Rather, it seems far more plausible to read the painting in its own terms; that is to say, an encounter between two highly seductive male protagonists whose very bodies suggest an incorporation of the feminine presence that the artist has quite deliberately and literally disembodied. Such a pictorial device seems less to embody Barthes's aporia of sexual difference than to evidence a wish to escape sexual difference altogether. *The Sleep* of *Endymion*, despite the androgyny of its protagonists, can thus be considered as fully in keeping with the masculinization of elite visual culture that is one of the characteristic features of Neoclassicism. By dispelling the goddess, who represents difference, the painting works to dispel the fantasmatic threat of castration that the fact of difference may invoke.

Exploring the modalities of homosociality in elite visual culture, however, does not necessarily depend on the depiction of male bodies. In this respect, paintings that feature female protagonists can also be read within its presiding terms. For example, and within the context of post-Thermidorian erotic and aesthetic sensibilities, it is of some significance to note that Girodet's *Burial of Atala* of 1808 (fig. 39) created at least as much of a sensation as did his *Sleep of Endymion*, one fueled by the immense popularity of Chateaubriand's eponymous novel of 1801. Where Girodet's *Sleep of Endymion* illustrates one circuit for homoerotic and homosocial desire, *The Burial of Atala*—an eroticized female corpse suspended between two men—can be viewed as its historical, structural and psychosexual counterpart. For although the female figure is central to the composition, the woman's body functions formally to link the two men, and the men, representing the claims of physical desire in the person of the beautiful, heathen youth Chactas, and those of religious renunciation in the person of the priest, Père Aubry, provide the meaning of Atala's life, as well as her death. As in the history of Brutus, relations between the men are relayed through the body of the woman.

Insofar as the central figure in the painting *is* a woman, the *Burial of Atala* constitutes something of a departure among the most popular and critically lauded history paintings in the revolutionary and post-Thermidorian period. With the possible exception of Gérard's *Kiss of Psyche* of 1798, few large-scale female figures that appeared in revolutionary or post-revolutionary Salons garnered such praise and enthusiasm. However, and as is frequently the case with history painting, one can find earlier precedents for the theme. Girodet was by no means the first artist to treat the subject; Pierre Gautherot, for example, had exhibited a *Funeral Procession of Atala* as early as the Salon of 1802.[55] Between the appearance of Chateaubriand's short novel (included, with the companion novella René in his 1802 *Le Génie du Christianisme*) and the next two decades, no fewer than thirteen paintings on the subject were produced, as were countless elite and popular prints, illustrated books, knick-knacks, clocks, fabric designs, wax dolls and puppets.[56] The extraordinary popularity of Chateaubriand's short novel, the corresponding fanfare that greeted Girodet's canvas, and the large-scale production of Atala-related memorabilia suggests that *Atala* spoke to its readers and spectators of 1808 in important ways. These were the post-revolutionary audiences of the Napoleonic empire, an empire that attempted to identify itself with an "accomplished" revolution while simultaneously implementing an imperial "*rappel a l'ordre.*"

As scholars of French literature such as Naomi Schor and Margaret Waller have argued, the enthusiasm which greeted *Atala* was fostered by the cultural and psychic resonance of an image of immobilized and deactivated femininity that significantly reversed the imagery of political militancy and energy previously represented by the revolutionary goddess of liberty, Marianne.[57] Indeed, it would be hard to imagine an image of femininity better suited to counter any lingering historical memory of the "furies" of the guillotine, or the rioting women of the insurrections of Germinal and Prairial of 1795.

Waller's discussion elaborates the ways by which René (the romantic male protagonist of Chateaubriand's novel of 1802) functioned as a subject of empathetic (masculine) identification, while Atala became a wholly commodified (and possessable) *image* of sanctified and extinguished femininity. In a complementary discussion, Schor characterizes the figure of Atala as a neutralized and disempowered counterpart to the image of the now-dethroned revolutionary Marianne. For Schor, the Indian maiden who kills herself rather than succumb to her desire for Chactas and violate her mother's deathbed dedication of Atala's virginity to God, emblematizes the "chaining" and immobilizing of the female heroine that is one of the dominant motifs of French nineteenth-century literature. This goes far to explain why artists such as Girodet preferred to depict Atala's death or burial rather than earlier incidents in the novel, such as Atala's freeing of Chactas after he is taken prisoner by her father. Such a choice permits both an eroticizing of the female body, and a containment of that eroticism (the heroine is dead, after all). Suspended between the heroically beautiful Chactas and the paternal figure of Père Aubry, Atala thus functions as a physical bridge between the two male figures, alluringly erotic, and poignantly dead.[58]

In art and in life, homosociality does not necessarily depend on the outright elimination of femininity, but rather, on the more powerful bonds that unite men to one another and which collectively operate to secure the subordinate position of women. *Atala* may thus be considered a liminal painting in a liminal period, looking backwards, as it were, to the presiding terms of homosociality in Neoclassical visual culture, anticipating, on the other hand, the new erotic paradigm of later nineteenth-century French culture, reinstating a passive feminine figure as the predominant and culturally sanctioned figure of desire.

Any consideration of images of heroicized or otherwise idealized masculininity in French Neoclassical art requires some explanation for their psychological appeal. Clearly, and by virtue of their status as ideals it seems reasonable to suppose that such images operate as much

39 ANNE-LOUIS GIRODET-TRIOSON The Burial of Atala, 1808

on the psychological level of narcissistic identification as they do on the level of homosocial desire. The beauty of the ideal male figure may thus solicit the male spectator's fantasmatic identification with an image of ennobled self-contained perfection that functions as a type of ego-ideal. Equally, icons of the masculine ideal—in either their feminized or masculinized versions—may provoke desires analogous to those at stake in the gaze of male spectators at the female nude. Neoclassical painting navigates these dangerous frontiers by furnishing the displayed male body with an ethical, a political, and most emphatically, an aesthetic alibi, thereby negotiating—however precariously—the actual social proscriptions against same-sex desire. Furthermore, the exemplarity of masculine beauty, like the exemplarity of the dramatis personae themselves, provides an ideal fiction for masculine identifications which, by virtue of their universalizing address and their distance from the world actually inhabited by French men and women elide very real differences and conflicts within class and gender. Images of ideal manhood therefore possess an obvious ideological utility insofar as an exalted personification of Man effectively overrides and subsumes the material actualities of economic and gender inequality. In this respect, we might recall that after establishing the distinction between "active" and "passive" citizens, the rhetoric of revolutionary culture acknowledged no differences between and among men other than those distinguishing aristocrats from republicans, and conspirators from patriots.[59] Needless to say, throughout the revolution, women remained defined as "passive" citizens, along with children, the mad, foreigners and the indigent.

Within the visual terms of ideal manhood, the cultural currency of two ostensibly opposed models of ideal masculinity, like the contradictions that can be identified within David's or Girodet's imagery of masculinity, is hardly a local, or narrowly historical contradiction. Indeed, the durability of these two models of ideal masculinity supports the observation that the ideology of masculinity, previously remarked, is at any given moment internally divided and split. An official aesthetic (and political) discourse of heroic, active, and phallic masculinity, a masculinity that is charged with the representation of public, civic, and indeed martial values and from which all traces of the feminine are deliberately expunged, can be seen to coexist with other visions of masculinity that figure very different visions of the ideal. These latter openly celebrate a vision of youthful and passive male beauty, quite detached from scenarios of stoic, patriotic resolve. In contrast to the nominal ideal of active and virile manhood, the feminized ephebe, often deactivated or disempowered, invites a relationship with the viewer that is essentially contemplative, private and hedonistic, and whose unworldly beauty, graceful *mollese*, and sensuous appeal were openly acknowledged and celebrated, even as a baleful and corrupting "effeminacy" was ritually denounced and condemned.

Such a recognition of these contradictions within Neoclassical art might serve us by "making strange," (in the meaning conveyed by the Russian formalist notion of *ostranenie*) representations of masculinity itself.[60] Thus, the act of defamiliarizing the familiar monuments of French Neoclassicism, as well as its more obscure productions, may permit us to see both the implacable and literally murderous visions of stoic manhood exemplified by David's Brutus (fig. 17) or Canova's Hercules (fig. 55)—Alex Potts's "quasi-totalitarian monism"—as well as the renditions of effeminate or otherwise disempowered manhood as equally problematic, equally fraught, and perhaps equally pathological indices of phallocentric psychic and political economies. In the former instance, femininity, representing the affective, "private" claims of love (familial or sexual) needs be sacrificed to the higher realms of the public, civic, and collective weal; in the latter, femininity, associated with eroticism, pleasure, and purely sentimental ties, is literally elimi-nated, but is nevertheless recuperated within an entirely masculine circuit in which active and passive drives and subject positions are respectively expressed in male bodies.

Although the elision of femininity and its reincorporation within an ideal masculine figure is a visual phenomenon characteristic of Neo-classicism and its historical moment, it is nevertheless the case that masculinization, considered as a psychic and social process, inevitably requires a repudiation of the maternal body, indeed its repression.[61] Nevertheless, and as the prevalence of feminized male bodies attest, what must be unconsciously expelled in the formation of male sub-jectivity does not by that token simply vanish into air. In Freud's theories of the formation of sexual subjectivity, an original (infantile, polymorphous) sexuality is variously shaped into the social mold of gender, and the nature of this process results in the repression of those desires and identifications that cannot be assimilated within the accepted norm of compulsory heterosexuality. At the same time, the bond to the mother and the initial identification with her must be violently repudiated. What I have called the feminized masculine and the masculinized masculine remain, nonetheless, both available possibilities within the organization of homosocial desire whether simultaneously or alternatively manifested. To the extent, however, that femininity is both differentially and negatively defined in relation to the masculine norm, and to the extent that women are positioned as Other (and lesser) within patriarchal systems, it is hardly surprising that a discourse of ideal masculinity, supported by philosophical as well as political rationalization, would inscribe conventional feminine attrib-utes and features covertly—or not so covertly—within the colonizing terms of its own narcissistic self-celebration.

It is for this reason too that homosocial desire rather than the more exclusive category of homoerotic desire has the greater explanatory force. Here it is important to recall that within Neoclassical culture the boundaries between a cult of male friendship (and male beauty) and what we would now consider as "homosexual" or even homoerotic rela-tions are not easily drawn. In keeping with this ambiguity, the life and work of J.-J. Winckelmann as it was perceived by the eighteenth and early nineteenth centuries suggests how the homoerotic may be subsumed within the homosocial. The nature of Winckelmann's personal, scholarly and psychosexual investments in the classical art that he studied and venerated need not concern us here (I will return to them in the following chapter), although many later commentators have understood him to be "homosexual" in the modern sense. Even his sordid murder—knifed by an adventurer in an inn in Trieste in 1768—has been thought to have had a sexual motive, "rough trade" *avant la lettre*. Despite the fact that Winckelmann did in fact have sexual relations with young men in Italy, if not before (they are discussed in certain of his letters to close friends), we do better, historically speaking, to consider Winckelmann's writing, friendships and sexual relations within the same context provided by Goethe in his memorializing essay of 1805:

> We react with astonishment when, with regard to two young men, we hear of passionate fulfillment of love's desire, the bliss of being inseparable, lifelong devotion, or the need to follow the other into death....Winckelmann felt born for friendship of that kind. He experienced his real self only in the context of friendship and could perceive himself as a whole only if he was complemented by another...[62]
>
> Winckelmann, by nature was receptive to such beauty [of the Olympian Jupiter]. He first became acquainted with it in ancient literature, but he encountered beauty more intimately in the visual arts, where one learns to recognize it before perceiving and appreciating its manifestations in nature.
>
> If the need for friendship and for beauty are both satisfied by the same object, then man's happiness and gratitude seem to know no limit. He will gladly give all he owns as a token of his devotion and admiration.
>
> Hence we often find Winckelmann in the company of beautiful young men. He never seems more alive and likable than in these often fleeting moments.[63]

Goethe's unembarrassed acceptance of eroticized male friendship is thus fully consistent with the conventionalized terms of Neoclassical homosociality. It may equally attest to Goethe's own acceptance of same-sex desire. Nevertheless, while the romantic male friendships of eighteenth-century culture were often implicitly understood by contemporaries as being erotically charged, this was categorically distinguished from more "public" forms of deviance—notably sodomy—associated with dissolute aristocrats, pederastic clergy, or male prostitutes. Furthermore, and in contrast to modern notions of "the" homosexual, effeminacy and even same-sex lovemaking were as likely to be considered evidence of dissolution and libertinage in general than to be perceived according to modern notions of same-sex exclusivity.[64] In eighteenth-century France, and with certain conspicuous exceptions, homosexuality, in the modern sense of the term, was officially condemned but rarely prosecuted.[65]

Sodomy and pederasty—however desultorily prosecuted—nevertheless constituted the juridical divide between licit and illicit male relationships. For aristocratic men of the *ancien régime*, even crossing this divide was generally tolerated. That said, there existed what could be called a homosocial continuum of intense and more or less romantic male friendships. That these were, unsurprisingly, far more common than male/female friendships was highly overdetermined, given such obvious factors as the lack of parity in men and women's education, the institutional segregation of the sexes (for instance, separate schools) and the severe constraints on women's mobility in general. Unmarried young women of the upper classes had virtually no public and social mobility insofar as decency, decorum and even marriage prospects depended on their sequestration and chaperonage. Although married women, particularly of the highest and lowest classes, enjoyed various degrees of autonomy—for aristocratic women, primarily in the domain of social life—relations of intellectual, economic, and sexual equality were possible only between men. In such circumstances, there was little to foster the development of non-sexual but intimate friendships between men and unmarried women, and much to discourage even their possibility.

The Roman Experience

The homosocial character of the republic of letters was, if anything, even more pronounced in the Roman artworld, "the Academy of Europe." The Roman sojourn of most history painters needs be considered as another tributary to the masculinization of French Neoclassicism, continuing young artists' aesthetic and cultural formation begun in the Ecole and within their teachers' studios. Eighteenth-century Rome was not only the *point de dissémination* for Neoclassicism, the place where Winckelmann became Winckelmann and David became

David, but also the revered site of a passionately invested, if largely imaginary antiquity. For the young artists who arrived at the Mancini palace for their state-supported sojourns, or for the many other artists who came on their own, such as Bénigne Gagneraux or Philippe-Auguste Hennequin (1762–1833), Rome was obviously the spiritual as well as the physical locus of what French art historians call *anticomanie* (a mania for the antique). By the 1770s, Winckelmann's writings were their aesthetic *vade mecum*, supplemented by the various illustrated collections of antiquities both classical and pre-classical, such as the folios of de Montfaucon and d'Hancarville, and the three volumes of Sir William Hamilton's collection of ancient vases illustrated by Tischbein. These were further supplemented by engraved reproductions of the art and objects excavated at Pompeii and Herculaneum. It was, moreover, a city in which the Vatican museums—the Pio Clementini and the Capitoline and the princely collections of the Giustinini, Barberini, Albani, Borghese and Ottoboni—were generally available to artists, both foreign and Italian. Within the cosmopolitan world of literary and artistic Rome, the cult of male beauty was a central, unanimously upheld tenet, and the Apollo Belvedere its unrivaled totem (fig. 66). The Roman experience seems also to have fostered intense and, as we will see, somewhat fetishistic viewing relations with antique sculptures, even as it provided other artistic influences such as sixteenth- and seventeenth-century Italian painting.

As in the world of the Ecole Royale in Paris and the various artists' studios where the young artists had received their previous training, in Rome the world of the Mancini palace was largely an all-male preserve. Although the directors of the Academy in the pre-revolutionary and revolutionary period (Joseph-Marie Vien, 1775–79; Louis-Jean Lagrenée, 1781–87; François-Guillaume Ménageot, 1787–90) were permitted to bring their families with them, the married students were not. Pensioners took their meals at the palace, under whose roof they had their studios as well as their lodgings, their lectures, their plaster casts, their library, and, of course, their (male) models. Like France, most European countries had colonies of resident artists and there was a considerable degree of fraternization. This occurred not only in the cafés and in the periodic exhibitions held at the French Academy, but in the local evening drawing academies run by Roman artists as well as the two "official" academies, the French Academy (which permitted foreign artists and non-pensioners to attend evening life-classes) and the Accademia di San Luca, which was open to students from all countries. Furthermore, after 1754, there were daily life-classes held at the the the

Accademia del Disegno, popularly known as the Accademia del Nudo, also open to students of all nations.[66]

Artistic Rome in the second half of the eighteenth-century was therefore not only the fulcrum of the Neoclassic style, based on the antiquities in the collections, the monuments, and the ongoing excavations, and based, as well, on the production of the living artists who either lived or temporarily worked there, it was also steeped in the study of male bodies in primarily all-male environments. Furthermore, the privileged aesthetic place of the ephebic youth in elite visual production had an interesting parallel in Italian musical life, specifically, in the institution of the castrati—vocal androgynes, so to speak (in France, however, the castration of boys to preserve their voices had always been forbidden).[67] In this respect, Roland Barthes's linking of Balzac's "heroine" Zambinella—a castrato who "passes" for a beautiful woman—to Girodet's Endymion is historically as well as psychically suggestive. Since Rome was a papal state, moreover, women were forbidden to perform publicly in theaters; male transvestite performers filled the breach and the most famous and beautiful among them dined with (and bedded) cardinals and princes. Recovering the ambience of artistic Rome requires consideration too of its transient as well as resident population—the well-heeled aristocrats or dilettanti, the antiquarians, pedlars and forgers of antiquities, the ciceroni of lesser and greater repute, renegade Freemasons and adventurers such as Cagliostro, and a constant parade of incognito royals.

As one of the principal cities of the Grand Tour, Rome was a sexual playground for foreign men, on leave from their estates, families, colleges, academies and associates in Germany, Britain and Scandinavia. Indeed, the Grand Tour, as G. S. Rousseau and others have argued, "could be a disguise for the 'erotic tour'—homosexual as well as heterosexual."[68] Looking at portraits of the young men who commissioned Louis Gauffier (who sat out the Revolution in Rome) to do their official Grand Tour portraits in the 1790s (this was a genre whose most sought-after specialist was the Roman Pompeo Batoni) it is under-standable why scholars have spoken of a "homosexualization" of Neoclassical culture (fig. 40 and pl. I).[69] Nevertheless, insofar as these are portraits and not living men, they are more usefully considered as collective and more or less idealizing self-representations, rather than statements of a particular sexual identity. Striking in their narcissistic self-display, as well as their seductive address to the viewer, such representations of male subjects became less and less acceptable after the Restoration period. A re-masculinization of male portraiture, with a concomitant de-emphasis of the sensual body (think, for example, of Eugène Delacroix's *Louis Auguste Schwiter* of 1830, fig.108)—parallels the eclipse of the desirable male nude of Neoclassical art.

However diligent and professionally ambitious the young artists at the French Academy and their cohorts might have been, the complex gender dynamics of the Roman art world was at least part of the social and cultural environment in which they were formed. Moreover, the Neoclassical style that had been formed in Rome by foreign artists (with the exception of Canova) was in full flower well before the arrival in Rome of the students of David, Regnault, or Vien. Rome, therefore, and the Neoclassical style it fostered and disseminated, was of central importance in promoting an erotics of manhood, while affirming a politico-ethical ideal of fraternal bonds and affiliations within which women had no place. This development was given its most sublime endorsement in Mozart's *The Magic Flute*, which had its première in 1792, an homage to the fraternal and patriarchal appeal of a rapidly growing Freemasonry, which the popes energetically, but vainly tried to extirpate.[70]

My argument here with respect to the terms for understanding male same-sex relationships in the Neoclassical period is therefore somewhat analogous to what Adrienne Rich termed a "lesbian continuum."[71] Describing the range of affective possibilities between women, Rich speculated that there is in fact no strict division between what distinguishes a sexual, that is, lesbian, relationship from intense and loving but non-sexual friendships. It is true that this viewpoint has been vigorously contested by other feminists for its essentializing of the category "woman" and criticized by many lesbian writers on the grounds that it unwittingly colludes with the discursive effacement of lesbianism by neglecting that which defines lesbianism and constitutes the particular subjectivity of lesbian women. Rich's formulation has also been criticized for its tendency to downplay the role of female sexuality overall, privileging instead a kind of feminine *agape* over a less utopian and far more gritty *eros*. Rich's formulation, however, may have greater descriptive utility, despite analogous problems, in a masculine context. The notion of a homosocial continuum, which extends from relatively de-eroticized forms of male bonding to lifetime sexual unions and all variations between, helps to explain why ostensibly "straight" artists like David and Gauffier, "homosexual" intellectuals like Winckelmann, sexually ambiguous figures like Girodet, misogynist *célibataires* like Quatremère de Quincy, and total sexual enigmas like Canova could have had an equal investment in the cult of male beauty,

40 LOUIS GAUFFIER An Officer of the Army of the Cisalpine Republic, 1801

in close male friendships, and in a concept of the ideal whose most fundamental theoretical precepts effectively precluded a place for femininity. Although images of ideal female nudes were, of course, produced by Neoclassical artists (notably Canova, there are relatively few in the paintings of David and Girodet), Neoclassical aesthetic treatises and aesthetic discourse, as we will see, tend to assume the masculinity of the nude *per se*. For although the French revolutionary period is characterized by particularly misogynistic tendencies, the actual position of most women within European culture was such as effectively to disqualify them not only from the republic of letters preceding the birth of the civil sphere, but from the fraternal orders of friendship and their reciprocal affective bonds that were its foundation.

Within the context of French revolutionary and post-revolutionary culture, these tendencies were doubtless facilitated by the masculine ethos of republicanism itself, one of whose justifications for the political exclusion of women (there were many) was the association of femininity with the corruption of the *ancien régime* and a venerable association of women with the forces of disorder and misrule. No doubt further contributing to the general distaste for female political militancy was the historical memory of the Fronde in which aristocratic women had been both active and prominent, inaugurating "a feminism of action if not of doctrine."[72] The pyschosexual analogue to the discursive and political exclusion and denigration of (female) femininity may accordingly have operated to promote its covert and symptomatic incorporation within reassuring representations of godlike youth or manhood. The coexistence of an excessive masculinity, as exemplified by the figures of David's Horatii (fig. 4), and on the other hand, a feminized version, such as Patroclus in Ingres's *Achilles Receiving the Ambassadors of Agamemnon* (fig. 10) or Girodet's Endymion (fig. 20), may be taken therefore, as testimonial to an internalized division inhabiting the patriarchal Imaginary within which the acknowledgment of sexual difference implies always a threat to the fictive—and fragile— integrity and unity of the male subject.

In a more strictly historical sense (and in keeping with analogous arguments made by other scholars and theorists for different times and places), there is reason to suppose that the lived experience of historical trauma plays a determining role in the intrapsychic mechanisms of subjectivity. Hence, in the fulcrum of revolution and counterrevolution, where traditional roles, structures, institutions and social relations are suddenly overturned, the terms for and of an idealized masculinity are unlikely to be either fixed or stable. In a world turned upside down, we may well ask what are the consequences for what Kaja Silverman terms the "dominant fiction" that serves to secure, among other things, the "natural" order of gender. Taking by way of example Lynn Hunt's description of the revolutionary overturning of a symbolic universe in which the monarchical father ruled his hierarchically positioned children/subjects to a new but volatile order defined as a fraternal (and parricidal) band of brothers, we may also ask how this transformation impacts upon the structure of male subjectivity. Finally, in a brief and condensed historical moment that not only witnessed the collapse of a venerable symbolic system, but produced as well the repetitive and public spectacle of bodies mechanically–depersonally–decapitated, an unprecedented, quasi-industrial mechanics of death, the belief in the integrity of the body was drastically subverted.[73] It may well be the case that the manifest preoccupation with perfect male bodies that are at the same time threatened, symbolically castrated, or dead speaks both to (and of) a defensive aggrandizement of masculinity and the concomitant acknowledgment of its vulnerability–the threats that assail it both materially and psychically. Hence, while the bodies of Endymion and many of his brethren are manifestly beautiful and self-contained, they are also dead, disempowered, or otherwise "in trouble." Such a diagnostic accords well with Delécluze's disturbing fantasy provoked by the sight of Mme de Noailles at her sketch pad. For what is united in this fantasy is the traumatic memory of the guillotine and the atmosphere of the Terror, both of which are deflected away from the world of men, of politics, of the state, coming to rest, instead, upon the woman, herself a locus of those primal masculine anxieties that Freud identified with unconscious fears of castration.

While it may not be possible to recover fully the mentalities that govern and underpin the infinitely complex and highly mediated forms of elite culture, it is nevertheless the case that these forms cannot but register the tidal changes in human consciousness within which gender is variously shaped. In the conviction that cultural texts manifest their own unconscious economies, we may thus attempt to interrogate the stakes that undergird their characteristic manifestations. Rather than privilege Brutus over Endymion (or *vice versa*), and in light of our contemporary recognition of the changing shapes of the masculine ideal, we therefore do well to try and identify those historical circumstances and determinations that variously promote one fantasy of masculinity over the other.

The feminine…is not outside the masculine, its reassuring canny opposite, it is inside the masculine, its uncanny difference from itself.

SHOSHANA FELMAN "Re-reading Femininity"[1]

Because the ephebic body was developed as a type within Greek classical art, and because classical art was a recurring influence in French history painting, one cannot pinpoint exactly when it became a significant presence in France. Certainly, charming shepherds and graceful adolescent deities are everywhere to be seen in the art of the early eighteenth century. Their numbers increased throughout the century, and their popular appeal was further bolstered by a parallel production of prints. Nevertheless, the appearance and role of the ephebic youth in Neoclassicism seems noticeably different from that of its earlier incarnations, a difference apparent in almost any comparison between Rococo and Neoclassical versions. The representation of the young god, for example, in Louis Lagrenée's 1769 *Psyche Surprising the Sleeping Eros* (fig. 42), despite the wings and unnaturally diminutive hands, is a fairly realistic rendering of an adolescent boy's body. Its greater degree of realism in comparison to the more conventionalized rendering of Psyche suggests, as do contemporary works by Joseph-Benoît Suvée (1743–1807), Jean-Baptiste-Henri Deshays (1729–65), Jean Bernard Restout (1732–97), Regnault and others, that the male figure inspired more empirical attention, consistent with the new institutional emphasis on working directly from the male model. Turning to a later depiction of Amor, Jacques-Louis Copia's engraving of *Sappho Inspired by Love* by François Devosge (1732–1811) from the Salon of 1795 (fig. 43), one can see immediately how the adolescent body has not only been more stylized, but unmistakably feminized, the hip arched and rounded, the thighs plumper, the abdomen fuller.

Exploring the Neoclassical predilection for androgynous ephebes, and the functions they served requires that we integrate the work of familiar artists like David, Girodet, and Prud'hon with work by less well-known artists such as François-Xavier Fabre, Bénigne Gagneraux, Jean-Baptiste Regnault or Charles Meynier, all of whom have remained outside the modern canon. Insofar as modern art historians have tended to consider such artists outside and apart from a retrospectively conceived great tradition—aesthetic non-contenders—they have precluded the possibility of developing either a theoretical or indeed an historical apparatus with which to recover their significance. There is also a tendency for scholars of French Neoclassical art to focus so exclusively on France as to miss the correspondences, influences and shared context—especially in the cultural crucible of Rome—that acted upon French artists, with the result that the prior examples provided by British artists such as Thomas Banks (1735–1805), John Flaxman (1755–1826), Gavin Hamilton and Benjamin West, Italians such as Antonio Canova, Germans such as Anton Raphael Mengs (1728–79), or Scandinavians such as Johan Tobias Sergel (1740–1814) and Bertel Thorvaldsen (c. 1770–1844) are ignored or only cursorily acknowledged.[2]

42 LOUIS LAGRENÉE Psyche Surprising the Sleeping Eros, 1769

43 JACQUES-LOUIS COPIA after FRANÇOIS DEVOSGE Sappho Inspired by Love, 1795

By way of exploring what I will inelegantly call the ideological value of the Neoclassical ephebe, I want to begin my discussion with several works featuring the ephebic god or hero, demonstrating how it fulfilled certain requirements (ideological, aesthetic, and psychological) for its makers and its audience. Such feminized and marmoreal but curiously eroticized male bodies might well be characterized as the Horatii's Other, and they are, interestingly, far more in evidence in the art of the 1790s than their martial brethren. In the guise of Amor or

Paris, of Abel or Ganymede—even as a "real" historical subject—these ephebic translations of the *beau idéal* became (arguably) the dominant visual emblem for the masculine ideal during most of the revolutionary and post-revolutionary period.

Although Charles Meynier (1768–1832) remains relatively obscure, his inclusion in the historic 1974 Grand Palais exhibition, "David à Delacroix," was instrumental in sparking renewed interest in his work, just as it did for the period it covered.[3] Like many of the other artists formed consecutively by the Ecole des Beaux-Arts, an established older artist (in this case, Joseph-Marie Vien), and finally, the Roman sojourn at the French Academy, Meynier proved himself a man for all seasons, adapting to the different aesthetic requirements of the Republic, the Empire, and the two Restorations. In like manner, Meynier's subjects were produced in obedience to the demands of the moment: encompassing narratives of Roman history as well as the classically derived *sujets gracieux* so fashionable in the 1790s; Napoleonic battle scenes ten years later; and finally, religious subjects for churches commissioned by the Restoration arts administration.[4] The painting that I want to consider here, however, is a product of the revolutionary moment, although, like Girodet's *Sleep of Endymion*, it was painted in the Mancini palace, the home of the Academy in Rome. Meynier dated his *Adolescent Eros Weeping Over the Portrait of the Lost Psyche* (fig. 1 and pl. II) to 1792, which makes it a near contemporary of Girodet's more familiar painting, but it was only exhibited in the Salon of 1795. In the absence of much documentation on the work before its Salon appearance, the relationship between the two artists, and indeed the two works, must remain conjectural. In his brief discussion of the work, the art historian Régis Michel assumes that the painting is directly modelled upon Girodet's, although there seems no reason not to assume the reverse influence.[5] What is more significant, however, is that whatever the qualitative and aesthetic distinctions one might wish to draw between the two paintings, the existence of Meynier's, as well as earlier works by other artists working in Rome, demonstrates that the cultural currency of the feminized ephebe not only predated the work of the young Davidians, but was an available iconographic type in circulation within Neoclassical visual culture.[6] To the extent that these distinctive icons of grace and beauty are both generic (the ephebic type was formalized in classical Greece) and historically specific (in the sense of their large-scale revival in Neoclassical art) an examination of their function in late eighteenth- and early nineteenth-century elite culture needs to consider both historical matrices.

With his serpentine contours, sinuously rounded left hip, and elegantly flowing limbs, Meynier's Eros might superficially appear more closely allied to the pneumatic female figures of the nineteenth-century Ingres than to his teacher Vien's Greek subjects. Moreover, Meynier's ambitiously scaled painting (153 x 202 cm, over 5 x 6½ ft), which was probably his official *envoi* from Rome, is, like Ingres's *Achilles Receiving the Ambassadors of Agamemnon*, intended as a virtuoso demonstration of theoretical, formal and aesthetic expertise. Like Ingres's painting too, this expertise is martialed to display his ability to produce an erudite and unmistakably Winckelmannian notion of the *beau idéal*. Meynier's Eros thus stands at the intersection of four overlapping aesthetic tributaries: classical art theory as it was codified within the pedagogy of the Ecole Royale and the Academy and within which the *beau idéal* was a central tenet; the Winckelmannian elevation of the ephebic youth to the apogee of ideal beauty; the Neoclassical predilection for male, rather than female nudes; and last, the vogue for those mythological subjects that French art criticism designated with the term "Anacreontism."[7]

Anacreontism refers to the sixth-century Greek poet Anacreon whose popularity after his mid-eighteenth century revival continued through the following century, acknowledged even by Gautier and Baudelaire, both of whom wrote homages to the poet. According to the French publisher D'Ambroise Firmin Didot:

> From the earliest time of antiquity, the name of Anacreon recalls the most gracious aspects of poetry. "The poetry of Anacreon deals entirely with love," said Cicero; and the Anacreontic name will always be associated with this pleasing genre, dear above all to the French, a happy people, living in a temperate climate where the vine flourishes, and who, like the Athenians, have the gift of enjoying life, with their inborn playfulness, liveliness and elegance of wit.[8]

In a more general sense, however, Anacreontism refers to the continued enthusiasm for all things Greek that by the last years of the eighteenth century more than rivaled the preoccupation with Republican Rome, a shift paralleled by the revival of Racine (whose plays had been censored under the "cultural revolution" of Year II) and the relative eclipse of Corneille.[9] It is, as Firmin Didot emphasized, further associated with the prevalence of romantic or erotic subject matter as opposed to civic or martial themes. Since its standard art-historical discussion in 1916, it has been described as a form of Alexandrianism:

Alexandrianism is for us, in the broadest sense, the taste for a mythology that is graceful, tender, and voluptuous, and consequently for a prettified form, prettiness extending even to mannerism. The inspiration comes from Asiatic Greece, whether from Anacreon of Teos and Sappho of Lesbos (who lived in the sixth century), whether from the Hellenistic and Greco-Roman epochs where the true Alexandrian spirit reigned.[10]

Predictably, the Anacreontic vogue of the revolutionary period has been attributed to the malign effects of women's power, patronage or proclivities:

Naturally, it was above all among women that this contagion raged: Canova, Chinard, Prud'hon, were the favorites of Mme de Groslier, Récamier, and Regnault de St.-Jean d'Angely. Gérard equally seduced them. For Mme Tallien in 1804 he painted ten pictures that Potrelle engraved, featuring Amors who represent *Departure, Arrival, Attack, Success, Regret*, and *Repose*....In sum, in all its tendencies, Alexandrianism is feminine. It was women who confined the art of the empire to the path that swept away, drum rolling, the triple caporalism—military, Roman, and Davidian...[11]

The assertion that the "contagion" of Anacreontism is the direct reflection of feminine patronage is, needless to say, extremely questionable. This is, of course, a familiar claim found in considerations of Rococo art, where Anacreontic themes also figure prominently, and where women were significant patrons. In fact, most of the paintings (as opposed to book illustrations and interior decorations) that comprise so much of this stylistic and thematic phenomenon were Salon paintings, usually commissioned by no one. In many instances they were purchased by the state after their exhibition, and, while women like Juliette Récamier, Joséphine Beauharnais, and Pauline Bonaparte did commission individual artists—occasionally on an important scale—few of them were patrons on the level of, for example, the Count Sommariva.[12] During the Directory and later the Empire, the power of patronage was largely concentrated among the newly wealthy *fournisseurs* and the important financiers of the Empire.[13] The charge of effeminacy and decadence in post-revolutionary art, for which the influential women of the Directory, Consulate, and Empire are held accountable, operates to obscure the far more complicated issue of the appeal of these themes and treatments to a male audience and to male patrons.

I LOUIS GAUFFIER Portrait of Prince Augustus Frederick, later Duke of Sussex, 1793

II CHARLES MEYNIER Adolescent Eros Weeping Over the Portrait of the Lost Psyche, 1792

III JEAN–PIERRE GRANGER Ganymede, 1812

Likewise, the conventional art-historical explanation of the profound differences between the art of the revolution and the art that succeeded it is largely based on the assumption that the former "reflects" the progressive and manly values of 1789–94, while the latter "reflects" the reactionary politics of the Directory or the contingencies of Napoleonic patronage. However, the significant presence of Anacreontic themes before, during, and after the revolutionary period suggests that the situation was more complex. What tends, in any case, to be ignored in such accounts is not only the ideologically productive role of visual representation, but more specifically, the many shades of meaning and significance in the shift from the (official) fantasy of Republican Rome to that of Hellenistic Greece.

By any reckoning, the literary and iconographic replacement of Republican Rome by ancient Greece as a locus of fantasy and desire is inadequately explained by invocations of the primitivizing and purifying urges of French Neoclassicism, or by reference to the politics of Thermidorean reaction. Republican Rome, so prominent in the revolutionary *imaginaire*, signifies not only the *vertu* of masculinity and the masculinity of *vertu*, but also a construction of ideal manhood closer to the Marlboro man than to Alcibiades. The Anacreontic idiom, in contrast to the asperities of Stoic manhood, celebrates a certain polymorphism (exemplified by the ephebe) as well as a demonstrable fascination with narratives of role reversal and gender ambiguity.

In this regard, it was also the case that Anacreontism included in its purchase the implicit recognition that beautiful youths, like beautiful nymphs, were equally desirable. Which is but another way of saying that one of the associations of Greece was, of course, "Greek love"—an association entirely familiar and available to artists of the epoch. In one sense, Greece stands to Rome as feminine to masculine, but Greece itself could be internally gendered; the warlike Sparta of Rousseau and St. Just's desire operating as the masculine counterpoint to the feminized Hellenism of Anacreon and Longus. In its most general configurations, however, where "Rome" signified the heterosexual casting of homosocial desire (its later "effeminacy" associated with the corruption of Empire, and its own form of Alexandrianism) "Greece" could represent, nowhere more memorably than in David's *Leonidas at Thermopylae* (fig. 19), an idealized vision of both.

In its most literal sense, however, Anacreontism refers to the revival of that aspect of classical literary culture consecrated to pastoral, romantic and erotic themes, including the revival and translation of poets such as Bion and Moschus and the production of modern pastiches such as the Abbé Barthélémy's *Voyage of Young Anacharsis* (1788) which was reprinted constantly. It includes new editions of Ovid, Pausanias, Apollonius, Longus's immensely popular *The Loves of Daphnis and Chloe*, as well as the production of new translations of the sixth-century poets Sappho and Anacreon.[14] The influence of these texts on French visual culture should not be underestimated. *The Voyages of Antenor (Les Voyages d'Anténor en Grèce et Asie, manuscrit grec trouvé à Herculaneum)* by E.-F. Lentier, (Didot l'ainé 1798), to take one important instance, was reprinted no less than sixteen times between 1798 and 1823. Modeled on the equally popular *Voyage of Anacharsis*, it became a much-used source book of themes and subjects for artists of the period. When such works were illustrated, as they frequently were, their illustrations were often appropriated by history painters who then reworked them into ambitious Salon paintings. For example, *The Voyages of Antenor* contained an engraving representing Sappho hurling herself from the rock, a subject which inspired no less than eleven painted or sculpted versions in the Salons of 1802, 1806, 1812 and 1814. Although François Gérard (1770–1830), Alexandre-Evariste Fragonard (1780–1850), and Prud'hon, among others, all illustrated Anacreontic themes at various times, it is Girodet who is the artist most closely associated with the poet's Neoclassical popularity in French visual culture as well as with the revival of other pastoral poets.[15]

A reading of "On Bathyllus," Ode XXII of Anacreon's *Odes*, and a consideration of its accompanying lithograph after Girodet's design (fig. 44) does much to explain the Neoclassical taste for Anacreon and what he represented. Within the cycle's span, the poet addresses himself alternately to both male and female lovers: Ode XXII is an impassioned eulogy to youthful male beauty:

> And now with all thy pencil's truth,
> Portray Bathyllus, lovely youth!
> Let his hair in lapses bright,
> Fall like streaming rays of light,
> And there the raven's dye confuse
> With the yellow sunbeam's hues.
> Let not the braid, with artful twine,
> The flowing of his locks confine;
> But loosen every golden ring,
> To float upon the breeze's wing,

Beneath the front of polished glow.
Front as fair as mountain-snow,
And guileless as the dews of dawn,
Let the majestic brows be drawn,
Of ebon dies, enriched by gold,
Such as the scaly snakes unfold.
Mingle in his jetty glances,
Power that awes, and love that trances;
Steal from Venus bland desire,
Steal from Mars the look of fire,
Blend them in such expression here,
That we by turns may hope and fear!
Now from the sunny apple seek
The velvet down that spreads his cheek;
And there let Beauty's rosy ray
In flying blushes richly play;
Blushes, of that celestial flame
Which lights the cheek of virgin shame.
Then for his lips, that ripely gem—
But let thy mind imagine them!
Paint, where the ruby cell uncloses,
Persuasion sleeping upon roses,
And give his lip that speaking air,
As if a word was hovering there!
His neck of ivory splendour trace,
Moulded with soft but manly grace;
Fair as the neck of Paphia's boy,
Where Paphia's arms have hung in joy.
Give him the wingèd Hermes' hand,
With which he waves his snaky wand:
Let Bacchus then the breast supply,
And Leda's son the sinewy thigh.
But oh! suffuse his limbs of fire
With all that glow of young desire,
Which kindles, when the wishful sigh
Steals from the heart, unconscious why
Thy pencil, though divinely bright,
Is envious of the eye's delight,
Or its enamored torch would shew
His shoulder, fair as sunless snow,
Which now in veiling shadow lies,

44 ANNE-LOUIS GIRODET-TRIOSON Ode XXII, "The Odes of Anacreon" 1869

Removed from all but Fancy's eyes,
Now for his feet—but hold—forbear—
I see a godlike portrait there;
So like Bathyllus! sure there's none
So like Bathyllus but the Sun!
Oh! let this pictured god be mine,
And keep the boy for Samos' shrine;
Phoebus shall then Bathyllus be,
Bathyllus then the deity![16]

For Neoclassical artists and literati, such effusions existed on a plane entirely apart from what, in terms of sexual behavior, was the inadmissible, if rarely prosecuted, activity of sodomy. Quite likely, many of them—certainly those who knew their Plato—were aware that the relations implied in the poem between the speaker and the beautiful youth were those between the *erastos* and the *eromenos*; the older, more powerful man and the youthful object of his desire.[17] Such relations must be distinguished from pederasty in the modern sense, insofar as they were highly ritualized, consensual and conventionalized roles within classical Athenian culture, fully codified by the fifth century BC, and in Neoclassical culture, familiar to all those with knowledge of Greek literature and poetry.

In Girodet's illustration, the artist is positioned as the mediating figure between the adult and the beloved youth. While the poet prompts the artist to produce the image that will speak his desire, Love himself, in the person of the winged putto, collaborates in its production. Ode XXII appears to have been particularly popular among critics and artists; Winckelmann makes reference to it in *The History of Ancient Art Among the Greeks*, and the art critics Auguste-Hilarion Kératry and Joseph Droz also allude to it. Moreover, one of the recurring motifs in Anacreontic art, going back to the Rococo, was the representation of the aged poet himself in the company of a youthful Amor, a subject treated by Jean-Baptiste Greuze (1725–1805) as well as by Bertel Thorvaldsen (fig. 45) and a motif that might carry pederastic implications. Significantly, Girodet's illustrations of the Anacreontic verses, produced in his most Neoclassical, Flaxmanian style, constantly reshuffle

45 BERTEL THORVALDSEN Anacreon and Amor, 1823

46 ANNE-LOUIS GIRODET-TRIOSON Ode IX "The Odes of Anacreon" 1869

the same repertoire of figures and poses, placing male and female figures in interchangeable formations (fig. 46).

While there is a tendency to assume that the art of the immediately pre-revolutionary and revolutionary period was crowded with Republican heroes and Stoic martyrs, an examination of the titles of works of arts listed in the Salon *livrets* indicates, on the contrary, that Anacreontic themes were far more prevalent, despite concerted efforts on the part of the royal arts administration, and later the revolutionary government, to impose more serious and edifying subject matter. Art historians have sought to distinguish the Anacreontic art of the *ancien régime* from that of the Directory or Empire, but its persistence in the revolutionary period is more suggestive of continuity than rupture.[18] The fact that David painted *The Loves of Paris and Helen* (fig. 47) as his own Anacreontic contribution in the years between his *Oath of the Horatii* (fig. 4) and his *Lictors Returning to Brutus the Bodies of his Sons* (fig. 17), with which, incidentally, it was paired in the Salon of 1789, suggests that even in a period of rapt identification with the masculine ethos of Republican Rome, a distinctly feminized Hellenism remained fashionable. Thus, where the painting of *Brutus* confronts the viewer with the austerities (ethical, political, and historical) of ancient Rome, *The Loves of Paris and Helen* provides an antique scenography

47 JACQUES-LOUIS DAVID The Loves of Paris and Helen, 1788

of *luxe, calme, et volupté*; where Paris and Helen risk and lose all in their surrender to physical passion, Brutus heroically violates the most "natural" of human bonds in deference to the higher service of the state.[19] The need felt by art historians to resolve this particular contradiction in David's oeuvre is doubtless accentuated by the desire to preserve, if not create, a coherent and satisfying authorial unity. In part, this is itself a function of the same individualistic bias of art history that seeks to map a coherent developmental trajectory for a particular artistic career, and within which—in the particular case of David—the painting's "hellénisme gracieux" finds little favor.[20] But David's figure of Paris of 1788, or his Bara of 1794, or his Telemachus (in *Telemachus and Eucharis*) of 1818 suggest, on the contrary, that the aggressively virile masculinity of the *Horatii* or the *Brutus* should not be assumed as normative, nor, for that matter, paradigmatic. The coexistence of such very different visions of ideal manhood within the career of a single artist, like the coexistence of these types within the cultural production of the period, suggests that while one model may at any given time be accepted and received as the dominant one, there exist simultaneously antinomies, reversals, alternatives, available to artists as a range of choices.

The Importance of Being Eros

Nowhere is the sensibility of this feminized Hellenism more clearly represented than in the enthusiasm for the story of Psyche and Eros (also called by his Latin names Cupid or Amor)—a major theme within Anacreontism.[21] Here was what French critics and academicians termed a *sujet gracieux*, a subject, needless to say, as remote as could be imagined from the cataclysms of revolution. The allegory is an episode in Apuleius's satire of the second century AD, *Metamorphosis* or *The Golden Ass*, but was given Gallic life in La Fontaine's 1669 retelling of the myth. François Noel produced another version in 1823. Between 1797 and 1814 there were at least twenty-seven paintings and sculptures produced by French artists representing the story in the Salon exhibitions, and this figure does not take into account the even more copious production of prints and illustrated books. The popularity of the theme increased in the Salons of the Restoration (the subject was represented in the Salons of 1819, 1822, 1824, and 1827) and includes several treatments by Angelica Kauffman, Gérard's *The Kiss of Psyche* of 1798, David's *Cupid and Psyche* of 1817, the 1824 *Psyche* of Jean-Jacques Pradier (1792–1852) and the 1819 *Amor and Psyche* of François Picot (1786–1868).

The visual popularity of the myth has many causes, and begins, moreover, in the Renaissance, but its frequency in Neoclassical visual culture is notable. Within the frame of Neoclassicism, the adulation accorded Antonio Canova's various renditions of the subject was also a likely spur to French artists of the 1790s and after (fig. 48). Gérard's version of 1798 was one of the resounding successes of that year's Salon, and his painting was almost immediately engraved for wider dissemination (fig. 49). Finally, the expropriation of the Capitoline *Eros and Psyche* by Napoleon and its exhibition in the Louvre (9 Thermidor, year VI) gave yet a further boost to the theme. (David had also made

48 ANTONIO CANOVA Cupid and Psyche, 1796–1800

49 HYACINTHE AUBRY-LECOMTE after FRANÇOIS GÉRARD
Cupid and Psyche, 1828

his homage to the work when he inscribed it behind the bed in *The Loves of Paris and Helen*, fig. 47).

The iconographic life of Cupid and Psyche is long, but here it is relevant to note that eighteenth-century depictions demonstrate considerable variety. In some cases, the lovers are represented as adolescents of approximately the same age; in some instances, Psyche appears older, taller, and relatively more mature physically. Prud'hon, for example, specialized in voluptuous, monumental, rather overscaled Psyches (fig. 50) and there was also a tradition of representing the two lovers as children. While the story's narrative licensed painters to focus on either the youthful couple (this was the most common motif) or on Psyche and her tribulations, Meynier chose to depict the ephebic god alone, accompanied only by putti mourning the departed Psyche.

Meynier's choice of subject, therefore, was anything but unprecedented and, like Girodet with his Endymion, he made his bid for originality by inventing a new iconography for the subject. Accordingly, the depiction of Eros tearfully contemplating a cameo relief of the departed Psyche occurs nowhere in Apuleius's text, nor does it seem to have had any earlier prototypes. Similarly, the crepuscular lighting, with its dramatic chiaroscuro effects of golden light and raking shadow announce the young artist's assimilation of the lessons of seventeenth-century Italian painting. Likewise too, the curly-haired putti, the *morbidezza* of Eros's flesh, and the compositional arabesques declare Meynier's acquaintance with—and ability to quote—Italian Mannerism. Formally and compositionally, Meynier's *Adolescent Eros* affirms his painterly accomplishments, his artistic erudition, his mastery of tradition and of his metier. Far more interesting than Meynier's artistic sophistication, however, is his bizarre exaggeration of the effeminacy of his Eros, an effeminacy whose morphological attributes are further underscored by Eros's dolorous passivity; for example, by his limp and enervated right arm from which his arrows and quiver have fallen. The rounded and undulating forms of the body, themselves a visual code evocative of femininity, are further emphasized by the arrangement of the embroidered mantle snugly secured between the columnar thighs, between which not even the barest hint of genitalia is suggested. Finally, bodily density, mass, and gravity are entirely denied. Weightless, Eros floats upon (or against) a vaguely defined shelf of what seems on the right of the canvas to be a billowing purplish cloud, and on the left, a more earthly-looking support. And while this impression of weightlessness, accentuated by the position of the lower part of the legs, may be read as a sign of ideality as well as a sign of Eros's divinity, it also functions to

50 HYACINTHE AUBRY-LECOMTE after PIERRE-PAUL PRUD'HON The Abduction of Psyche, 1824

heighten the effect of girlish grace and delicacy. This attenuated and serpentine figure reappears regularly throughout the period, as in paintings such as the *Hylas and the Nymphs* of 1812 of Pierre-Jérôme Lordon (1760–1838), or the *Sappho and Phaon* of Pierre-Claude-François Delorme (1783–1859) of 1834 (figs. 72 and 51).

Although the story of Eros and Psyche had a long tradition of allegorical interpretation (immediately apparent in the etymology of the protagonists' names—Love and the Soul), on a purely literal level the narrative does in fact focus on a male/female couple. It is therefore of some moment that Meynier's androgynous Eros weeps over a cameo portrait that is a virtual double of his own *néo-grec* head; the tight curls and the top part of the coiffure, as well as the profile, are almost identical. In spite of the narrative, it is as though the look at the cameo is the look in the mirror; the absorption in the image of the beloved woman belying an amorous fascination with the self. Sexual difference, supposedly represented by Psyche, appears in the painting as a

51 PIERRE-CLAUDE-FRANÇOIS DELORME Sappho and Phaon, 1834

52 After ANNE-LOUIS GIRODET-TRIOSON
Self-portrait with Julie Candeille, c. 1807

solipsistic doubling of the same. Although this is an uncommon pictorial device, such visual doubling is equally evident in Girodet's portrait
of himself and Julie Candeille (fig. 52) where there too sexual difference
is diminished if not altogether obscured.

In the case of Meynier (who, like so many Neoclassical artists, was
as adept in producing images of heroic manliness as ephebic grace, as
in his *Death of Timolean* of 1791 (fig. 53), we must not discount the fact
that what we consider to be the manifest eroticism of such paintings
was not perceived as such by contemporary viewers. Rather, the
seductiveness of the ephebe was subsumed under the more elevated
rubric of the *beau idéal*. Nevertheless, even if we assume that critics as
well as viewers found nothing especially provocative about the beautiful ephebe and that such bodies had already become conventional
signs, we still require some kind of schema of identification that
accounts for their general appeal. This, I would suggest, resides in a
form of empowerment by which the male viewer is affirmed in *his*
masculinity *vis à vis* the effeminacy and beauty of the youth. For
surely that languorous, pallid, and swanlike body is fashioned to evoke
the feminine it appears to somatically incorporate. This "recuperation"
of an eroticized femininity deemed inimical to the public weal suggests
the ways by which sexual difference—traditionally embodied in representations of femininity—can be seen to haunt the art of Neoclassical

painters and sculptors. In this reading, the ubiquity of the androgynous ephebe, exemplified by Meynier's Eros or Girodet's Endymion, is fostered not only by the homosocial, or even homoerotic tenor of Neoclassical (elite) culture, but by the very cultural and political discourses concerned to expel (or contain) sexual difference itself. Such insistently feminized bodies can thus be interpreted as a return of the repressed, such that the feminine returns like a symptom, covertly inscribed, upon or within the body of the ideal youth. Notwithstanding the feminization of the body, however, Meynier's Eros (and his brethren) were undoubtedly perceived as avatars of the male ideal; contemporary criticism (Winckelmann excepted) rarely evokes the androgyne, much less the hermaphrodite, in characterizing the ephebic body, despite the aesthetic prestige of the Hellenistic *Sleeping Hermaphrodite*. When such language enters art criticism—as it does in the Empire in the writing of Kératry, Miel and others—it heralds a new discomfort about gender ambiguity, and a new concern about the appropriateness of androgynous bodies to stand for the *beau idéal*.

That the ephebic body should have become one of the period's most frequently deployed versions of the *beau idéal* is itself significant. In theory, the concept of the *beau idéal* was not gendered. Indeed, the mythic origin of this aesthetic and philosophical principle hinged on *female* beauty. As recounted by Pliny the Elder and Cicero, the great Athenian artist Zeuxis was commissioned by the town of Croton to do a painting of Homer's Helen. Her beauty being divine rather than mortal, Zeuxis could find no living woman whom he judged beautiful enough to act as his model. Consequently, he chose the most beautiful features from six of the most beautiful girls to produce an amalgam of feminine perfection; hence the principle of beauty as an imaginative synthesis of discrete and individual parts. Despite the narrative tale of its mythic origins, French theory and criticism nevertheless understood the *beau idéal* to be male. Claude-Henri Watelet's entry in his *Dictionary of the Arts of Painting, Sculpture and Engraving* of 1792 is a paradigmatic formulation:

> The *beau idéal* is today, in our opinion, the uniting of the greatest perfections that certain chosen individuals can in part provide. If one wants to conceive the *beau idéal* in a manner relating more to the ideas of Greek artists of the time of Pericles, it is necessary to imagine the beautiful as it would exist if Nature formed its products, and man above all, with the most exquisite selectiveness, with all its general and particular perfections...[22]

53 CHARLES MEYNIER Death of Timolcan, 1791

As an emblem of the *beau idéal*, the ephebe was officially supposed to embody the ideal—the pure and disinterested form of abstract perfection—not to provoke carnal desire. Given the existence of homosexual proscription (be it in legal or social terms) we may speculate that the artists producing such feminized or androgynous youths had to navigate the "problem" of a too-blatant homoerotic address. Furthermore, those qualities evocative of debility, passivity, impotence—even castration—which further functioned to feminize the ephebe needed to be refigured so that they did not contradict its harmonious perfection. To a certain extent, eighteenth-century elite culture did in fact provide precedents that linked debility and passivity with sanctioned—even venerated—forms of male subjectivity (notably, that of Jean-Jacques Rousseau and, of course, Goethe's Werther). But what appears to have been the preferred strategy of Neoclassical artists was to cloak their various forms of male trouble under the rhetorical sign of pathos (pathos: from the Greek word for suffering, expression, and emotion). Indeed, "patheticized" male figures such as Meynier's tearful Eros are a commonplace in Neoclassical painting and sculpture. Moreover, where the attribute of pathos elevated ephebic weakness to tragedy, it also worked to leaven–to soften–the opposing type of stoic, warrior, or patriarch. Accordingly, the dying warrior types, as figured in paintings such as those by Drouais and Lafitte, or in sculptures such as the *Achilles* of Jean-Baptiste Giraud (1752–1830) were rendered poignant by virtue of their mortal wounds (figs. 31, 32 and 54); the murderous Hercules–as in Canova's *Hercules and Lichas*–made pitiful in his helpless madness (fig. 55). Similarly, the blind Oedipus or the blind Belisarius, the eviscerated Cato or the stoic Socrates simultaneously evoke authority and vulnerability, yet another version of the troping of pathos. Such highly charged depictions are not only indices of a crisis in authority, but signs of the untenability of an overly patriarchal ideal of masculinity.

54 JEAN-BAPTISTE GIRAUD Achilles, 1789

55 ANTONIO CANOVA Hercules and Lichas, 1795–1815

François-Xavier Fabre's *morceau de réception* is an interesting and not uncommon example of the formulae for pathos that David would himself employ in his 1794 commemoration of Joseph Bara (fig. 61). In addition, it provides another example of the appeal of the disempowered ephebe in the revolutionary period. It demonstrates too the internationalism of Neoclassical art, insofar as Fabre's painting, produced in Rome, is inspired by a Swiss poet, writing in German, translations of whose work appeared within a short time in Paris, in London, and in New York. Like the later Meynier's *Adolescent Eros* and Girodet's *Sleep of Endymion* (fig. 20), the critical reception of the *Death of Abel* (fig. 56) suggests such renditions of masculinity were promoted institutionally and fully approved by academicians and the royal arts administration.

The painting was completed during the winter of 1790–91, the third year of Fabre's tenure as royal pensioner at the French Academy in Rome. Life-size in scale, the *Death of Abel* was warmly received when it was exhibited in the Salon of 1791.[23] Even before its enthusiastic reception by the Salon critics, d'Angiviller had sent a personal letter of congratulation to Fabre and it was strongly endorsed by the Academy's judging committee when the painting arrived in Paris at the end of February, 1791:

> We cannot deny ourselves the pleasure of giving deserved praises to the figure of Abel by M. Fabre. It is of a good tonality, beautifully painted and of beautiful form, all the accessory parts are executed with taste; lastly, its gracefulness accords with its truthfulness, and we can only exhort him to follow the road that he has taken.[24]

This was, by comparison with the committee's usual perfunctory two- or three-sentence remarks on students' work, strong praise indeed. As is the case with the great majority of Salon criticism of this period, the professionally formulaic language makes it difficult to understand why, for example, Fabre's *Abel* should be considered so obviously superior to the *Diogenes* of his fellow-pensioner Etienne-Barthélémy Garnier (1759–1849):

> The *Diogenes* of M. Garnier is of a truthful tonality; fine and luminous; all the parts are well harmonized according to age and character, [with] the head [which] is truthfully rendered. We call upon him particularly to concern himself with its correction, without, however, neglecting the feeling he shows for color and harmony.[25]

56 FRANÇOIS-XAVIER FABRE The Death of Abel, 1791

Fabre had been the second of David's students, after Drouais, to win the prestigious Grand Prix de Rome, and had spent several years working under David before his arrival at the Academy in Rome in 1787.[26] But while this latter work observes the codes and formulae of Davidian Neoclassicism far more closely than Girodet's *Sleep of Endymion*—indeed, is in no obvious way concerned to subvert them—the dramatically isolated image of a beautiful annihilated male body has a more than adventitious resemblance to later variations on this theme. Furthermore, this (relatively) de-narrativized icon of passive and disempowered beauty can be considered, like all the paintings under discussion, as an iconographic ancestor of the nineteenth-century female nude, presaging its characteristic codes of presentation, display, and address.

The *Death of Abel* was one of the four required works painted for the Academy during Fabre's residence at the Mancini palace. This requirement, implemented in 1787, specified that pensioners produce four life-size figures after the model. In keeping with the tendency in the period to complicate and elaborate these nude male figures, one of the innovative features of the youthful Fabre's painting resides in its elevation of an *académie* into a history painting. Thus, while the dominant feature of the work remains an individual male figure, the provision of a few contextual elements—the landscape, the burning altars, and the discreet puddle of blood—serves to transform it into a narrative, bringing it into a far more ambitious category. The daring of such a compositional and narrative reduction was apparently not lost on his fellow pensioner Girodet; it had, as we have seen, been anticipated by Drouais with his *Dying Athlete* of 1785 (fig. 31), and succeeded by others, such as Garnier's *Ajax Shipwrecked* (fig. 57) and Louis Lafitte's *Dying Warrior* (fig. 32), both exhibited in the Salon of 1795. Fabre's own *Roman Soldier at Rest* (fig. 33), completed in 1788, was also presumably inspired by Drouais.

That Fabre should make his official artistic bid in the most exalted realm of sacred history painting, but with such a radical reduction of plot and décor, further supports the assertion that the *Death of Abel* is structurally closer to the female nude of the later nineteenth century than it is to a classical prototype such as Poussin's *Echo and Narcissus* of c.1628. (Interestingly, Poussin's version of the myth includes the pining nymph Echo, a central character in the Ovidian myth; in keeping with my larger argument, it is notable that later versions, particularly from the Neoclassical period, often eliminate her.)

Detached from the frame of classical antiquity which provided for the possibility of explicitly political or moralizing interpretations geared to a broad contemporary audience, the *Death of Abel* occupies a different discursive space from a "public" painting such as David's *Death of Joseph Bara*. Furthermore, the spectator addressed by the *Endymion* or the *Abel* is not the same as the one addressed by the *Bara*. As a devotional patriotic image, the *Bara* was designed to speak to the people as a political collectivity, not to the more elite Salon visitor, arts administration bureaucrat, or cultivated connoisseur. Its appeal was calibrated for collective rather than individual consumption. In contrast to David's painting, Fabre's operates on a far more subjective, even privatized realm of reception despite its official status (that is, an obligatory *envoi* from a Prix de Rome recipient, subject to the approval of the academicians and the institution they represented).

Another interesting aspect of Fabre's painting is its departure from the prevalent antique scenography; it manifests a kind of pastoral

57 ÉTIENNE–BARTHÉLÉMY GARNIER Ajax Shipwrecked, 1791

primitivism *avant la lettre* which accentuates its atmosphere of revolutionary *chic*. Although Old Testament themes were comparatively rare
during most of the revolutionary and immediately post-revolutionary
decades, the theme of Cain and Abel experienced new popularity,
reflecting, when not literally illustrating, Salomon Gessner's wildly
popular poetic retelling of the Biblical story. (Six French editions of

Gessner's book appeared between 1760 and 1793). Gessner's prose poem, a recasting of sacred history as *pastorale*, imagines Cain as a tormented malcontent, but also describes him as "austere," "savage," "rigorous" and "stern." Abel, on the other hand, is condemned by Cain for his "effeminate weakness," his "soft and effeminate" nature: "I never hated my brother. No, never. I saw instead with pain, that he, by his softness and effeminacy, stole from me the affection of Adam and Eve. Could I be insensible to this?"[27] Consequently, artists and sculptors, if they took their inspiration from Gessner, were narratively prompted to envision Abel as the "feminized" brother. Prior to Gessner, however, Abel had featured in sculpture throughout the eighteenth century, and had precedents in seventeenth-century art, including works by Philippe de Champagne, Salvator Rosa, Guercino, Charles Le Brun and Poussin.

Fabre's *Death of Abel*, however, like his earlier *Saint Sebastian* of 1788 (fig. 58), is also notable for the way its beautiful victim so completely dominates its visual field, filling nearly three-quarters of the painting's space. The flaming altars in the wilderness of a landscape (still Claudian nonetheless) provide both the backdrop and rationale for the exquisite young corpse, whose slender white fingers, curled up in death, accentuate the element of pathos on which the painting's emotional effect depends. Insofar as the other protagonists are absent, the immediate effect of the picture is located in the distilled drama of the lifeless but sensually beautiful male body. It is in this sense that it manifests its affective similarity to David's later *Bara*; pathos and eroticism are integrally linked and work together to mobilize the painting's affective charge. Where the absence of genitalia, if anything, accentuates the eroticism of Bara, in Fabre's painting, the small patch of pubic hair and the presence of the fur between Abel's loins—at the very center of the composition—draws attention to what it is supposed to veil.

The tendency to dramatize and make into narrative what begins as an *académie* is arguably far more widespread than my examples might suggest. Whether or not this is the case, Fabre's Abel and his St. Sebastian have a distinctly characteristic form. The standard conventions for the representation of the ephebic as opposed to the mature male body depended upon softer and more subtly articulated transitions between muscle groups as well as a more slender bodily frame. In the parlance of Salon criticism, the body was characterized by the qualities of *grâce*, *mollesse*, and *morbidesse*; the Gallic equivalent of the Italian *morbidezza*. As a type, Fabre's figures are more more closely related to the Praxitelean model of the Apollo Belvedere, than, for example, the Capitoline Faun (figs. 66 and 9).

58 FRANÇOIS–XAVIER FABRE Saint Sebastian, 1789

59 After PIERRE-PAUL PRUD'HON Winged Youth Leaning on a Herm, after 1791

Nevertheless, while Fabre's Abel is a far less androgynous rendering of the ephebic male body than Girodet's Endymion or Meynier's Eros, it can nevertheless be read in similar structural terms as a feminized body; that is to say, a body whose *raison d'être* is to be displayed and contemplated, divorced from any heroic or elevated ideals. Appreciably more effeminate male bodies were, however, on offer well before Fabre, Girodet, and Meynier made their Salon debuts. For example, in the Salon of 1791 (the last to be held under the *ancien régime*, and the first one open to non-academicians), Pierre-Paul Prud'hon exhibited his black chalk drawing, *Winged Youth leaning on a Herm* (fig. 59), and as we have seen, androgynous ephebes were familiar subjects in the international artistic culture of Rome.

The Ephebe as Revolutionary Martyr

Obviously, the copious production of dead Hectors, Patrocluses and other Homeric warriors from the 1770s and after were important precedents for the dead ephebes of the 1790s. Furthermore, countless such examples exist in the sculpture of this period, French and British as well as Italian: Thomas Banks's 1773–74 marble relief, *The Death of Germanicus* (fig. 60) provides a good example of this type, with the slender, sensuous and highly polished corpse presented, like the dead Christ, as a kind of sacerdotal offering. Accordingly, an examination of the feminized version of the (male) *beau idéal* in Neoclassicism requires that attention be paid to the non-canonical works of the period as well as to related cultural and historical phenomena. For it is only in relation to these works by relatively obscure artists that the imagery of David, for all his undisputed originality and aesthetic quality, can be given an aesthetic as well as historical interpretation. This is not to dispute the

60 THOMAS BANKS The Death of Germanicus, 1773–74

relative singularity of David's depiction of the newly minted young martyr, Joseph Bara (fig. 61), for alone among Neoclassical artists, David presented an ephebic body whose physical torsion entirely elides the genitals; without recourse to coy strips of ribbon, or drapery cloaking an absence (*vide* Meynier, pl. II), David combined an empirical realism of bodily pose (in the twisted body and legs) with a stylized language for femininity (the arabesque of Bara's hip, his streaming hair and delicate face) in order to produce...what? For surely the body of Bara prompts a reading in terms of castration—male trouble *par excellence*—yet why would a revolutionary martyr be so figured?

Unlike the other paintings thus far discussed, David's *Death of Joseph Bara* is a specifically political commission, the unfinished third and last of his revolutionary martyr paintings (succeeding the *Death of Le Pelletier de Saint-Fargeau* and the *Death of Marat* of 1793). Commissioned by Robespierre on behalf of the Convention after the thirteen-year-old boy's death in a skirmish during the counterrevolutionary insurrection of 1793 in the Vendée, the painting was therefore part of the propaganda program of the Committee of Public Safety and was meant to feature in an elaborately choreographed fête of public commemoration.[28] Following the events of 9 Thermidor and the overthrow of Robespierre and the Committee, the fête never took place and the painting was never publicly displayed.

Like Girodet's *Sleep of Endymion*, David's *Bara* seems to have also been a personally significant work for him; it remained in his studio until his death. Whether Girodet's painting was a primary "influence" on David's astonishing conception of the boy martyr is no more important for my purposes than any other of David's possible sources; for example, the Borghese Hermaphrodite that David, like most artists, knew from his years in Rome (later triumphantly installed in the Louvre with Napoleon's other artistic booty in 1798). Unlike the *Sleeping Hermaphrodite*, much admired by David's contemporaries, Bara has no sex, which is not to say that he isn't highly sexualized. Rather, it is more to the point to consider the implications of depicting Bara in so emphatically feminized a manner, to the unprecedented extent of hiding the genitals between the compressed thighs, a feminization further accentuated by the flowing curves of the body, the girlish face and ecstatic expression.

Among the array of Neoclassical ephebes, it is the Bara which most closely conforms to the three possible meanings of the epicene (from the Greek, *epikoinos*): that is, "having but one form to indicate either sex" or "having characteristics typical of the other sex" or "lacking

61 JACQUES-LOUIS DAVID The Death of Joseph Bara, 1794

characteristics of either sex." However, like the "hermaphroditic" connotations of Bara's body, his manifest emasculation need not necessarily be read as a visual sign of impotence. Indeed, as the feminist scholar Tania Modleski has suggested, the appearance of weakness may be another ruse of power.[29] In keeping with her suggestion, it is necessary to distinguish the visual rhetoric of masculine disempowerment from its political reality, and the actual circumstances surrounding this particular painting. For however we may wish to interpret the manifest effeminacy of Bara's body, the delicacy and pathos of the expiring boy martyr are themselves generated from a locus of considerable political and artistic power. This was, after all, an artistic commission originating from Robespierre himself and produced at the height of David's artistic and political authority. If nothing else, we can assume that if David indeed intended the work to function in a ceremony of public mourning and patriotism he wished it to be an empowering icon. The text of David's address to the Convention on 23 Messidor (*rapport sur la fête héroïque pour les honneurs au Panthéon—Barra* [*sic*] *et Viala*) puts an interesting spin on the painting's actual appearance:

> Thus withers and dies a new flower cut by the furrowing of the plough; thus the poppies, beaten by the storm, bend their heads weighted down by the rain; Barra [*sic*] and Agricole Viala! Thus were you harvested in the flower of your youth!
>
> And you, infamous oppressors of the earth – you who attribute your language to the creator of liberty, and imagine that you derive from him the right to govern the world, where are your heroes? Let them show themselves! How can you compare our young republicans to these vile courtiers nurtured in the breast of voluptuousness, these effeminate sybarites whose corrupt soul has no notion of virtue, and whose enervated arms are burdened only with their conquests, immodest tokens of their adulterous loves; these courtiers who, finally, carry their arrogance and cowardice into the heart of their camps, fleeing at the least hint of danger, and flying to hide their shame in the arms of debauchery.[30]

The language of the *rapport*—highly rhetorical, overheated, if not overwrought—was by no means exceptional by the standards of the Convention in 1793, but the gendered aspects of its invective are undeniable, although these too can be considered standard features of republican discourse. Thus, the connotative chain which begins with vile courtiers, and generates voluptuousness, effeminacy, sybarites, enervation, immodesty and debauchery demonstrates how a language of sexual attributes or behavior was mapped upon the political language of militant, and in this instance, Jacobin republicanism. The nature of this sexualized language, moreover, reveals a set of overlaps between the notion of effeminacy (a perversion of masculinity) and sexual profligacy, which could be imputed to male or female subjects. What is particularly striking, however, is that David's hysterical evocation of effeminacy and debility in his characterization of the enemy describes rather well the physical attributes of his painted Bara. We confront, therefore, in the production of Bara, the apparent contradictions mobilized in the fabrication of an icon of feminized pathos engendered, as it were, from a site of state and artistic power; a remarkably androgynous and seductive body on offer, produced in a discursive environment distinguished by considerable misogyny and homophobia.

Since *Bara* was not a Salon painting and therefore not subject to aesthetic (as opposed to political) commentary, it is hard to reconstruct the responses of the painting's contemporary viewers. For Delécluze, there seems to have been nothing especially shocking about the figure: "This work, which the painter never completed, is without contradiction, one of the most delicate that he made and the most graceful."[31] For P.-A. Coupin, David's biographer of 1827, the *Bara* was simply "a masterpiece of sentiment and expression."[32] It is only relatively recently that the sexual and affective specificity of the painting has been directly confronted. Thus, in arguments similar to those made for the political meaning of Endymion, Crow and Michel claim that Bara's virginal but violated body can be politically interpreted as the sensual casing for the utopian aspirations of Jacobin ideology. For both scholars, the explanations offered to account for Joseph Bara's distinctive appearance are based on three principal arguments: Crow argues that Robespierre effectively dictated to David the boy martyr's artistic form (there is, however, no concrete evidence extant for this assertion); both scholars claim that Jacobin ideology required the use of an ideal, utopian body; and third, that David straightforwardly availed himself of existing, admired prototypes such as the *Sleeping Hermaphrodite* to fulfill these artistic and political requirements. As for the genitals, Crow interprets this "suppression" (his word) as a device to denote the hero's "innocence" without explaining why visual castration would work to such an end. Furthermore, the manifestly unnatural position of the supine body—its discomfiting torsion—is for Crow both a sign of the body's decorously omitted violation (bayonet wound to the abdomen), an aesthetic choice of pose that obscures the genitals without recourse to shading or drapery, and a formal means to express the body's suffering.[33] Hence, the singularity of the body—as a body, as a painting, and as a revolutionary icon—is interpreted as the result of fully conscious and deliberate choices (by Robespierre, by David).

Such positivist explanations, however, are not in themselves sufficient to account for the painting's singularity: moreover, they serve to rationalize the image and to expel the issue of Bara's feminization, both politically and iconographically. This mode of interpretation further precludes the possibility that visual culture may be shaped by unconscious forces and investments, both personal and collective. What seems therefore to be at stake in these art-historical encounters with the *Bara* is the unspoken, but implicit assumption that there exists an unproblematic or normative model (represented, perhaps, in David's other work) against which this blatantly feminized model needs be reconciled. This assumption, however, has more to do with the *mentalités* of modern art historians than with those of the revolutionary period. Overall, it would seem that for many modern scholars of David, the sexual ambivalence and effeminacy of the *Joseph Bara* require explanation (as it apparently did not for early nineteenth-century commentators), thus prompting the desire to resolve the painting's contradictions, whether by invoking Jacobin adoptions of the *beau idéal*, or the propaganda requirements of the Jacobin dictatorship, or David's receptivity to the prior model of the *Endymion*, and so forth. On the one hand, then, the *Bara* is considered to be an anomalous production within David's oeuvre, but on the other, it is duly accounted for, explained, and rationalized.

In striking contrast to such voluntarist readings, Alex Potts has interpreted the painting in relation to the exclusion of women from the public sphere and has described the ideal, androgynous nude as the product of "a radical middle-class imagination besieged by contending populist and revisionist pressures."[34] Bara, like other androgynous ephebes produced within the period, thus functions as an appropriation of the femininity elsewhere banished from political and cultural domains. Figured as a presexual ephebe (which also accounts for the elision of the genitals), the *Death of Joseph Bara* may consequently be understood as an imaginary resolution of real social and sexual contradictions and conflicts, a point I will elaborate below.

Such an approach, which brings into light a somewhat different set of issues, is premised instead on the preservation of these contradictions. Instead of attempting to stabilize the meanings of the *Bara*, we may do better to accept and explore those contradictions as an index of the inherent instabilities that underlie the revolution's single-sex model for spiritual and corporeal beauty, heroism, and virtue—*la vertu mâle et républicaine.* Indeed, it may well be that a consideration of the contradictions themselves will enable us to glimpse unacknowledged and (at the time) unspeakable exigencies, fantasies, investments that are deeply socially and culturally embedded and thus only partially the "invention" of any individual artist.

Consequently, it would seem more useful to assume that masculinity in either its phallicized or feminized guise is chimerical—an image, a fiction, variously inflected by the needs, the desires, the context, and the political unconscious of the moment of its making.[35] Hence, while it is certainly true that David's conception of Bara fits the propaganda needs of the Committee of Public Safety (for whom dictatorship, the suppression of the *sections*, and not least, the Terror itself were justified by the plight of a besieged and vulnerable France, threatened by hostile states without, and counterrevolution and conspiracy within), there are other factors determining David's artistic choices. Moreover, and from whatever vantage point one might want to interpret the treatment of the figure, I think it is more important to stress that the currency of both the feminized masculine and the masculinized masculine in visual culture (like the parallel interest in Anacreontic and Roman Republican subjects) is jointly shaped by the expulsion of femininity, the privileging of male fraternal bonds, and—ironically enough given the sensual appeal of ephebic youth—a moralistic repudiation of the eroticism associated with the sensuality of the despised Rococo.

Bara should therefore be seen not only as an icon of Jacobin revolutionary politics, but as a statement of its gender politics. As an ideal male body, Bara stands for the manly values and virtue of Jacobin Republicanism; as a "patheticized", innocent, and child-like body it rationalizes the Terror, figuring Republican France as a vulnerable and violated victim; as a utopian body (devoid of signs of rank or station) it papers over actual class conflicts; and finally, as a feminized body, it recuperates and contains a carnal femininity that Jacobin culture was concerned to expel.[36] Perhaps most important, as a universal body, it was nominally masculine but could be fashioned in ways whereby femininity could nevertheless be seen to "inhabit" it. Such an interpretation provides a framework for understanding why artists like Meynier, Fabre, Girodet, Prud'hon, Gagneraux, Regnault and a host of others would find the androgynous ephebe so well suited to the contradictory requirements of a heroic masculine ideal that nominally abjured sensuality, and a culturally embedded homosociality that nominally proscribed homoeroticism. Regnault's *Liberty or Death*, probably painted during the Terror and exhibited in the Salon of 1795, and Bénigne Gagneraux's *Spirit of Peace Halting the Horses of Mars* of 1794 (figs. 62 and 63) provide further instances of the deliberate political uses to which the ephebic body was put. In Regnault's painting, originally destined for the Legislative Assembly, the genius is isolated spatially, suspended against the intense blue of allegorical non-space. Arms outstretched, the genius confronts the viewer to whom the "choice" of the painting's title is narratively addressed. This choice is both an abstract concept—Liberty or Death—and alarmingly literal: the perfunctory trials held under the Terror allowed only for innocence or death. The Christ-like presentation of the genius has doubtless been calculated; like David's dead martyr Marat, revolutionary artists appropriated Christian iconography and its formal devices for secular purposes.

62 JEAN–BAPTISTE REGNAULT Liberty or Death, 1795

63 BÉNIGNE GAGNERAUX The Spirit of Peace Halting the Horses of Mars, 1794

Despite its variety of iconographic roles, and despite the variety of its renditions, the ephebe may nevertheless be characterized as an essentially fetishistic figure, acknowledging and denying sexual difference simultaneously. In this sense, its widespread currency provides visual evidence of the ways that femininity, as Shoshana Felman has described it, can be seen to exist "inside the masculine, its uncanny difference from itself."[37] Even as political, medical, or moral discourse increasingly insisted on the absolute boundaries dividing male and female beings, even as femininity was progressively defined in terms of of a strict and biologically grounded difference, cultural production testified continually to an internal division, a pervasive and haunting difference within the same. Fetishistic and magical (these are allied features), artists' deployment of the beautiful ephebe may be viewed as imaginative attempts to resolve the conflicts between genders, sexes, even classes. And to the extent that the ephebic body failed at this imaginary resolution, it ritually enacted its own form of male trouble, perpetually wounded, *in extremis*, expiring, cast in roles of limp surrender. As an icon of erotic polymorphism, it was furthermore capable of soliciting many kinds of erotic projection. This is undoubtedly why male artists and viewers of all known proclivities—and probably women as well—were enchanted by the figure, and why it retained its appeal during three generations of artmaking.

All of which is to say that David's dramatic rendition of the ephebic body was only possible—that is, politically and aesthetically legible— because it was situated within its horizon of reception; culturally familiar, officially sanctioned, and already endowed with "revolutionary" significance.

This level of significance was, to a considerable extent, the achievement of Johann-Joachim Winckelmann, whose aesthetic influence was both international and, for the half-century or so after his death, virtually unrivaled. Most art historians who have dealt with Winckelmann tend to locate his influence too narrowly. Anton Raphael Mengs, as is well known, was Winckelmann's preferred contemporary painter, and few scholars can muster any enthusiasm about Mengs's art (fig. 64). But, as I will argue, Winckelmann's celebration of the ephebe, and indeed male beauty in general, provided the political as well as aesthetic authorization of the representation of the ephebe for several generations of French artists. By the time the ephebic male body became a significant presence in French history painting and sculpture its meanings, its forms, and its various mythological guises were, thanks to Winckelmann, fully assimilated and altogether familiar to artists, critics, connoisseurs, and dilettanti. While the androgynous ephebe could explicitly denote a homoerotic identity, for example, a Ganymede or a Hyacinthus, the iconographic range of the ephebe was, a we have seen, far wider and more inclusive.[38] Eros or Amor, for example, in his ostensibly heterosexual role as Psyche's lover, belongs to the same genus as do the youths beloved by Zeus or Apollo. Consequently, the figure can be seen to migrate, from role to role, from painting to painting: for example, the nude equerry in David's *Intervention of the Sabine Women* (fig. 96) reappears in one of Alexandre-Evariste Fragonard's illustrations for the Didot edition of *Amor and Psyche*; many other such iconographic migrations can be demonstrated in the period.

What Winckelmann (and later, his successive exegetes and epigones) had taught the European art world, including the well-heeled pilgrims and connoisseurs of the Grand Tour, was that the Beautiful

64 ANTON RAPHAEL MENGS Perseus and Andromeda, 1777

was to be located—pre-eminently—in the graceful adolescent bodies of the Capitoline Faun (fig. 9), the Belvedere Antinous, the Apollo Sauroctonos (fig. 65), the Capitoline Antinous, the Capitoline Cupid and Psyche, and so forth. Crowning this aesthetic Parnassus of classical perfection—for the most part, and unbeknown to its idolaters, late Roman copies of lost Greek originals—was the Apollo Belvedere, acme of Winckelmann's Beautiful style, and radiant incarnation of the *beau idéal* (fig. 66). Although Winckelmann's historiographic system proposed two aesthetic summits of the Greek achievement, one characterized as the temporally anterior "severe" style and the other as the later, beautiful style, it was the latter, exemplified by the Apollo Belvedere and the Belvedere Antinous for which he reserved his most intense and passionate prose.

For Winckelmann, whose rhapsodic descriptions of antique art definitively stamped Neoclassical sensibility, and whose *Reflections on the Painting and Sculpture of the Greeks* (1755), *History of Ancient Art Among the Greeks* (1764) and *Monumenti antichi inediti* (1767)[39] functioned as breviaries for the history painter, the image of desire was principally drawn from the ephebic ranks. It was the ephebe who most perfectly embodied his notion of grace, and it was this quality of grace that above all else constituted the morphological identity of the beautiful. But, for Winckelmann, it was not merely the beauty of male adolescents that exceeded all other forms of beauty, it was an explicitly effeminate version of it. His florid descriptions of various fauns and Bacchuses as well as his commentary on individual works such as the Belvedere Antinous dilate on those aspects of form, expression and modelling that are most expressive of effeminacy, and in fact Winckelmann claimed that the most beautiful of classical statues had been modelled on eunuchs:

> The second kind of ideal youth is drawn from the conformation of eunuchs. It is represented, blended with masculine youth in Bacchus. He appears under this form at different ages, until he attains his full growth, and, in the most beautiful statues, always with delicate, round limbs, and the full expanded hips of the female sex, for according to the fable, he was brought up as a maiden....The forms of his limbs are soft and flowing, as though inflated by a gentle breath, and with scarcely any indication of the bones and cartilages of the knees, just as these joints are formed in youths of the most beautiful shape, and in eunuchs.[40]

Winckelmann's attention to the minutiae of bodily delineation—the

65 Apollo Sauroctonus, copy of bronze original by
Praxiteles

66 Apollo Belvedere, copy of bronze original by
Leochares

articulation of kneecaps, the depth of navels, the indication of nipples,
the undercutting of testicles, and so forth—inescapably suggests the
fetishist's obsessive gaze. Indeed, Winckelmann's taxonomy of ideal
body parts extended to the size and shape of the genitalia.[41] But
however great the temptation to read Winckelmann's own sexuality
through his texts, it is far more apposite to note that the loving
intensity with which Winckelmann scrutinized every aspect of the
statues and reliefs he examined was shared by his contemporaries as
well as his post-revolutionary successors:

...the muscles swell very much but they run quick or sharp against each other with great attention to contrast such as small nipples and navel, the sides full of small muscles opposed to the large masses of the breast, small knees, long threads of drapery opposed to the mass of the body of limbs.[42]

As Francis Haskell and Nicholas Penny note in their fascinating study, *Taste and the Antique*:

We sense [Winckelmann's] influence immediately when we read in Goethe of a group of German art students discussing the Apollo's ears, or when we hear of a French connoisseur pointing out that the merit of the Capitoline Antinous was demonstrated by the fact that the undercutting of the testicles was so fine that a paper slipped between them and the thigh would be held in place...[43]

In France, and by the time of the Revolution, Winckelmann's writings on antique art had been given an explicitly political interpretation.[44] Insofar as Winckelmann had directly linked the cultural achievement of classical Greece with its development of political democracy, his writings had an immediate relevance for those concerned with the creation of a revolutionary republican culture. Despite the fact that the period that Winckelmann considered the finest of Greek art did not correspond to its period of greatest democracy, his association of political freedom with artistic excellence was a valuable argument for republican aesthetics. In this respect, the strong political reading of Winckelmann, propounded, for example, by Jacobins such as Athanase Détournelle and the other members of the Revolutionary Society of the Arts, made of Winckelmann a kind of authorizing patriarch *cum* prophet.[45]

What formally distinguished the severe and beautiful styles in antique statuary was for Winckelmann a question of what, in his French translations, was characterized by the latter's more pronounced qualities of *grâce* and *mollesse* (*Anmut* and *Weichigkeit* in the original German); softer, more nuanced modelling, suave articulations between muscle groups, more lithe and slender, but distinctly rounded bodily proportions. These were the qualities identified with certain female nudes; for example, the Medici Venus, who could be said to have functioned throughout the eighteenth century as the female equivalent to the Apollo Belvedere, although even a cursory survey of late eighteenth-century commentaries on antique statuary suggests that far more ink was spilled on the latter. Furthermore, Winckelman was especially taken with antique physiognomies that merged male and female attributes, and this unisex approach to ephebic facial character was also assimilated into Neoclassical practice.[46]

Doubtless one of the appealing aspects of Winckelmann's vivid evocations of male beauty was the way they blurred the boundaries between life and art (Winckelmann believed that the classical statues he venerated more or less faithfully reflected the real bodies of real Greek men and youths), as well as the high-minded moralism accompanying their voluptuary raptures. And despite the fact that Winckelmann privileged the "beautiful style" over the "severe style," grace over muscular strength, ephebic youth over virile manliness, what mattered was that Winckelmann's vision of antiquity and the superb bodies with which it was supposedly populated was a world untroubled by sexual difference. As much for their celebration of Athenian freedom, it seems likely that the homoerotic and homosocial aspects of Winckelmann's writing were factors in their extraordinary influence, providing the authorizing political, as well as the aesthetic terms by which the ephebic body was integrated into French elite visual culture.

If, however, Winckelman provided the theory, Canova—far more than Mengs—provided the practice, and in this respect, the figure of Bara is unthinkable without the prior examples of Canova and Thorvaldsen. It is important to recall that Antonio Canova, whose sculptural production provides many instances of graceful ephebes (figs. 67 and 68) was not only a contemporary of David, but was unquestionably the most important artistic figure internationally from 1779 until his death in 1822. Committed Davidian critics, such as T. B. Eméric-David, A. C. Quatremère de Quincy, Baron T. C. Neergaard, and H. de Latouche were themselves worshippers of Canova, as were Napoleon and virtually all the important patrons of the Napoleonic era. The nude adolescent youths so frequent in his work, and in those of his younger contemporary Thorvaldsen, are clearly close kin of the erotically charged ephebes produced by French painters and sculptors in the following decades. In some instances, painters such as Jean-Pierre Granger (1779–1840) used such sculptures as models (compare for example, Thorvaldsen's 1804 Ganymede (fig. 69) with Granger's 1812 Ganymede (pl. III). This Roman as well as Winckelmannian context is thus crucial for understanding how the androgynous ephebe became a central trope in French Neoclassicism, because it was in the Roman art world that French artists were made familiar with the ephebe's aesthetic/political potentialities which were then integrated into revolutionary and post-revolutionary art practice.

67 ANTONIO CANOVA,
Genius (Tomb of Pope
Clement XIII, 1783–92)

68 ANTONIO CANOVA,
Genius (Tomb of Maria
Christina, 1798–1805)

69 BERTEL THORVALDSEN
Ganymede Offering the Cup,
1804

70 JEAN–PIERRE FRANQUE Angélique and Médor, c. 1816

In the wake of Abel, Endymion, and Bara, French history painting provides countless examples of images of idealized ephebes which connote effeminacy, passivity, debility, helplessness and impotence, and, at the same time, are charged with an eroticism rarely matched in contemporary images of femininity. René Schneider provides an encapsulated list of the kinds of mythological subjects so prevalent in the Neoclassical period:

> Our artists borrow from this compilation [Ovid's *Metamorphoses*] or from his *Heroides* the sad and tender fables of Narcissus, of Cyparissus, of Adonis, of Salmacis, the nymph of the Carian spring, of Hylas, whose Asiatic legend was Grecianized by the Alexandrians Apollonius and Apollodorus....Musaeus's charming romance gave us the voluptuous myth of Hero, priestess of Aphrodite, and Leander of Abydos...[47]

These themes, all of which feature ephebic protagonists, fall into three general categories: role reversals in which the male subject is the passive object of female desire, as in the myths of Salmacis and Hermaphrodite, Hylas and the Nymphs, Aurora and Cephalus, Iris and Morpheus, and Diana (or Selene) and Endymion; narratives that are more or less explicitly homoerotic, referring as they do to the love between gods and youths; and, third, narratives that explicitly engage my theme of male trouble and feature male protagonists, like Leander, gravely menaced, wounded, expiring or dead, but not in military or heroic contexts. To this latter category were added characters from contemporary literature such as Médor (fig. 70) from Gentil Bernard's 1772 *Phrosine et Mélidor*, and Mazeppa (figs. 41 and 71) from Lord Byron's 1819 *Mazeppa*. It is further significant that certain of these narratives—especially Hylas and the Nymphs and Salmacis and Hermaphrodite—were rarely represented before this period despite their availability in standard classical sources.

The story of Hylas, for example, comes from Apollonius's *Argonautica*. Hylas, the squire of Hercules (his beloved, in Bullfinch's version), while searching for water for his shipmates on the island of

71 HORACE VERNET Mazeppa, 1826

72 PIERRE-JÉRÔME LORDON Hylas and the Nymphs, 1812

73 BERTEL THORVALDSEN Hylas and the Nymphs, 1833

74 JULES-ÉTIENNE LENEPVEU Hylas and the Nymphs, 1865

Cius, approaches a fountain inhabited by the Naiads. So overcome are they by his beauty that they drag him below the water to be their companion. Hercules vainly searches for his friend and the ship departs without him. In François Gérard's version of the subject (pl. V), which was intended to be paired with his *Daphnis and Chloe*, only one nymph is depicted. Her gesture—forceful, insistent—is contrasted with Hylas's panicked helplessness and disarray. The aggressive nymph, however, is of secondary interest: it is Hylas's face, a scrupulous rendering of Lavateresque *passion*, mixing fear and surprise, that is presented to the viewer; the nymph's face is reduced to *profil perdu*. In the version by Pierre-Jérôme Lordon (fig. 72), there are several nymphs engaged in this male rape although, it must be said, the victim seems relatively more willing. As the three nymphs pull at his arms and billowing cape, Hylas gazes meltingly at the nymph who embraces him. Thorvaldsen's marble bas-relief depicts the nymph of the spring coyly filling his pitcher with her spring's water (fig. 73).

A very late treatment of the same subject in 1863 by Jules-Etienne Lenepveu (1819-98) provides an instructive contrast to these earlier versions and graphically illustrates how a given motif is transformed when the erotic locus shifts from a masculine to feminine protagonist (fig. 74). In Lenepveu's painting, it is the central nymph whose body is most prominently displayed: one finger hooked into Hylas's clothing, the other fondling his curls, the nymph has metamorphosed into a Second Empire tart and Hylas has become her hapless foil. By the time Lenepveu produced his Salon entry, the graceful ideal of Winckelmann and the school of David had long been displaced by the re-eroticization of femininity; the erotic focus of the myth has been reversed into familiar and modern terms.

Salmacis and Hermaphroditus, whose story comes from Ovid's *Metamorphoses* (4:285–388), is an especially rare motif, possibly because it thematically poses the issue of a sexuality neither male nor female, but a melding of both. Unlike all the other metamorphoses Ovid describes, the story concerns not one being transformed into something else, but two beings merged into one another, a violent dissolution of boundaries between male and female. In Ovid's version, Hermaphroditus, the beautiful son of Hermes and Aphrodite, comes upon the spring presided over by the nymph Salmacis. Hermaphroditus is described as androgynous even before his metamorphosis: "...in his face he showed/ Father and mother and took his name from both..."[48] Seized by irresistible desire for the youth, Salmacis offers herself to him and is summarily rejected. Mortified, she hides herself and when Hermaphroditus

75 CHARLES DE CHATILLON after ANNE-LOUIS GIRODET-TRIOSON
Hermaphrodite and Salmacis, 1825

bathes in the waters of the spring, she wraps herself tightly around him, draws him into the depths of the waters and prays that they never be parted. The two beings are instantaneously merged, becoming the new composite being thereafter called hermaphrodite: the spring becomes associated with softening, emasculating properties.[49] Although rare, there were other treatments of the subject throughout the Napoleonic and Restoration periods. François-Joseph Bosio (1768–1845), for example, sculpted a *Salmacis*, exhibited in the Salon of 1819, a companion piece to his 1817 reclining *Narcissus* (without nymph).

It is, perhaps, Girodet's version of the story (lithographed by Chatillon) that is the most provocative and psychologically charged of the various Neoclassical versions (fig. 75). Salmacis, in keeping with her greater sexual aggression, is the larger and more physically mature figure; it is her ardent face we see, while the youth, whose body faces the viewer, twists his head almost entirely backward at the engulfing (but standing) nymph. This is clearly a physically impossible pose. Body against body (and there is at least the suggestion of anal penetration), and the open mouth of the fountain from which the water spews accentuate the sexual subtext, while the "impossibility" of Hermaphroditus's position has multiple meanings. In this respect, the death by drowning that figures in the stories of Hylas, Leander, and (in a certain sense) Hermaphroditus is a highly evocative motif: such deaths, given the traditional feminine associations of water, imply an extinction of self in a regressive return to the maternal body. Indeed, certain artists, such as Delorme in his *Hero and Leander* or Jean-Nicolas Laugier (1785-1875) in his *Death of Leander* of 1816 (fig. 76), portray the hero's death as a near-ecstatic abandonment to the element. Given such imagery of masculine surrender (of a tenor not usually found in earlier stages of Neoclassicism) there is some temptation—and more than a little justification—to read such works through the prism of their political moment, that is, the repression and eventual repudiation of radical Jacobin aspirations; the failure of the *sans-culottes* uprisings of Ventose Year II and Germinal and Prairial Year III; the new political order of Empire, and so forth. Such a reading, however, risks a crude reductionism insofar as these elite cultural products may then be thought to "reflect" the traumas of the Revolution and later the collapse of its democratic and utopian aspirations under the Empire. But insofar as the feminized ephebe emerges on the artistic stage well before the revolutionary decade and persists through the Restoration, it would seem to be the case that its ideological and psychological appeal (like that of Anacreontism) overarches the day-to-day political tumults, shifts, and transformations associated with the period 1789–99. It thus needs to be considered in relation to the larger social and cultural determinations of the Neoclassical period. Consequently, it would seem to be the case that to the extent that one of the defining features of Neoclassicism is its containment and/or denigration of femininity, and to the extent that its gender politics evolve towards increasingly rigid boundaries, the ephebe can be said to function as a figure of difference within an economy of the same. As such, the imagery of passive and androgynous manhood bears a dialectical relation to official ideologies (and moralities) of gender which such imagery constantly subverted, complicated or transformed, refusing the fixities that were central to republican programs for moral and political regeneration.

76 JEAN-NICOLAS LAUGIER, Death of Leander, 1816

Pierre-Narcisse Guérin's two pendant paintings of *Aurora and Cephalus* and *Iris and Morpheus* of 1810 and 1811 respectively (figs. 77 and 81), are perhaps the most extreme examples of both the iconography of role reversal and the morphological effeminacy of the male figure. These were originally part of the collection of Giovanni-Battista Sommariva, whose influence as a patron and collector in the Neoclassical period was considerable. Cephalus is given a plumper, more undulant body than one generally sees in depictions of the adolescent ephebic body, a body which floats weightlessly on its billowing cushion of clouds. While Cephalus floats horizontally, unconscious and inactivated, Aurora springs up dynamically, pushing back the veil of night, while gazing languidly down at the supine body beneath her. With her hubcap breasts, metallic curls and enameled face, Aurora is a somewhat alarming presence, but it is worth noting too that the narrative's role reversals are inscribed on the bodies of the protagonists. Thus, where the body of Cephalus is obviously feminized, Guérin has also phallicized the figure of Aurora, whose taut and upright body can be read as a displacement of the potency that Cephalus lacks.[50] A preparatory drawing (fig. 79) makes this even more explicit. Holding a limp hand in hers, Aurora not only appears to surmount the unconscious Cephalus, but to be poised to mount him as well. Other preparatory studies for the painting (figs. 78 and 80) indicate how Guérin progressively feminized the initial *académie*; the bony structure of the mandible in the drawing becomes rounded and fleshy in the painting, the pectorals are smoothed out to a waxy planar surface, the flexed right arm repositioned not only to enable the putto to grasp the hand, but to expose the torso as well.

In Guérin's *Iris and Morpheus*, both figures are nude, the Iris given the doll-like features and *chic* coiffure of Gérard's Psyche of 1798 (fig. 49), the Morpheus figure positioned, as with Girodet's Endymion of 1791 (fig. 20), towards the spectator rather than towards the goddess. Like the iconography of Cupid and Psyche, highly stylized versions of masculine and feminine desirability are put on display, consistent with visual (and libidinal) regimes that while privileging the erotics of masculinity, is equally able to purvey its feminine equivalent. Here too, contemporary critical commentary deploys a highly conventionalized language that gives no hint that such imagery constitutes a dramatic departure from either earlier prototypes or from more typical representations of gender: "Cephalus, delivered to sleep, is slackly stretched out on a cloud which appears to rise gently towards the heavens…the body of the goddess is slender and graceful…the composition of the painting is tasteful, the drawing is correct, the flesh-

77 PIERRE–NARCISSE GUÉRIN Aurora and Cephalus, 1810

78, 79 and 80
PIERRE-NARCISSE
GUÉRIN Three studies for
Aurora and Cephalus,
before 1810

tones are brilliant..."[51] Similarly, when one encounters criticism written in a spirit of strong partisanship and with enthusiasm, criticism that can fairly be called Winckelmannian, it is clear that the voluptuousness and sensuality of Guérin's male figures could be openly celebrated:

> It is good sense, energized by a poetic sentiment, ennobled by an elegant and pure taste that I find there and which charms me in the compositions of M. Guérin: there is reason, poetry and beauty in his painting of Aurora carrying Cephalus away; the beautiful sleeping hunter is borne up by the clouds; his arms, one hanging down, the other supported by a little Amor full of grace, express his surrender to sleep; above him is the svelte and celestial figure of Aurora, who pushes back the veil of night with both hands, letting fall on the youth the flowers that it is her delightful power to scatter upon the earth. I know of nothing more beautiful than Cephalus: in the midst of sleep his drooping head maintains an expression of nobility and sweetness; his hair is arranged with graceful negligence; his body offers an admirable union of youthful beauty and heroic form. Here, the nude is not out of place: the artist, far from employing a facile, detailed display of the anatomy of the torso, has shadowed, softened, married with an exquisite sensibility the joints and muscles in their full and vigorous roundness of the flesh: no flaccidity, nothing indeterminate; no harshness, nothing peremptory or labored; these are male beauties and feminine graces: this recalls the Meleager, the Hermaphrodite...[52]

81 PIERRE–NARCISSE GUÉRIN Iris and Morpheus, 1811

82 JEAN BROC The Death of Hyacinthus, 1801   83 JEAN-PIERRE GRANGER Apollo and Cyparissus, 1817

I quote at length to demonstrate that what seems to be an erotic invest-ment in the male body had become by the Empire also a rhetoric, a form of literary speech, that was highly stylized, codified, and rendered "innocent" of any equivocal subtext. Between the rigors of Davidian *dureté* and *roideur*, and the sensuality of Prud'honian *douceur* and *mollesse*, the post-revolutionary art critic, imbued with the *beau idéal*, could find harmoniously joined in Cephalus's youthful beauty and heroic form.

In contrast to the sharply differentiated and enameled forms of Guérin's version of the myth, Pierre-Claude-François Delorme's 1822 treatment of the subject (pl. IV) is organized to produce a softer, more tender, more patently emotional effect, one further reinforced by the darker, shadowy palette and diffused and mysterious lighting. In keep-ing with the more rhetorically emotional address of such works, Cephalus is posed Pietà-like on the lap of the goddess who cradles him tenderly while surrounded by a bevy of putti. A former student of Girodet, Delorme was clearly influenced by the example of the *Endymion*, a too-evident borrowing for which he was criticized.[53] Like

Girodet's Endymion too, the head of Cephalus was separately litho-graphed larger than life size. That these beautiful male heads were produced as lithographs (fig. 21) is a further indicator of their popular appeal (the new technology of lithography was invented in Germany in 1798 and enthusiastically adopted by French artists after 1813). Lithographers purchased the rights to make and sell such images only if they had some idea of their likely success in the print market. Delorme occupied that area of post-revolutionary painting that was critically identified with the legacy of Leonardo and Correggio (*sfumato*, erot-icism, emotionalism, "painterly" effects, etc.) and whose most promi-nent adept was Pierre-Paul Prud'hon. There is a lengthy art-critical and art-historical tradition of viewing Prud'hon's work as representing a kind of Rococo revival, clothed, however, in the more elevated (and fashionable) trappings of the *grand goût* informed both by the antique and by Michelangelo. Such a reading depends, however, on a prior assumption that true Neoclassical can be neatly distinguished from this putative neo-rococo, but as I have argued, such distinctions obscure shared preoccupations and themes operative within different stylistic formations.

In this respect, a consideration of three paintings illustrating the Apollo/Hyacinthus and Apollo/Cyparissus couple demonstrate how artists of two generations, and with quite different artistic formations, could avail themselves of culturally sanctioned homoerotic subjects. While the 1801 *Death of Hyacinthus* of Jean Broc (1771–1850) is self-consciously primitivizing in its stylistic construction (fig. 82), alluding to Peruginesque prototypes with its high-keyed color, relative flattening of the figures and decorative linearity (deemed "Etruscan" by a number of the Salon critics),[54] Claude-Marie Dubufe's (1790–1864) work of 1821 (pl. IV) remains recognizably within a Neoclassical framework (the Apollo himself a two-dimensional translation of the Apollo Belvedere). This is equally the case with Jean-Pierre Granger's *Apollo and Cyparissus* (fig. 83), from the Salon of 1817, whose Apollo derives from the same source.[55] That said, all these painters chose subjects from Ovid that unabashedly presented the male loves of Apollo, orchestrating the poignant spectacle of the dying ephebes with the meltingly tender ministrations of the sun god. As with the circulation of the Endymion figure, once an artist had established a successful new version of the subject, it was frequently appropriated for the same or a related narra-tive. Granger's *Apollo and Cyparissus*, for example, is clearly modelled on Broc's *Death of Hyacinthus*, even though he has rejected Broc's primitivizing Barbu stylistics.[56]

IV PIERRE–CLAUDE–FRANÇOIS DELORME Cephalus and Aurora, 1822

V FRANÇOIS–PASCAL–SIMON GÉRARD Hylas and the Nymphs, c. 1826

VI CLAUDE–MARIE DUBUFE Apollo and Cyparissus, 1821

As we have seen throughout, pathos is the rhetorical trope, and while it is an open question as to why the homoerotic was acceptable in history painting even after sodomy was recriminalized, it is probably the case that the cultural prestige of classically derived subject matter trumped, as it were, actual homosexual proscription.[57] Here as elsewhere, Salon commentary demonstrates no particular discomfort with an explicitly homoerotic subject. François-Antoine-Marie Miel's discussion of the painting, like Guizot's discussion of Guérin's *Aurora and Cephalus*, employs a critical language that has fully assimilated the *doxa* according to Winckelmann. It is as conventionalized in its consideration of the homoerotic as the painting itself is a conventionalized depiction of it:

> It is with all the abandon of friendship that Cyparissus has thrown himself into the arms of Apollo, where he expires....This composition is simple and touching; there is nothing of the bustle that attracts the mob and it will not have a faddish success; but if one contemplates it with attention, one feels moved and penetrated. The unity of the subject strengthens the interest that it inspires; there reigns in it a grace and a simplicity which recall the Italian school. The entire upper body of the young Cyparissus is worthy of the greatest praise. The neck is perhaps a little swollen; but the chest, the line which traces the contour of the torso, the line which indicates the direction of the arm, offer all the perfection of the model. The body of Apollo has a certain stiffness; perhaps it is a little heavy. The hips also seem heavy. With as much fullness, the antique statue is nevertheless more svelte...[58]

As one might expect, the figures of Narcissus and Ganymede were also popular, but since both had featured regularly in Renaissance, Baroque, and Rococo art, it is more difficult to interpret their specific relevance to post-revolutionary culture. Indeed the figure of Narcissus appears throughout the later nineteenth century, sometimes in quite startling incarnations, such as Jehan Georges Vibert's (1840–1902) piece of 1863 (fig. 84). In any case, by the time Granger and Dubufe were exhibiting their homoerotic ephebes, the first inklings of a general discomfort with the celebration of male youthful beauty were apparent, as in the criticism of Kératry. I will return to this in the next chapter, but it should also be noted that the vogue for ephebic youth was further disseminated through the new technology of lithography as well as traditional intaglio processes. In Aubry-Lecomte's *Young Neapolitan Shepherd* (fig. 85), a pretty Italian boy naps on the ruins of the classic world, indicated by the fragments of columns on which he reclines.

84 JEHAN GEORGES VIBERT Narcissus, 1864

85 HYACINTHE AUBRY-LECOMTE after R.P.J. MONVOISIN Young Neapolitan Shepherd, 1826

86 ADOLPHE CARON after AUGUSTE VINCHON Cyparissus, 1824

This is one instance of the transformation of classicizing motifs into a broader and more popular syntax. Similarly, engravings such as Adolphe Caron's *Cyparissus* after Auguste Vinchon (fig. 86) were geared to a less elite audience, and operated both to disseminate the critically lauded works in the Salons, as in the engraved version of Gérard's *Cupid and Psyche* (fig.49), and to popularize the subjects that Neoclassical artists had been purveying for decades.

The Ephebe as Liminal Figure

The androgynous ephebe should be taken, I believe, as the presiding, if liminal emblem of the Neoclassical period. Its liminality is defined by those attributes it inherits from the past, and those that herald the new dispensation of modernity, where femininity would henceforth prevail as the sign of the beautiful and the erotic. Accordingly, the ephebic body is shaped, on the one hand, by its roots in older cultural forma-tions—the mid-century cult of *sensibilité* with its privileging of pathos and its models of "soft" masculinities, the sartorial exhibitionism and bodily self-display of courtly masculinity—and, on the other hand, by its anticipation of new aesthetic models for the display of a re-eroticized femininity that would dominate most of the nineteenth century. The femininity incorporated in the bodies of passive youths would then be rechanneled—reinstated—in female figures. Before this happened, however, the incorporation of femininity within a masculine ideal served a number of expressive functions. It allowed for, indeed promoted, the psychosexual "monism" that Potts described in David's *Leonidas* (fig. 00), thus lending support to the argument that the femi-nized masculinities of post-revolutionary culture represent the ultimate flight from sexual difference and are, if anything, the logical extension of the "real" historical event of women's expulsion from the public sphere. One might claim too that the resurgence of a poetics (and erotics) of feminized masculinity represents an implicit repudiation of a previous model of masculinity that may not only have been experi-enced as oppressive by male subjects, but more importantly, no longer conformed to the needs of a new or changing collective imaginary and symbolic order.

Here it is worthwhile to refer back to the pre-revolutionary cult of *sensibilité* and the *âme sensible*, the models of ideal masculinity pro-moted by writers such as Richardson (*Clarissa Harlowe* was translated into French in 1751; *Sir Charles Grandison* in 1777), Bernardin de

Saint-Pierre in his *Paul et Virginie* (1788), and most famously, in the hapless and poignant figure of Goethe's *Werther* (translated into French in 1776).[59] As for Rousseau, it would be difficult to overestimate the extraordinary influence of Rousseau's own mythic self-representation and the astonishing identifications it provoked, within both pre- and post-revolutionary culture.[60] Saint-Preux, especially, provided an immensely appealing model of ideal masculinity, one that was considered by readers (of both sexes) to be an alter ego of Jean-Jacques himself. In Richardson's novels and in Goethe's *Werther*, as Louis Hautecoeur remarks:

> Sensibility became the virtue of the honest man, and the taste for morality, reverie, and nature were its signs. But these sentiments, whose morals, ideas and new beliefs and literary styles had enriched the French soul, still lacked their expression in popular form: this was the work of Rousseau.[61]

Although elements of pre-revolutionary *sensibilité* remained a significant part of the cultural environment of the 1790s, largely legitimized and mediated through Rousseau, one of the shaping determinations of revolutionary culture was its uncompromising repudiation of that aspect of *sensibilité* associated with the feminine. As feminist scholars have argued, the revolutionary veneration of exemplary Stoic figures, such as Cato and Brutus, implied, among other things, an overthrow of a once-shared (by men and women) emotional universe of affect. As the historian Dorinda Outram has observed:

> What the Revolution did was decisively to force the abandonment of the *sensibilité* which had united men with women in their reactions to novels, to drama, and to real-life events in the late eighteenth century. Men and women had sighed and wept together over the novels of Rousseau, Richardson and Goethe. Now that kind of reaction was confined to one sex only. Whatever "feminization of the public realm" had been accomplished before 1789, by these means were decisively reversed after 1789.[62]

Hence, the post-revolutionary reappearance of literary and iconographic manifestations of sensibility and sentiment, of sensual, erotic and homoerotic themes, and most significantly, the phenomenal success of Chateaubriand's *René* (1801) and its literary progeny expressing the *mal de siècle* lend support to two interpretative formulations. On the one hand, these "soft" masculinities of Neoclassicism and preromanticism may represent a return of the repressed; not only the return of a repressed femininity—the difference within—but, also, a cultural reinscription of that part of masculinity that revolutionary gender ideologies attempted to foreclose. It is as though the very excess of the prior model of Jacobin *vertu* engendered its own antithesis whereby the repression and denigration of the feminine, the puritanical rejection of the erotic and the sensual, returned in the culture of Thermidor and Empire but in a form of classical drag.

Hence, when the iconographic expressions of male trouble are integrated with literary productions that similarly thematize masculine debility, impotence, distress, and failure to take an effective, active (and procreative) role in society, it seems possible to argue that the roots of male trouble as represented in art lie in a crisis of masculinity itself, a crisis both generally historical in the sense of the *longue durée* (the delegitimization of the aristocratic ideal of manhood and the birth pangs of the refurbished bourgeois model), and specifically historical in terms of the new economic and political realities of Empire and Restoration. Indeed, and as the literary scholar Margaret Waller has argued, "the malady (*le mal*) that is said to characterize an entire age (*le siècle*) afflicts only the male segment of the population…the *mal de siècle* novel recounts a son's alienation from the patriarchal *status quo* as a tragic tale of male disempowerment."[63] Whereas Pierre Barbéris and other scholars of literary romanticism have interpreted its texts as indices of the economic and class dislocations and conflicts attendant on the rise of the bourgeoisie and the new social relations of capitalism, Waller has persuasively demonstrated the equal importance of sexual politics within these texts. The problematic masculinities of the literary protagonists contemporary with the imagery of late Neoclassicism (Chateaubriand's René or Constant's Adolphe, Senancour's Oberman, Stendhal's and Musset's Octaves, Balzac's Félix) are therefore symptomatic not only of the oppressive political and professional circumstances of the Restoration period, but also, of a profound uncertainty about the nature and terms of masculinity itself. The official and elite visual culture of this period consequently presents a Janus aspect; in one sense, its designated cultural "work" is to give expression to a public, institutionally sanctioned, and elevated statement of ideal masculinity; in another sense, it cannot but manifest the internal contradictions, the fissures, the difficulty of a cultural fantasy that is as much subverted by external circumstance as it is by its psychological impossibility; specifically, the denial of sexual difference. For insofar as revolutionary discourse worked to shut out, contain and expel a femininity felt inimical to the free and autonomous expression of masculine subjectivity, its reappearance may be seen in the culture's most exalted and prestigious representations of the masculine.

This "symptomatic" eruption of the feminine within ostensibly masculine imagery is obviously more evident in some artists' work than in others, but it seems especially prevalent in the first twenty years of the nineteenth century. Guérin's paired portraits of the Rochejaquelein brothers–heroes of the Vendéen counterrevolution–provide a good example of how the feminine may be covertly inscribed within the most "manly" themes and subjects. Formally speaking, these paintings are neither conventional portraits nor battle scenes featuring the principal hero. They anticipate–if only generically–the isolated, dramatic and anonymous soldier portraits of Géricault (who briefly worked in Guérin's studio), and follow the model–without the fiery steed–that David developed for his depiction of Napoleon at the St.-Bernard pass. This genre of portraiture spans the earliest stage of Neoclassicism through its Romantic revision and represents yet another articulation of an erotically invested masculinity, deployed here in the service of counterrevolutionary politics.

The earlier of the two paintings, *Henri du Vergier, Comte de la Rochejaquelein*, Salon of 1817 (pl. VIII), depicts the wounded count in the midst of battle. On his left and behind him are two fighting Vendéens, musket and pitchfork poised in such a way that the left edge of the painting consists of a ladder of weapons, starting with La Rochejaquelein's pistol and descending to the points of the bayonets and then to the wielded musket and pitchfork of the fighters. On the right, and behind the count, is the standard bearer, evidently in the act of planting the billowing white flag–*vive le roi*–of the counterrevolution. In the background and along the edges of the hill that they mount is the glow of battle-fire, and, above, the massing clouds of smoke and dust. In the midst of this manly and heroic world of warfare and weaponry is La Rochejaquelein himself, whose porcelain features and silken blond curls, white sash, rose ribbon and tight yellow trousers operate to theatricalize the scene, transforming the rough soldiers behind him and the furor of battle into a scenic backdrop unrelated to his graceful and elegant figure. Quite suggestive here is Guérin's attentiveness to his crotch: defying anatomical verisimilitude, no less than two separate bulges are carefully delineated. These may possibly be interpreted as an (unconscious) compensation for the lapidary prettiness of the hero himself. Although clothed, the image of La Rochejaquelein is recognizably akin to the ephebic ideal, and therefore manifests similarly fetishistic features, manifest, for example, in a

87 PIERRE-NARCISSE GUÉRIN Louis de La Rochejaquelein, 1819

rift between the bulges. To the degree that Guérin's painting fails as a convincing and serious icon of warring manhood it is because his symbolic purpose resides elsewhere, functioning as a kind of elegant pin-up to whom the martial masculinity of the painting refuses to attach itself.

In the later portrait, *Louis du Vergier, Marquis de la Rochejaquelein* (fig. 87), the image of combat, and indeed the Vendéen fighters themselves, have become even more disembodied and distinct from the hero. As doll-like and prettified as his brother the count, the marquis, looking towards his right, gestures to the dark and indistinct clump of soldiers. Given the ghostly flag that floats above them and their somewhat spectral aspect, one may surmise that Guérin intends an allegorical commemoration of the defeated Vendéens rather than an actual battlefield representation. But whether the painting is defined as allegory, (contemporary) history painting, or commemorative portrait, here too one finds on the body of the hero the marks of femininity; specifically, the vagina-like fold above the right thigh.

In the work of Guérin and of so many of his contemporaries, the male spectator can be said to have it all ways; the edifying and culturally sanctioned universe of male *vertu* and beauty, but leavened, as it were, with a femininity contained, interiorized, and incorporated. Despite the fact that discourses of sexual difference are based on a binarism that presumes the stable opposition of male/female, the appearance of the Rochejaquelein brothers, like that of the androgynous ephebe, is testimony to the instabilities inhabiting the binarism itself. Accordingly, the inscription of femininity upon the male body bears symptomatic witness to what has been repressed—a difference within—that official discourses of masculinity had at all costs to disavow. The ephebe, the androgyne, the feminized *beau idéal*, the pretty warrior, in none of these cases should we assume a harmonious integration of masculine and feminine, a utopian expression of wholeness, integration, and reconciliation. On the contrary, the ephebic figure, no matter how ostensibly feminized, is as much a masculinist icon as is its martial and virile Other. Where the latter ideal depends on the literal evacuation of the feminine, the former depends on its no less triumphalist assimilation.

Le Nature y respire partout: malheur à qui la trouve idéale. J'aime à croire et je sens alors avec orgueil que je suis homme, j'aime à croire qu'il a existé des êtres aussi parfaits.

PIERRE CHAUSSARD "Sur le tableau de Sabines"[1]

A man who has exchanged his narcissism for homage to a high ideal has not necessarily on that account succeeded in sublimating his libidinal instincts...As we have learnt, the formation of the ideal heightens the demand of the ego and is the most powerful factor favoring repression; sublimation is a way out by which the claims of the ego can be met *without* involving repression.

SIGMUND FREUD "On Narcissism: An Introduction"[2]

Lacan's distinction between the phallus and the penis, briefly discussed in Chapter One, is a useful point of departure for a consideration of the conventions of the ideal male nude. The disparity between the symbolic power of the former and the mortal, corporeal status of the latter may be likened to the difference between the authority of patriarchy as a social and psychic edifice and the contradictions, difficulties and frailties (historical and psychic) of masculine subjectivity. The less than heroic status of the penis in relation to an abstracted and elevated ideal of a sovereign masculinity also underpins the story—possibly apocryphal—of the day that a major American museum decided it was time for the fig leaves to be removed and the penises returned to the classical statues on exhibition.

The curator responsible for the classical statuary (so the story goes) had for years kept all the detached penises in a shoe box, each one numerically labeled to match it with its body. At a certain point, the curator's assistant, who was doing the actual work of reattachment, protested that one of the statues had been given a wrong part. The

88 FRANÇOIS-JOSEPH HEIM Theseus Slaying the Minotaur (detail), 1807

curator, taken aback by this challenge to her scholarship and record keeping, insisted that her numbers were accurate, her matches correct, until the assistant showed her that the part in question was, in fact, a thumb.

True or not, this anecdote points to one interesting but politely unacknowledged aspect of the classical male nude—the modest size of the genitals, a convention firmly established by the fifth century BC and never modified, either by those artists, like Michelangelo, who so powerfully imprinted the nude with their own idiosyncratic and visionary imagination, or by those like David, who sought to re-animate the antique model through the devoted study of nature. Penises, while obviously not as individual as faces, do come in various sizes, colors, and shapes, and while the standardization of the representation of genitalia can be considered part of the standardization of all body parts that is conceptually integral to the *beau idéal*, that this particular attribute of the ideal should have been determinedly modest in size requires explanation.[3]

Insofar as the phallus is by definition a symbolic representation and the penis an anatomical reality, an investigation of the codes of the idealized male nude is necessarily concerned with the misfit between the overweening authority of the phallus—possessed, we are told, by no one—and the biological organ. For notwithstanding the ontological distinction between penis and phallus, it would seem far more reasonable to expect that the desirable male body of the patriarchal imaginary, in whatever epoch, should be equipped with more impressive organs, just as phallic emblems, such as Hindu stone lingams, often dwarf mere human proportions.

It is, of course, precisely the distinction between penis and phallus that accounts for such an apparent contradiction. For to whatever extent the penis can be said to represent the phallus, its bodily equivalence is at best provisional, if for no other reason than that the organ is flaccid more frequently than not. Although Lacan has himself been charged with phallocentrism, his insistence on differentiating penis and phallus parallels the distinction between biology and culture, between male human beings and the symbolic order of patriarchy. Accordingly, while the authority of the phallus may well be vested in the image of ideal masculinity, the power of patriarchy is so much in excess of its anatomical representative that the actual organ fails to carry its symbolic weight.

Consistent with this disparity, French history painting (and a great deal of heroic sculpture) provides numerous examples of penises busily

89 FRANÇOIS-JOSEPH HEIM Theseus Slaying the Minotaur, 1807

"supplemented" by scabbards, swords, swirling drapery and other pictorial devices, as in the 1807 *Theseus Slaying the Minotaur* (fig. 89) by François-Joseph Heim (1787–1865). It is as though the symbolic importance attributed to genitals, which the genitals do not themselves announce, must be visually indicated somewhere and somehow. Although in some cases resort to strategic bits of cloth or even strips of ribbon may have been compelled by considerations of modesty and decorum, Neoclassical French history paintings, such as the 1812 *Telemachus and Odysseus Slaying the Suitors of Penelope* by Léon Pallière (1787–1820) feature unembellished male bodies as well as veiled groins (pl. VIII). What is suggestive about these veiling devices, however, is that they serve to accentuate rather than diminish. Power is thus displaced from the genitals themselves to various martial paraphernalia—the sword or scabbard—or to the drapery whose color or forms attract the eye to the site of male power and potency.

Any accounting for such pictorial conventions is necessarily speculative, as no *traité* or pattern book I am familiar with specifies either the pictorial recipes or their rationales. But if nothing else, the merit of the penis/phallus distinction provides some explanation for conventions that are otherwise enigmatic but remarkably pervasive. The distinction, moreover, may account for another convention of the ideal male nude, namely, the diminutive scale of the genitals on bodies intended to express not only god-like physical perfection, but the patriarchal values that body incarnates. This discrepancy has recently been addressed by Norman Bryson, who attributes to it an essentially reassuring function for the (male) viewer:

> The convention is so familiar that it is still possible to overlook its aspect of the bizarre; for idealization here entails that the discrepancy between the viewer's sense of his own sex and the ideal, as well as the accompanying anxiety, be resolved by so diminishing the genitalia that no anxiety concerning discrepancy will arise…as the sculpture's genitals are diminished relative to actual genitals, so the sense of the male's genital self-possession and sexual power stands in relation to the masculine imago.[4]

However, another, more historical explanation of the disparity between phallic power and small genitals might lie in the absolute and unquestioned authority of the classical model for later European artists. This authority, after all, underwrites the literal meaning of a canon, and for the artists of the eighteenth century, as for those of the Renaissance or Imperial Rome, the ancients had once and for all discovered the immutable laws and proportions of ideal physical beauty. In much the same way that the basic protocols of the female nude (elision of the genitals, no body hair, small round breasts) were rarely altered, so too were the aesthetic protocols of the male nude rigorously respected. Unlike later manifestations, however, Athenian conventions governing the representation of male sex organs were themselves structured by the beliefs, preferences and social and sexual practices specific to Attic culture and society. Athenian men considered genitalia beautiful when small and taut, possibly because the socially sanctioned object of desire was an adolescent, not a mature man (fig. 90). Thus, it was uniquely the ithyphallic satyr who was provided with an exaggerated, even caricatured, penis, almost always in a state of erection (fig. 91). For the male god, hero, or athlete the small, pointed and dainty penis was the rule,

90 BERLIN PAINTER Ganymede (detail of red figure Attic krater) early 5th century BC

91 PHINTIAS Satyr and Nymph (detail of red figure cup) c. 510 BC

reflecting the cultural/sexual preferences of aristocratic Athenian men.[5] Moreover, as the classicist Eva Keuls has noted, this aesthetic/erotic preference was even provided with a biological rationale, by no less an authority than Aristotle himself, who theorized that the small penis was more fertile than the large one because the distance for the seed to travel was shorter, and therefore had less time to cool.[6]

Finally, the spectacular size of the satyr's genitals was an index not of his masculinity, but of his animality; cause for mockery rather than admiration. Indeed, and as classicists such as François Lissarrague have demonstrated, it was not the glorious figure of Hercules who was endowed with large genitals, but rather Geros, the emblem of decrepitude, or monstrous Pygmies. But where the depiction of penises may have been relatively unproblematic for the classical world, this was surely not the case for Christian Europe. Debates—ecclesiastical, aesthetic and institutional—about the propriety or justification of nudity recur regularly in European art history, most famously perhaps in the deliberations of the Tridentine Councils. In the post-classical world, the body itself was a problematic entity, and the cultural desire to invest it with the most elevated and exalted values existed always in a certain tension with its potential to disrupt or trouble them. Just as Freud argued that the products of civilization result from the sublimation and rechanneling of primitive drives and desires, so is the nude the aesthetic/cultural sublimation of the material stuff of the human body. The reluctance of post-classical artists to modify the canonically fixed dimensions of male genitalia is thus not only indicative of the remarkable and enduring power of aesthetic convention, but also of the anxiety that constellates around the genitalia itself and its representation.[7]

My initial anecdote about the statues' penises is thus intended to frame several issues under the rubric of the political economy of the (male) nude: first, the ways in which the distinction between penis and phallus informs the representation of ideal masculinity; second, the roles played by images of ideal masculinity (mature or youthful) in bridging the symbolic space between the phallus and the actual political and social realities in which male subjectivities are shaped; and third, the vicissitudes of ideal masculinity in the wake of the new political and cultural order of bourgeois civil society.

It goes without saying that the classical body is a male body, and it also goes without saying that it is a body thoroughly saturated with ideological significance. It receives its characteristic attributes through a series of differentiations: from the female body, obviously and centrally, but no less definitively from the grotesque body.

VII PIERRE–NARCISSE GUÉRIN Henri de La Rochejaquelein, 1817

VIII LÉON PALLIÈRE Telemachus and Odysseus Slaying the Suitors of Penelope, 1812

For Mikhail Bakhtin, these two radically opposed fantasies of the body (located respectively in the ideal and the grotesque) corresponded to the worlds of elite and popular culture. The distinction between classical and grotesque bodies was, as we have seen, already operative in the ideal Greek nude, whose small genitals, in contrast to the satyr's, were one of the markers of its ideality, its luminous transcendence of the bestial or "low." In their study of "transgressive bodies," and in keeping with Bahktin's formulations, literary scholars Peter Stallybrass and Allon White point out that "the classical body denotes the inherent form of high official culture and suggests that the shape and plasticity of the human body is indissociable from the shape and plasticity of discursive material and social norms in a collectivity."[8] The classical male body is "the radiant centre of a transcendent individualism, 'put on a pedestal,' raised above the viewer and the commonality and anticipating passive admiration from below."[9] Accordingly, one important aspect of the ideology of the classic male nude is its ability to signify both reason and law:

> Taking its formal values from a purified mythologized canon of Ancient Greek and Roman authors…the classical body was far more than an aesthetic standard or model. It structured, from the inside as it were, the characteristically "high" discourses of philosophy, statecraft, theology and law, as well as literature, as they emerged from the Renaissance. In the classical discursive body were encoded those regulated systems which were closed, homogeneous, monumental, centred and symmetrical.…Gradually these protocols of the classical body came to mark out the identity of progressive rationalism itself.[10]

In French classical art theory, and most specifically in the corpus of theory that in aggregate formed the aesthetic foundation of the *beau idéal*, the ideal male nude was the very linchpin of the system.[11] Mastery of the representation of the male ideal was considered the most formally and intellectually demanding aspect of art practice, combining as it did the labor of mimesis with the requisite imagination to ennoble the raw material of brute nature. This mastery further required the assimilated knowledge of those abstract proportions and regularized relationships believed to have been once and for all established by the ancients and thus teachable and perpetually reproducible. As Quatremère de Quincy tirelessly, tendentiously, and authoritatively propounded these dicta in his writings, the gist of the matter was that it was held that the ancients had provided the immutable rules, regulations, and proportions, which alone could guarantee "the perfection of the ensemble."[12]

Academic teaching in France was basically divided into two types of excercises, practical and theoretical. Practical studies were themselves grounded in the body; the student began by copying the *académies* of the masters, including recognized moderns such as Edmé Bouchardon (1698–1762, fig. 92); moved on to *l'étude d'après la bosse où l'antique,* (studies from classical sculptures or casts of them) and eventually graduated to the living model.[13]

One of the fundamental elements of an artist's formation was therefore the assimilation of schemata for the depiction of bodies; these were supplied by the *traités,* pattern books and drawing manuals which included engraved plates of the body taken from antique statuary, or modern masters (such as Raphael). The engraved plates of the human body that one finds in collections such as those by Girard Audran, Sebastien Le Clerc, Charles-Nicolas Cochin, Louis Bonnet Gilles Demarteau, Gérard de Lairesse, Charles-Antoine Jombert and others are striking in their conventionality; noses, eyebrows, kneecaps, buttocks–all are ascribed their correct and mandated shapes, proportions, ratios, based, of course, on classical statuary (figs. 93 and 94). Which is to say that even as the artist positioned himself in front of the living model, the body had *a priori* been envisioned as an antique sculpture or an engraving from a Renaissance master. The referent thus remained the world of art, which mediated between the artist and the world of real bodies.

Herein lies one central paradox of academic theory; the representation of the human body is the centerpiece, so to speak, of the system, both theoretically and practically, but that body is itself always and already absent, displaced by an abstraction that is anterior to the living model. Quatremère de Quincy's formulation may be taken as paradigmatic:

> You delude yourself curiously when you take the study of the model for the study of nature. The model is of course within nature but it doesn't follow from that that nature is in the model. Nature is the species, the model is only an individual of the species. Obviously, this study cannot be confined to a single individual, at least insofar as this individual is not granted every beauty and every perfection....Nature, in its generation of beings is exposed to too many accidents. Add to this those of upbringing and all the circumstances which surround man in society, you will have the proof that the perfection of the model is a chimera of the

92 EDMÉ BOUCHARDON Standing Male Nude with Staff

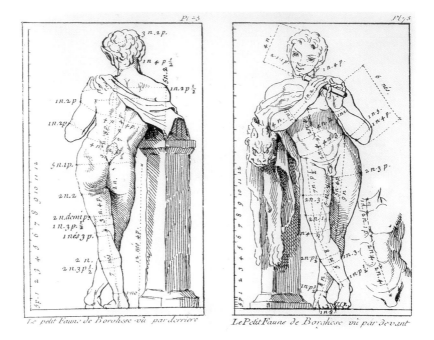

93 CHARLES-ANTOINE JOMBERT Borghese Faun, 1755

imagination. Art can only realize this chimera through the reunion of all the beauties dispersed in the individuals of the species, and this endeavor or the study of what operates to produce this reunion that is perfection is truly the study of nature.[14]

Invocations to "nature"—one of the rallying cries of Davidian theory and practice, which, it should be noted, derived its polemical force from its profound anti-academicism—had little to do with the material reality incarnated in the living model. In Neoclassical art theory "nature" was, on the contrary, an ideal deduced and extracted from its individual representatives; it was conceived as a derivation from the individual type that existed in no single representative.[15] Nevertheless, the zeal with which access to and control of the model were jealously guarded by French state institutions gives some notion of the symbolic stakes involved. After 1663, even private life-classes were forbidden by the government, and, although the Academy of St. Luc managed to acquire the right to the model in 1730, in 1776 Turgot dissolved the guild altogether.[16]

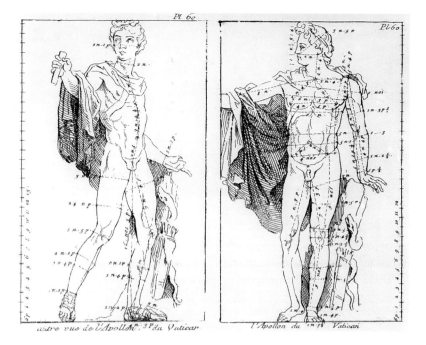

94 CHARLES-ANTOINE JOMBERT Apollo Belvedere, 1766

The central role of the living model within French academic theory and practice and the Academy's continuing efforts to maintain its monopoly on life-drawing suggests the strength of the institutional investment in the body, which like Bakhtin's classical body, incorporates the entire panoply of law, authority, and culture. In this respect, we may recall one of Foucault's central arguments in *Discipline and Punish*:

> But the body is also directly involved in a political field; power relations have an immediate hold upon it; they invest it, mark it, train it, torture it, force it to carry out tasks, to perform ceremonies, to emit signs. The political investment of the body is bound up, in accordance with complex reciprocal relations, with its economic use;…the body becomes a useful force only if it is both a productive body and a subjected body.[17]

It is in this profound sense that the Academy can be said to inhabit the *académie*; the values and beliefs of the institution quite literally embodied and inscribed in the image of ideal and universalized manhood. Given this freight, it is anything but surprising that the living model was male, and remained so until almost the end of the nineteenth century, when female models, actively and rigorously proscribed from the very inauguration of the École Royale des Beaux-Arts, were reinstated. Even for the competitions, such as the Grand Prix de Rome, where the works were produced *en loge*, female models were strictly forbidden; for the depiction of female figures, students had recourse only to their own previous sketches or to engravings.[18] Furthermore, at the acme of the Academy's control of elite cultural production, the male model was himself invested with the *mana* of monarchical power. As the French art historian Jean Locquin vividly reconstructed this royal employee, the role of the official male model in the *ancien régime* was in marked contrast to that of the working-class female models employed by individual artists in their studios:

> As for the model himself, the man who was charged with the task of personifying nature in front of this attentive crowd (400 students after 1764) everything converges equally to give him an exalted idea of the important role he plays in the school. Chosen to represent the figure of Apollo or of Hercules, "the model" as one calls him, is a real somebody. This is no part-timer who poses in an occasional and intermittent fashion and whom one pays at the end of the session. He is a royal functionary. He carries the sword and wears the livery of the king, he is lodged in the Louvre where he has two bedrooms, and he receives a pension ranging from 200 to 500 livres, revertible to his widow. He is a man of substance, who can, like the "good Deschamps" be connected for his whole life to the service of the Academy.[19]

Insofar as it was uniquely the male body which could furnish the artist with the material for the act of distilling and perfecting "nature," the use of male bodies for the depiction of female bodies was a standard feature of academic practice, and, once one is made aware of the fact, it becomes obvious that many images of women are based on male bodies modified with the addition of breasts and a supplementary upholstery of flesh. Even an artist like David, whose aesthetic and pedagogical reforms were based on a return to nature, routinely used male models for female bodies; the grieving servant in *The Lictors Returning to Brutus the Bodies of his Sons* (figs. 17 and 95) is obviously based on a male model. There are many implications that follow from this practice, but as far as the Academy was concerned, an actual female nude was by definition indecent, presumably because it was thought only a dissolute and immodest woman would remove her clothing and pose for men as a

way to earn a living. Engravings such as Pierre-Antoine Baudouin's 1752 *The Honest Model*, which depicts a modest young woman being undressed and displayed by her mother, imply that such virtue is highly exceptional. Female models of course existed, and were employed in artists' studios. But at least one artist—Taillasson—is quoted as having found female models "horribly costly" and necessarily, if regretfully, expendable.[20]

Within the official precincts of the Academy and its school, the *only* situation in which female models were employed was for the *tête d'expression* competition, one of the many in which the students of the Ecole regularly participated. This had become a part of the curriculum in 1760, inaugurated by the Count de Caylus to redress that aspect of physiognomy that was thought to have been neglected in classical statuary. Although fully dressed, the female model chosen to pose for the competition was one whose "good morals" had been confirmed in writing. That it was a female head thought most appropriate for the representation of emotion (anger, fear, ecstasy, pity, and so forth) was fully in keeping with an ideology of gender that located the capacity for reason in the male subject and emotional expressivity in the female one.

The classical codes regulating the depiction of the male body as they were codified by the end of the eighteenth century insistently suggest a repressive operation marshalled to keep at bay the body's Other; the leaking, excessive, boundary-breaking specter of the grotesque. Indeed, one scholar has suggested that the Neoclassical privileging of linearity, exemplified by the contour line illustrations of Flaxman, Gagneraux, Girodet, and others, may be interpreted as a heightened insistence on the body's boundaries, the line functioning as a containment between self and Other, self and world.[21] Quatremère's formulae leave little doubt as to what must be eliminated in the quest for the ideal:

> The ideal image of the ideal man should possess all the types of regularity which it includes. The forms will be modeled with simplified, purified of all individual detail, of all accidental imperfections; the proportions and the relations between the parts will be fixed with all the rigor of a mathematical equation. Finally, all its essential character will be made evident by the accentuation, even by the exaggeration of its features and made to stand out through the subordination of its appendages and secondary features... [The artist's] mission, if one can so put it, is to distill reality, in

order to show us its essence. He should thus guard against trying, under the vain pretext of animating his figures, to imprint upon them the characteristics which in reality denote life: the suppleness of living flesh, the moisture of the skin, the elasticity of the muscles. He should avoid allowing one to perceive what lies below the exterior envelope, the outcroppings of the bony structure, its muscles and its veins, for all that is only the *animal* detail. [Quatremère's italics][22]

But the classic male nude of academic theory is never only an embodiment of elevated cultural values, nor are its meanings entirely circumscribed through its discursive difference from the grotesque body, nor, for that matter, the female body. Inherent to both are psycho-sexual investments that operate on both conscious and unconscious levels. Within the homosocial and homosexual (visual) codes of fifth-century Athenian culture, for example, the ideal male nude was an acknowledged object of sensual desire and pleasure (as was the female nude, despite its greater rarity), whereas in post-classical culture and within the constraints and proscriptions of post-classical morality, masculine sexual investment in the body was necessarily disavowed.

Furthermore, the volatility and difficulty of the male nude *qua* nude is amply documented in the history of debates it periodically engendered in French academic discourse and theory. French artistic culture, from the reformist arts administration of d'Angiviller through the Empire and the Restoration, was founded on the classical male body as the principal signifier for elevated public values (civic, ethical, heroic) as well as the most exalted aesthetic productions. Nevertheless, it could not but be a knot of contradiction: not only was heroic nudity a periodically contested aesthetic value, its sensual appeal was permeable to sensations, desires, and fantasies in excess of its "official" and nominally transcendental representational task. Throughout the eighteenth century there were periodic challenges to the propriety of the nude *per se*. At certain times, it was the female nude that became the object of condemnation and censure; Diderot's reservations in his later writing about the eroticism of the female nudes so abundant in Rococo art were part of a larger critical and moralizing tendency recognizable in the second half of the eighteenth century. As he wrote in 1769:

I am no Capuchin monk; I admit however that I would gladly sacrifice the pleasure of looking at beautiful nudes if I could hasten the time when painting and sculpture, having become more moral and decent, would unite with the other arts to inspire virtue and to purify morals. It seems to me that I've seen enough tits and buttocks; these seductive objects vex the soul's emotions by throwing the senses into turmoil.[23]

But where the erotic address of female nudes could be readily admitted, even if to be deplored, the male nude was considered, by definition, to exist on another level entirely. Its corporeal beauty was conscripted to a different discursive order such that it would have been unthinkable to attribute to it the capacity to "throw the senses into turmoil." That this was unthinkable was not only in consequence of heterosexual presumption, and concomitantly, homosexual proscription, but just as important, the result of an ideology that dissociated maleness from the province of sexuality. No matter how blatantly carnal, sensual, or provocative the male nude, it was effectively purified of licentious intent— then as as now—by a dominant fiction of gender in which it was female persons designated as "the sex" and female bodies assigned for the representation of the erotic, indeed, for the representation of sexuality itself. Even when Neoclassical critics waxed effusive over the beauty of the male bodies depicted in paintings and sculpture, deploying such adjectives as "ravishing," "exquisite," "charming," etc., by virtue of the fact that the bodies were male, the fiction prevailed that such raptures were prompted exclusively by aesthetic and formal considerations. Furthermore, the theorization of ideal nudity had long since assimilated a certain Platonism—evident in Winckelmann's work—and apparent in Canova's own formulation of the issue:

> The nude, when it is pure and instinct with exquisite beauty, takes us away from mortal perturbations and transports us to those early days of blessed innocence: all the more so because it comes to us as a spiritual and understood thing, and lifts our soul to the contemplation of divine things, which, since they cannot be made manifest to the sense by their spirituality, can only be indicated to us by excellence of form, to kindle us with their eternal beauty and detach us from the imperfect and fleeting things of the earth...[24]

Hence, and as a consequence of all these factors, the critics and art administrators like d'Angiviller who promoted a morally elevating return to the "grand style," exemplified by seventeenth-century classicism—pre-eminently the art of Poussin—made an implicit distinction between the values represented by female and male nudity in art. Accordingly, the new moralism of the 1770s, encouraged by Louis XVI and fully supported by state arts administrators like d'Angiviller, had the effect of promoting the representation of male bodies rather than female ones, and placed even greater emphasis on drawing and painting the male nude. This emphasis on male bodies was, as we have seen, fully dispersed within the larger framework of Neoclassical culture and in part promoted by the anti-Rococo reaction itself. But as we have also seen, the primacy of the male body was highly overdetermined insofar as it was uniquely the male body that could represent those civic and humanist ideals that celebrated "Man," while providing covert expression to those homosocial (and homoerotic) investments that so powerfully informed the masculinist ethos of the republic of letters.

Whereas the ideal female nude could and did do allegorical, as well as mythological service, a female human being was ontologically disqualified to represent the values of a transcendent and sovereign subjectivity, endowed with reason and judgment, a self-mastering *cogito*. And while female figures had long been used to express abstract qualities or attributes such as "justice" or "fortitude," in keeping with the conventional mode of allegorical depiction, this in no way implied any relation between actual women and the qualities the female figure might represent. If anything, it was the perceived distance between the abstract attribute and the putative nature of real women that facilitated emblematic indentification. Just as the Revolution adopted Marianne, the goddess of liberty, as its emblem, as Lynn Hunt as noted, "The proliferation of the female allegory was made possible...by the exclusion of women from public affairs. Woman could be representative of abstract qualities and collective dreams because women were not about to vote or govern."[25]

But if female nudes were (positively or negatively) associated with carnal desires and sensual appetites and male nudes with lofty or heroic values, it was nevertheless the case that at a certain juncture within French Neoclassicism questions about the "decency" of the male nude were raised. Such adverse criticism, with a few important exceptions, seems to have been limited to its painted incarnations if for no other reason than statuary, apart from portraits and certain religious subjects, was effectively synonymous with the nude, from whose classical prototypes it took so many of its cues. (This is also why male nudes remained a common subject in sculpture long after they had disappeared in painting). Thus, at the same time that Canova's and Thorvaldsen's male nudes were enthusiastically received, David's *Intervention of the Sabine Women* (fig. 96) of 1799 prompted sufficient negative comment as to require his specific address ("On the nudity of my heroes," which David appended to his printed pamphlet that accompanied the work). Pierre Chaussard, an enthusiastic Davidian, also felt it necessary to justify and explain David's decision to render his warriors nude in his explanatory essay, "Sur le tableau des Sabines par David":

> David has represented, in conformity with the Greek manner, the two heroes entirely nude, except for their helmets and a drapery which flutters around their shoulders. People have loudly protested its indecency; they have spoken of its inappropriateness. David has made this a general question by falling back upon the ancients. One has responded with reason, that indecency does not reside in nudity, and that it can only come from an attitude of mind; that, for example, the Meleagers, the Dioscuri, etc., and in general all the statues, all the bas-reliefs of antiquity represent their gods and heroes nude, and in no way shocking to modesty, whereas, on the contrary, it is those figures veiled from feet to head which express actions contrary to decency."[26]

Only a few years later, the controversies that erupted around Dejoux's monumental nude statue of General Desaix erected in 1810 in the Place des Victoires were of such intensity that less than two months after the statue was unveiled, it was boarded up.[27] It remained under wooden wraps until 1814 when under the Bourbon Restoration it was dismantled and melted down. The bronze was then used for Lemot's (clothed) statue of Henri IV erected on the Place de Pont-Neuf.[28] These incidents, as well as the rash of "defenses" of heroic nudity in statuary produced by the likes of Vivant Denon, Nicolas Ponce, Alexandre Lenoir and a veritable host of Neoclassical propagandists, all attest to the existence of conflict and unease around the subject, intensifying in the first decades of the new century.[29]

The emergence of a critical discourse concerned to rationalize what had hitherto appeared as a self-evident artistic principle (particularly after the institutionalization of Winckelmann's writing), like the surprising protests about the display of male nudity, are perhaps to be understood as presentiments of a changing order. This new discomfort with an aesthetics and an erotics of masculine grace, sensual beauty, and bodily display can be interpreted as a sign of cultural transition; it marks the passage, one might say, to sexual modernity where such attributes were henceforth to be limited to feminine representations. Such discomfort may also signal a belated, if implicit acknowledgment that the beautiful bodies of heroes and youths were capable of generating or provoking meanings apart from their official ones, that they

96 JACQUES-LOUIS DAVID Intervention of the Sabine Women, 1799

could in fact be capable of "vexing the senses," prompting voluptuary rather than purely aesthetic responses. Such an acknowledgment suggests the advent of a more rigorous albeit internalized policing of homoeroticism in elite culture, consistent with the more rigid terms of bourgeois gender ideology. And in this respect, it is also worth remarking that by the first decade of the nineteenth century it was the abstracted, geometricized and planar forms of Bertel Thorvaldsen that began to be critically preferred to the more sensual, polished and seductive bodies of Antonio Canova (compare, for example, Thorvaldsen's *Jason* of 1828 with Canova's *Perseus* of 1801, figs. 97 and 98). If, by the turn of the new century, David's nude Greeks provoked uneasiness, or if the heroically nude General Desaix was considered ridiculous, if not indecent, there is reason to suppose that their "horizon of reception" was in the process of alteration. It would seem as though male nudity

97 BERTEL THORVALDSEN Jason with the Golden Fleece, 1828

was losing its transparency, so to speak, or alternatively, forfeiting that effect of nudity that Quatremère famously likened to a form of dress: "Nudity is considered to be a form of costume."[30] Such a shift in the perception of male nudity signals an anxiety with those aspects of male bodily display that previously appeared not only entirely appropriate, but aesthetically laudable, confirmation of an elevated and ennobled concept of Man.

But whatever the components of this new discomfort signaled by the apologetics of Denon, Lenoir, Ponce, Chaussard, *et al.*, it cannot be considered apart from the fact that the image of Man was always

98 ANTONIO CANOVA Perseus, 1801

intended for the consumption of men. This is not to deny the existence of women spectators or even the rare female critic, but rather, to insist on the overwhelmingly masculine character of the artistic sphere in its widest sense. Thus, the beautiful painted or sculpted male body, in principle geared to a universal spectator, was in practice addressed to a rather specific one; an adult white male subject usually, but not exclusively, a member of the dominant class. As a result, the male nude, whether of antique or European manufacture, was in almost all instances produced, received, commissioned, sold, discussed, celebrated or criticized within entirely male formations. The effective exclusion of women artists from this highly specialized cultural arena further guaranteed that visions of ideal masculinity would be articulated only by men. As quite literally a man-made artifact, the male no less than the female nude was forged in the masculine imaginary. It is therefore to the requirements and the expression of both homosocial male desire and narcissistic identification that we must look in attempting to understand the privileged place of the male nude, mature or ephebic, in Neoclassical visual culture. Especially in the case of those paintings featuring feminized or androgynous types of masculine beauty, we should jettison once and for all the traditional view that associates the work of, for example, Prud'hon or Guérin with either the "decadence" of Directory and Empire culture or, even more egregiously, the post-Thermidorian power and patronage of women. Such a view of post-revolutionary French culture has an art-historical legacy going back at least as far as the Goncourts who did much to establish the belief that the transition from the martial and masculinist ethos of 1789 to more epicene productions of later decades could only be explained by the restoration of female influence:

> The Thermidorian revolution was the victory of women. The Terror was an entirely virile tyranny and was the personal enemy of woman in the sense that it took away her influence and gave her back only rights. The Terror overturned, women returned to their eternal role: they softened hearts in order to guide souls; they made of the political revolution a sentimental one.[31]

Many of the most prominent connoisseurs or collectors of Neoclassical work that featured images of eroticized male youth, from the 1770s through the Napoleonic Empire (Lord Hamilton, Count Sommariva, Joachim Murat, for instance) were men. Furthermore, as I have indicated, the ephebic body was fully in evidence in the revolutionary Salons of the 1790s, and had been an iconographic commonplace in European and British Neoclassical sculpture for decades. Based on such evidence, and given the relatively marginal role of women as patrons, it seems indisputable that the appeal of the ephebic male body is in the first instance directed to men.

This is one of the reasons why the cult of heroic nudity, the ubiquity of the ephebe, and the intensely eroticized atmosphere of post-revolutionary painting must be integrated into a consideration of the framing terms of masculinity operative in the period. Acknowledgment of the historically specific viewer of the ideal male nude therefore suggests that the viewing relations between the (post) classical spectator and an idealized masculine figure must themselves be interrogated with reference to the operations of homosocial desire and narcissistic identification. And once these considerations have been introduced it becomes immediately apparent why the male nude, far more than the female nude, is a fulcrum of contradiction. On the most fundamental level, the production and consumption of desirable images of masculinity took place within a changing social and cultural context that could hardly afford to acknowledge its own erotic investments, whether on the register of the individual artists or that of the culture. In this respect, it would seem to be the case that as the visual language of homosocial desire became increasingly subject to more stringent distinctions between what was deemed appropriately manly (or womanly), the more fluid, polymorphous and sexually ambiguous renditions of Neoclassicism fell out of favor. For this reason too, the male nude in post-classical culture can be seen to function as a sensitive register of those distant rumblings in the sex/gender system that presage shifts in the *status quo*.

Such rumblings may also be identified in a new uncertainty about the significance of the androgynous ephebe, in contrast to the Winckelmannian enthusiasm for its *grâce équivoque*. In a critical essay published in 1822, Kératry, who had earlier sung the praises of Prud'hon's feminized ephebes, expressed certain reservations, now couched in terms of moral degeneration:

> Applying philosophical notions of the ancients to several of the masterpieces of statuary that have come down to us through the centuries, sculptors were persuaded to discern there a particular type of beauty. This seemed to reside, as a principal mode of [the works'] success, in making all effortful movement, all roughness in the forms, disappear, but they failed to see that the result of this process would be to confuse what nature made distinct; the Mercurys, the Apollos, the Dianas, and the Cyparissuses and the Daphnes of the Greeks offer only the slightest differences, the distance that should separate them has disappeared under the chisel which prompts the imagination audaciously to overcome [this difference]; thus, we have justly observed that having arrived finally at the Hermaphrodite, whose origin in moral degradation perhaps escaped them, the artists called to Rome under the reign of Hadrian descended to the level of the Antinous, for the alteration of the signs which establish without equivocation the distinction between the sexes, has the serious fault of tending to corrupt the

taste....Surely, the antique Ganymedes and Bacchuses had too much resemblance to the most beautiful women....From a certain point of view, what we call the *beau idéal* in formal terms has been the effect of a degeneration in morals, if it has not been its cause...[32]

That Kératry should view Winckelmann's adored Belvedere Antinous as an index of moral decline was part of a larger argument concerned to reinstate the "natural" boundaries between male and female, to insist upon the unbridgeable and divinely sanctioned division of the sexes. In Kératry's Restoration texts, we can perceive the hardening of gender lines that was emerging at the same time in medical and psychological discourse. Despite the fact that it was the *androgynous* male body that was the subject of Kératry's reservations, it would be only a matter of time before the nude male body would itself be perceived as an inappropriate object for admiration and critical desire.

To this point, it has been the coding of the male body on the side of the feminine that has most concerned me in the period under discussion. As we have seen, a French painter schooled in any of the important studios who had passed any time in the École des Beaux-Arts possessed a mental pattern book of ideal bodies, as well as number of actual ones, which pre-existed his direct work from the living model.[33] The joint influences of the *beau idéal* within the aesthetic/pedagogical system, the reverence for antiquity, and the substantial visual reservoir of prototypes of antique beauty collectively insured that a history painter, aspiring or established, had a range of possibilities that were, however, to be used in more or less prescribed ways. In keeping with these formulae, the body of Ganymede or Narcissus would not be employed for Cato or Brutus or *vice versa*. The feminized masculine, as I have been designating it, was therefore merely one of a number of available types in the lexicon of ideal bodies, appropriate to, for example, the representation of ephebic characters, or alternatively, for certain types—geniuses, amors, fauns, and so forth. As we have seen, this feminized male body had a venerable pedigree in antiquity: hermaphrodite, androgyne, faun, all of which comprised overlapping categories on a spectrum that fell within the genus ephebe. All were modalities of the feminized masculine and each had its own myths, associations, and representational history.[34]

The frequent representation of the ephebe in European Neoclassicism, bred in Rome and imported to France by resident French artists, was the result of one set of cultural and psychological determinations, but its later popularity in France, particularly in the revolutionary and post-revolutionary period had others. To grasp the appeal of the eroticized ephebe, we need, therefore, to consider its virilized "Other." For if the ephebic body can be said to negotiate sexual difference through a process of incorporation, its excessively masculinized alternative can be seen as the product of emphatic expulsion. These psychological processes were given literal expression in the brief period, beginning in 1793, during which the Jacobin government attempted to replace the allegorical figure of Marianne with the unambiguously virile figure of Hercules.

To understand fully this revolutionary initiative, we must return to one of the most conspicuous features of revolutionary culture, namely its celebration of a constellation of values and attributes associated with manliness and at the same time a segregation (and devaluation) of those associated with femininity. As I have suggested throughout, the masculinization of visual culture in Neoclassicism must be considered dialectically in relation to the period's attitudes toward femininity and toward women. Homosocial desire itself must be seen as requiring an abject feminine Other whose expulsion secures masculine sovereignty. Thus, the anti-Rococo reaction, which virtually every scholar acknowledges as one of the most conspicuous features of Neoclassicism, must be considered as root and branch a gendered phenomenon, a ritual purification of the political and social order whose mechanisms, at its most extreme, suggest the psychological structure of paranoia.

If the ephebic body represents one form by which Neoclassical artists responded to the masculinization of elite culture, the manly, mature, and even brutish Jacobin Hercules, was, far more obviously, another. Insofar as both avatars of masculinity were characterized by excess, they are equally eloquent of male trouble, recalling that aspect of masculinity that Lacan likened to *parade*—meaning a form of display, of show—even burlesque. Where the androygnous ephebe was frequently depicted in situations of disempowerment (or worse), the revolutionary use of Hercules required the display of his unfettered strength and power. But where the imagery of ephebic youth was in evidence for decades before the revolution, and retained its importance well after it, Hercules' turn in visual culture was relatively brief. Precisely because it was a product of revolutionary politics, the Hercules figure permits us to understand more clearly why we may speak of the political economy of the male nude, and why, as in the case of the ephebe, the distinctive appearance of both is shaped by the presiding terms of gender and gender conflict.

The Virile Icon

Needless to say, the ideological substrate preceding the advent of Hercules (and all the other incarnations of more or less ferocious emblems of manhood) is itself related to the ways in which the bourgeois civil sphere, forged in the revolution itself, was in part constituted by and through the exclusion of women from public space and public life.[35] As feminist historians such as Joan B. Landes and others have argued, the constitution of the bourgeois public sphere relies, in the first instance, on the exclusion of all interests deemed particularistic in favor of those deemed universal. In contrast to the sovereign good, women's interests were defined as particular. Furthermore, the concomitant separation between public and private domains, and the ensuing identification of the latter with domesticity, femininity, reproduction, and nurture operated to exclude the feminine, virtually by definition, from the purview of the public:

> ...none of this was the accidental consequence of the lesser status of women in pre-liberal society, to be amended in a more democratic order. Rather, the resistance of enlightened liberal and democratic discourse to femininity was rooted in a symbolization of nature that promised to reverse the spoiled civilization of *le monde* where stylish women had held sway and to return to men the sovereign rights usurped by an absolute monarch. Furthermore, when women during the French Revolution and the nineteenth century attempted to organize in public on the basis of their interests, they risked violating the constitutive principles of the bourgeois public sphere: In place of one, they substituted the many; in place of disinterestedness, they revealed themselves to have an interest. Worst yet, women risked disrupting the gendered organization of nature, truth, and opinion that assigned them to a place in the private, domestic, but not the public realm. Thus, an idealization of the universal public conceals the way in which women's (legal and constitutional) exclusion from the public sphere was a constitutive not a marginal or accidental feature of the bourgeois public from the start.[36]

The demise of the old order and collapse of a premodern patriarchal organization, symbolized by the overthrow of the monarchy and the abolition of divine rule, consequently inaugurated a far more pervasive gendering of the public sphere. Ideologies of gender were insistently inscribed throughout the revolution, most obviously in the constant association of the corruption of the *ancien régime* with the (unnatural) power and depravity of women. Nowhere is this more vividly illustrated than in the pamphlets and *libelles* attacking Marie-Antoinette in the 1780s and '90s. It is scarcely an exaggeration to view her trial as a ritual enactment of this associative chain. Where Louis XVI was accused and condemned on grounds of treason, that is to say, on political charges, the trial of the queen was marked by accusations of incest (with her son), lesbianism (with her companions) and promiscuity (with everyone).[37] Moreover, the insistent masculinization of the concept of *vertu*, one of the dominant tropes in revolutionary (and Rousseauiste) discourse, did much to insure that when the time came juridically and institutionally to expel women from the civic sphere, the philosophical and moral justification was already fully established. Language itself was mobilized in ways that excluded women from the polity of patriots, as in such frequent locutions as *la vertu mâle et républicaine*. Vice and corruption, however, were insistently associated with femininity.[38]

The credit for much of this lies with Rousseau who perhaps more than any Enlightenment figure provided the philosophical rationale for the elimination of women from the nascent civil sphere. By promoting a highly seductive vision of compliant and breast-feeding women and virtuous and sensitive men (exemplified by Jean Jacques himself) whose diametrically opposed roles were consecrated by the very imprimatur of nature, Rousseau provided the philosophical rationale that underpinned successive elaborations of this view from the fields of medicine, physiology, psychology, and jurisprudence. This idyllic notion of the Happy Mother, felicitously restored to her edenic estate of wife and mother was, as Carol Duncan famously demonstrated, massively purveyed in print culture as well as in all forms of elite cultural production.[39] Rousseau's passionate conviction that virtue and happiness could be achieved by women only through submission to nature's intent, that is, exclusion from intellectual and public life and exclusive devotion to children and husband, was, in one scholar's phrase, "a bold and daring provocation in the eighteenth century, where an egalitarian attitude toward women had become fashionable in enlightened and aristocratic circles."[40] This is perhaps to overstate the case, for with the exception of a few *philosophes* such as Condorcet, De Laclos, or (arguably) Helvetius, theoretical discourse on women during the Enlightenment can hardly be characterized as egalitarian.

Nevertheless, even before the establishment of the Jacobin Republic, the status of women as citizens was already equivocal; the constitution of 1791 had distinguished between active and passive citizens, and women (along with the insane, minors and condemned criminals) were relegated to the latter category. Throughout the revolutionary years, the government used the word "man" to stand for "human" in areas such as tax or criminal laws that applied to women as well as men, and used the word "male" where it was a question of political, educational and social rights, from which women were explicitly excluded.[41] The symbolic languages of republicanism were therefore preordained to equate citizenship with masculinity despite the fact that from 1789 until 1793 the symbolic figure of the Revolution—Liberty, the Republic, or Marianne—was a female effigy. However, the use of a female allegory, either in its pre-revolutionary applications (where, for example it could symbolize the monarchy) or after, implies little or nothing with respect to the actual status of women. The usefulness of female allegories, as already remarked, lay in the distance between the symbolized attribute and the female representing it. Moreover, the members of the Convention may well have been motivated by the desire to chose a symbolic form as far removed as possible from the physical form of the deposed male monarch.[42] Nevertheless, despite the fact that a female allegory is unrelated to views about, or the actual status of women, the desire to replace it with a virile icon is directly related to the gender politics of Jacobin culture.

As the Revolution mobilized languages of individual freedom, rights and popular sovereignty, so too did it foster the active and militant participation of women, who in certain instances, particularly in the *journées* of 1789, 1792, 1793 and 1795, were the spearheads of direct revolutionary action. Animated by both the revolutionary language of rights and popular sovereignty and by the actions of militant women, what might be described as the first modern feminism (that is to say, a feminism both pluralist and internally divided) was generated. Throughout the revolutionary years, however, as women increasingly established their political presence, either through direct action or through various political entities such as women's political clubs, they were, as we have seen, simultaneously effaced in history painting. In this context, it is worth noting that among the broad range of classical subjects deployed by French artists in the revolutionary period, images of Amazons, Judiths or other martial women were conspicuously rare. Instead, French artists of the revolutionary period preferred to depict virtuous mothers (such as Cornelia, mother of the Gracchi) when they undertook to create patriotic subjects.

The climax of these parallel developments occurred at the very crest of Jacobin political consolidation as women were definitively expelled from the space of public speech and action.[43] The specific pretext for this expulsion was the market riot that occurred in early October 1793 when the Jacobin women of the Club des Citoyennes Républicaines Révolutionnaires led by Théroigne de Méricourt marched on the market women in Les Halles with the intention of enforcing the decree that citizens wear the revolutionary cockade. The ensuing riot, including the beating of de Méricourt by the market women, was used as justification by the Jacobin delegates to ban officially women's political clubs, to prohibit their speech in the Convention, and even to prohibit women meeting in groups larger than five. In his *discours* in the name of the Committee of Public Safety given on 9 Brumaire 1793 addressing the questions: (1) Must political assemblies of women be accepted? (2) Can women exercise political rights? and (3) Can they deliberate in political or popular gatherings? The deputy J. B. André responded thus:

> This question is tied to morals, and without morals, no republic. Does the reputation of a woman allow her to show herself in public? In general, women are hardly capable of lofty conceptions and serious meditations; and if, among the ancient peoples, their natural timidity and modesty did not let them appear outside the family, do you wish, in the French Republic, to see them in court, at the podium, in political meetings like men, casting aside reserve, the source of the sex's virtues, and the care of the family?[44]

The men, of course, did not.

As the historian Lynn Hunt first argued in 1982, it is for this reason that the project to establish a colossal statue of Hercules as the official emblem of the Republic, replacing the now well-established Marianne has such resonance. The specific proposal, made in early November of 1793 was David's—then a deputy to the Convention—and the statue's form was to be a colossus:

> I therefore propose to situate this monument on the Place de Pont-Neuf. It will represent the people—the French people—[as a] giant. And this image, which will be imposing by virtue of its force and simplicity, will bear in large letters on its forehead: Light; on its chest: Nature, Truth; on its arms, Force, Courage. And in one of its hands the figures of Liberty and Equality, one nestled against the other, and ready to travel the world, showing that they rest only on the genius and the virtue of the people! And this upright image of the people, holds in his other hand the terrible club with which the ancients armed their Hercules.[45]

This was a newly resurrected emblem (Hercules had earlier functioned as the mythological representation of French kings, the *Hercule gaulois*, and in classical iconology was linked to the rhetorical arts as well as to godlike strength) but its utility as a radical effigy had multiple determinations. Hunt has speculated that one element in the Hercules' appeal was its masculinity, permitting the Jacobin deputies to signal their difference from the Girondins, but another, even more important element was its "virilizing" of the concept of popular sovereignty. Accordingly, she argues, "the masculinity of Hercules reflected indirectly on the deputies themselves; through him they reaffirmed the image of themselves as the band of brothers that had replaced the father-king. In addition to supplanting the king, Hercules dwarfed his female companions. In this way, the introduction of Hercules served to distance the deputies from the growing mobilization of women into active politics."[46]

During the relatively brief period of Hercules' deployment as a revolutionary emblem (for all intents and purposes he disappeared as a political symbol from the scene by the end of the century) he was deployed in both classical and popular guises.[47] For example, he appears in an anonymous pen-and-wash allegory of the French Republic, *The Triumph of the French Republic Under the Auspices of Liberty,* 1789 (fig. 102). He appears in classicizing form in David's 1793 drawing *The Triumph of the French People* (fig. 101) and in the 1794 design of Jean Guillaume Moitte (1746–1810) as *The French People Crushing the Hydra of Royalism, Fanaticism, and Federalism* (fig. 99). Equally classicized, he draws the chariot of the Republic in Joseph-Marie Vien's ink-and-wash drawing *The Triumph of the Republic* (fig. 103) also produced for the competition of the Year II. He features too as the personification in the clay *Project for a Monument of the French People* (fig. 100) produced by Joseph Chinard (1756–1813) for the competition of the Year II (November 1793) to replace the statue of Henri IV on the Pont-Neuf. He dwarfs Alcestis in Regnault's painting of 1799 (fig. 25). And he also features in David's monumental tableau for the Festival of the Supreme Being (8 June 1794) where, as in David's project for the monumental statue, he holds two tiny effigies of Liberty and Equality in his hand. In his popular incarnation, Hercules appeared as a brutish *sans-culotte* (the People as pure force) in prints and engravings. And from the evidence of at least one contemporary print, he was the giant personification in David's tableau for the festival of 10 August.

That the Hercules—a man for all seasons—could be depicted either in classicized forms or in "low" incarnations of militant populism was a measure of the adaptability of the figure. More important, however,

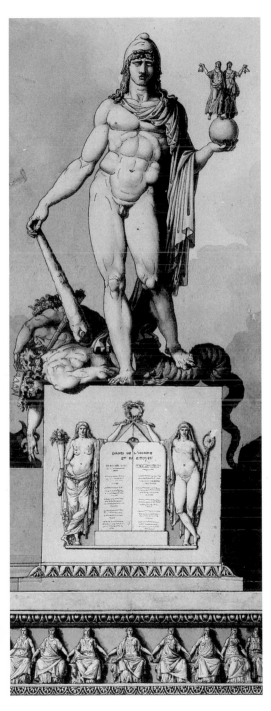

99 JEAN-GUILLAUME MOITTE The French People
Crushing the Hydra of Royalism, Fanaticism and
Federalism, 1794

100 JOSEPH CHINARD Project for a Monument to the
French People, 1793

101　JACQUES-LOUIS DAVID
The Triumph of the French People, 1793

102　ANONYMOUS The Triumph of the
French Republic Under the Auspices of
Liberty, 1789

103　JOSEPH-MARIE VIEN
The Triumph of the Republic, 1794

were the ways by which the masculinization of symbolic visual language could function to camouflage conflict between different classes of French (male) citizens. This, as I have argued, was the ideological use-value of the ephebic body, but the hero warrior, or the stalwart Hercules can be seen to perform a like function. In this respect it bears repeating that the worship of masculine ideals—ephebic or virile, classical or plebeian—has historically operated to obscure a broad range of differences and conflicts *between* men. One might well be an impoverished laborer rioting for bread and *le maximum* (state control of grain prices) but as a man, one was nevertheless allied in fraternity with one's bourgeois brethren in the Convention. The honorific of male citizen, in revolutionary France as in classical Athens, could therefore function to invoke a specious equality symbolically ratified by the shared prerogatives of masculine supremacy and feminine subordination.

Classical Precedents

Despite its temporal distance from the gender politics of revolutionary France, the work of the classicists John J. Winkler and David M. Halperin on the sexual politics of Athens in the time of Cleisthenes provides an important explanatory model for the intensified phallicism of revolutionary French culture exemplified by the reinstitution of the Hercules figure.[48] In his discussion of the disenfranchisement of male prostitutes and the polis's provision of female ones which accompanied the democratization of Athens in the sixth century BC under Cleisthenes, Halperin comes to certain conclusions that seem applicable to the psychosexual and political organization of France in the 1790s. He points out, for example, that the Athenian production of a democratic political body was accompanied by an increasingly strict demarcation of the public realm as a male citizen's preserve. The absolute distinction between *oikos* and *polis*—while by no means the same as the eighteenth-century distinction developed between private and public—bears certain resemblances to the latter insofar as it delineates the space (literal and discursive) occupied by male citizens from that occupied by their inferiors (women, slaves, children). Furthermore, the disenfranchisement of male prostitutes and the official support of female prostitution may be taken as twin correlations of an masculinist ideology that wishes to downplay social and economic distinctions between male citizens. Citing an expression by which adult males of the Kabyle people of Morocco indicate their "inalienable and irreducible masculinity"

("I, too, have a moustache"), Halperin sees an equivalent formulation in the symbolic language of democratic forms in Athens along the lines of "I, too, have a phallus." Specifically he locates the signs of this privileged fraternity in such sixth-century innovations as the state's curbs on male prostitution (and subsidization of female prostitution) and the erection of ithyphallic herms as doorkeepers and guardians of each citizen's household. All these, he argues, are markers of a masculine egalitarianism from which all non-citizens were necessarily excluded.[49]

The herms (quadrangular posts with a carved head of Hermes and an erect penis carved at the base) did not appear on vase paintings until 520-500 BC, the same period from which the earliest surviving stone herms are dated. John Winkler interprets them as "levelling signs," tokens of both democracy and masculine hegemony.[50] While it would hardly be accurate to consider the Attic herms as strictly analogous with the Herculean emblem, or, for that matter, with the exaggerated virilism of Jacobin discourse, what is striking here is the congruity between an expanded democracy for male citizens, the strategic use of phallocratic symbolism and the more stringent confinement of women, all of which combine to sustain and foster the bonds of homosocial organization. It was the historian Joan Kelly, in her classic essay of 1984 "The Social Relations of the Sexes: Methodological Implications of Women's History," who pointed out that the historical periods singled out by liberal historians as those marked by progressive developments—such as the expansion of individual freedoms, exemplified by Athenian democracy, the Renaissance, and the French Revolution—were those in which women's estate, if anything, worsened.

> Let me merely point out that if we apply Fourier's famous dictum—that the emancipation of women is an index of the general emancipation of an age—our notions of so-called progressive developments...undergo a startling re-evaluation. For women, "progress" in Athens meant concubinage and confinement of citizen wives in the gynecaeum. In Renaissance Europe it meant domestication of the bourgeois wife and escalation of witchcraft persecution which crossed class lines. And the Revolution expressly excluded women from its liberty, equality and fraternity.[51]

In the context of what Margaret George termed the "world historical defeat of women" at the apex of Jacobin consolidation and the cultural dominance of virile and stoic models of masculinity, how then do the passive and androgynized masculinities of post-revolutionary painting factor in?

As I have been suggesting throughout, ideologies of gender, like ideology *tout court*, are historical complexes and therefore may manifest their own forms of uneven development. New models of sexed subjectivity, spawned in the revolution, were very much in process, revealing in some aspects the emerging order of bourgeois hegemony, in others, the residual traces of the old order. If for a few decades the stoic masculinities of Cato and Brutus, the Horatii and Socrates, were briefly proposed as ego-ideals, if, for a brief moment, the muscle-bound Hercules was promoted as an ideal icon, such models may well have proved too oppressive to masculine subjectivity to endure for long.

But notwithstanding its diverse articulations, the imagery of ideal manhood—addressed in all instances to male spectators—can be seen to serve several overlapping functions: first and foremost, it perpetually secures the equivalence between man and human, ensuring that female persons will remain categorized as other and lesser, and will be identified with difference, alterity, the domain of the body, sexuality, and reproduction; as masculine representatives of the *beau idéal* such imagery can evoke narcissistic identification (along the track of what the subject would like to be); as feminized (or infantilized) images of masculinity, they could mobilize fantasies of possession and mastery, standing in, so to speak, for the absent feminine; as feminized or masculinized icons of desire, they permit different forms of erotic projection (whose identity as male figures absolves them from being considered as grossly sensual or carnal); finally, in the form of androgynes, "unstable" images of ambiguous gender, they could generate a fantasmatic free play, an escape from the uncompromising fixities of gender ideology that revolutionary, and later, Napoleonic culture was concerned to resecure. In all cases, however, the masculinity of the spectator is effectively shored up and affirmed, a bulwark against actual historical and psychic circumstance and their inescapable tribulations and traumas. The imagery of ideal manhood is thus—to use Freud's term, *apotropaic*—averting and warding off what assaults and threatens it.

There is here at work in the Neoclassical worship of beautiful masculinity a structural homologue to Freud's theorization of mechanisms of the ego-ideal:

> The formation of an ego ideal is often confused with the sublimation of instinct, to the detriment of our understanding of the facts. A man who has exchanged his narcissism for homage to a high ideal has not necessarily on that account succeeded in sublimating his libidinal instincts. It is true that the ego ideal demands such

sublimation, but it cannot enforce it; sublimation remains a special process which may be prompted by the ideal but the execution of which is entirely independent of any such prompting....Further, the formation of an ego ideal and sublimation are quite differently related to the causation of neurosis. As we have learnt, the formation of an ideal heightens the demand of the ego and is the most powerful factor favoring repression; sublimation is a way out by which the claims of the ego can be met *without* involving repression.[52]

Equally germane to these arguments is the fate of femininity—its constitution as pure difference—in the forge of revolution. In this respect, one of the salient features of the epoch was an emerging paradigm of sexual difference, developed by Georges Cabanis, among others, that insisted on the radical differences between male and female human beings. This more rigid reconceptualization of sexual difference was expressed in clothing styles no less than in the new physiologies and psychology. Where pre-revolutionary clothing (for the upper classes) was conspicuous in opulence and display for both sexes, revolutionary styles were not only more sober, they manifested increasing divisions between what was acceptable self-presentation for men and women. In the court culture of the *ancien régime*, men and women both wore wigs and/or hair powder, high heels, rouge, jewelry, perfume and the like.

> The new "minimalist" clothes of the Revolution, and the forbidding to men of disguise, display and artifice in dress and body adornment, meant that Revolutionary fashions echoed the new political culture's emphasis on sharpening differentiation between the sexes and insisting that members of each sex appear for what they "really" were. At the same time, it is interesting to note, *class* lines in dress were often deliberately blurred, as ardent male middle-class revolutionaries donned the trousers identified with the working man and escaped the knee breeches associated with the aristocracy. The clothes expressed the profound truth that while the line between middle-class men and working-class men might, on strategic occasions be blurred, that between men and women had at all costs to be made visible.[53]

In the classic account by the psychoanalyst J. C. Flugel of what he termed the "great masculine renunciation," the tidal shift from aristocratic to bourgeois masculine subjectivity occurred by the middle of the eighteenth century, at least in England. Remarking on the shift in British male fashion that originated in the 1740s, Flugel reasoned that as the components of what might be termed the collective ego-ideal were altered historically, so too were masculine subjectivities correspondingly adjusted. In abjuring previously masculine prerogatives such as lavish and richly decorative clothing, wigs, make-up, high heels, and instead accepting "bourgeois" garb (more closely linked to the dress of the working man; hence, a signifier of equality) the well-to-do men of Europe and America had also to repress their exhibitionism and narcissism—two fundamental drives in all human subjects (hence the renunciation). These qualities could, however, be massively projected outward upon women, the "muted other," and masculine exhibitionism transformed into voyeurism:

> Thus we can see that, in the case of the exhibitionistic desires connected with self-display, a particularly easy form of conversion may be found in a change from (passive) exhibitionism to (active) scoptophilia (erotic pleasure in the use of vision)—the desire to be seen being transformed into the desire to see. This desire to see may itself remain unsublimated and find its appropriate satisfaction in the contemplation of the other sex, or it may be sublimated and find its expression in the more general desire to see and know.[54]

In essence, Flugel is here describing the transition from the visual economy of pre- and post-revolutionary elite culture in which the masculine occupies—perhaps for the last time until now—the position of specular object of desire, to the new order of bourgeois culture where such a position may only be occupied by the feminine. The domain of specularity, exhibitionism and display comes therefore to be both designated and identified as the domain of femininity, an association for which there were, in any case, venerable cultural and religious precedents.

In the same way that clothing operated to accentuate sexual difference but lessen class difference, by the early years of the new century, there was another development in the refashioning of gender ideology; namely, new epistemological, medical, and psychological models of gender that insisted on the absolute alterity of the female body. As women were expelled from the public sphere, femininity itself was retheorized as pure otherness. The gradual replacement of an older one-sex model for reproductive and genital biology (in which female anatomy was understood to be an internalized and imperfect analogue of the male's) had important implications for the conceptualization of gender across the board. Once science had established a biological paradigm of incommensurability and difference, all other discourses in the human sciences would be correspondingly organized around this unbreachable divide.[55] As Thomas Lacquer has argued, the prior paradigm of sexual difference, based on various classical and Renaissance authorities "whose telos was male, gave way by the late eighteenth century to a new model of radical dimorphism, of biological divergence. An anatomy and physiology of incommensurability replaced a metaphysics of hierarchy in the representation of woman to man."[56]

In the wake of the Revolution, the reinstitution of monarch as emperor, and not least, the charismatic power of Napoleon and the production of the myth of the New Alexander, can be said to have also contributed to the depletion, if not the deflation, of the mythic masculinity of the revolutionary moment, doubtless another factor favoring the iconography of male trouble. The "band of brothers," in Hunt's terms, was replaced again by the governing patriarch. Seen within this new politico-symbolic universe, the relative impotence and narrative passivity of Chateaubriand's René or Stendhal's Fabrizio del Dongo and Julien Sorel (constantly described in *Scarlet and Black* as physically "girlish" and "delicate") contrasts tellingly with the overweening stature of a mythologized Napoleon, whose phallic *mana* overshadows the age. Similarly, and following fast upon the heels of Thermidor, new masculinities can be seen to emerge, masculinities that would henceforth be associated with the purview of the feminine. For as Flugel understood, the sartorial display and narcissistic exhibitionism of aristocratic manhood was to be contradicted by newer, emerging models for masculine subjectivity. The extravagant posturing and flamboyant costume of the *jeunesse dorée* was thus—in Raymond Williams's terms—a residual phenomenon.

In fact, contemporary descriptions—textual and iconic—of the *merveilleux* and the *incroyables*, (themselves descendants of the eighteenth-century *fats* and *muscadins*)[57] convey the sense of a masculinity, like that of the *ancien régime*, expressed through exhibitionistic and unabashed display. Although satirical in intent and rendering, drawings such as the anonymous *Game of Lotto* of 1800 (fig. 104) and engravings such as Godefroy's *The Parisian Tea* of 1801, Naudet's *The Parisian Seraglio or the Fashionable World of 1802,* and the anonymous *Waltz* of 1802 (fig. 105) and *Purposeful Promenade* of 1803 (fig. 106) provide a vivid sense of these new styles of comportment and self-fashioning. Consistent with the heightened emphasis on sexual difference, the women's clothing reveals all or part of their breasts, their arms, and the

104 ANONYMOUS The Game of Lotto, 1800

105 ANONYMOUS The Waltz, 1802

106 ANONYMOUS The Purposeful Promenade: the Montansier Theatre, 1803

light transparent fabric of their dresses reveal the body underneath. And while the men's clothing exposes less flesh, the breeches are skin-tight and drawn high at the waist, thereby accentuating the crotch. Around 1802 the more extravagant of the *incroyables* adopted baggy-seated breeches, but for the most part, the style was for form-fitting, striped and light-colored pants. Furthermore, the men's elaborate coiffures (albeit unpowdered), complicated neckcloths, and delicately slippered feet are not so much markers of sexual difference as they are equivalents of feminine display, drawing attention to various parts of the body, while remaining nominally within the bounds of the new requirements for bourgeois male costume. Although mocked as "effemi-nate" in contemporary graphic imagery and literary and epistolary accounts, there was as yet no "homosexualization" of these *fashion-ables*, this *jeunesse dorée* or the dandies. Portraits such as Louis Gauffier's *Prince Koudacheff* of 1796 (fig. 107) are even more revelatory of this transitional period in masculine self-representation. Compared to Eugène Delacroix's (1798–1863) comparatively disembodied portrait of Louis-Auguste Schwiter—a later, and greater example of this portrait

107 LOUIS GAUFFIER Portrait of Prince Koudacheff, 1796

108 FERDINAND-VICTOR-EUGÈNE DELACROIX Portrait of Louis-Auguste Schwiter, 1826–1830

genre (fig. 108)—the prince is far more of an embodied spectacle. Despite his somewhat portly trunk, the tight silk trousers and dainty slippers accentuate his fashionability and *chic* aplomb. Similarly, the come-hither expression and the posing of the body declares the prince's actively seductive and highly self-conscious identity as *fat* or *fashionable*. Nor was such self-fashioning the exclusive purview of the aristocracy, for this final efflorescence of masculine exhibitionism was not limited to the Thermidorian right and the *jeunesse dorée*: the Barbus— the primitivizing dissidents within David's post-revolutionary studio—

were themselves spectacles, something like Neoclassical Beatniks, parading through the streets of Paris in antique costume and sporting beards and sandals.

Following the stylish reign of the *incroyable*, and with the end of the Napoleonic wars, came the new avatar of dandyism—a British import—whose various incarnations would reverberate throughout the rest of the nineteenth century. In keeping with Baudelaire's classic characterization—"Dandyism appears above all in those transitory epochs when democracy is not yet all-powerful, and when the aristocracy is only partially tottering and disgraced"[58]—historians and literary critics have interpreted the phenomenon largely in strictly materialistic terms. But dandyism and its earlier incarnations demand to be understood within the larger framework I have described; like the desirable male nude of the post-revolutionary Salon, dandyism too is the last gasp of an archaic model of masculinity, already marginalized and headed for (official) cultural extinction.

For male viewers, a category to be strictly distinguished from a mythic and universal "beholder," the pleasures provided by the spectacle of the male body in the works I have discussed throughout these chapters celebrate masculine sovereignty while registering its tensions, its frailties, its element of masquerade. Ironically enough, these pleasures provided by Neoclassical manhood are integrally related to their narrative and iconographic "pains." Thus, the representation of male trouble, which in many instances constitutes the manifest content of the art can be interpreted at one and the same time as both the expression of the problem and its fantasmatic solution. Whether femininity is effectively banished and expelled, assimilated and interiorized within the image of masculinity, or itself metamorphosed into a hybrid gender, the common denominator remains the flight from difference and its recuperation under the sign of the same. It is in this sense that the uneven development of gender ideology is given visual expression. Thus, the legions of feminized youths that populate the art of Neoclassicism are alike inhabitants of a liminal space in which homosocial desire is unselfconsciously articulated in relation to the masculine. When this paradigm shifts, as it does in the period between the Restoration and the July Monarchy, the attributes of an idealized and erotically charged masculinity will henceforth be projected on to femininity, minus, of course, all the heroic, ethical, and institutional values that had been mapped upon the classical male body.

For the generation of critics, intellectuals and belle-lettristes who came of age in the Restoration, the generation for whom the new art

109 HIPPOLYTE FLANDRIN Theseus Recognized by his Father, 1832

was heralded under the banner of romanticism, the *beau idéal*, exemplified by the beautiful bodies of men and youths was the fossil of a bygone age: "We are on the eve of a revolution in the fine arts," wrote Stendhal in his Salon of 1824. "The large pictures composed of thirty nude figures, copied from antique statues and heavy tragedies in five acts and in verse, are doubtless quite respectable but whatever one says about them, they are beginning to be boring."[59]

While there is obviously no strict line of demarcation dividing these two iconographic regimes, I would propose by way of symbolic closure two works from the July Monarchy that respectively signal the decisive collapse of the older paradigm. The first, an artifact of elite culture, is Hippolyte Flandrin's Prix de Rome winner of 1832, *Theseus Recognized by his Father* (fig. 109). The distinction between penis and phallus with which I opened this chapter is given here particularly delirious expression in Flandrin's unfortunate use of the rib roast to mask Theseus's genitals and the contiguity of the knife to both. Although some critics made mocking reference to this device ("We would also say that the plate of cutlets used to hide the natural parts of Theseus, standing in front of the table, is a pretty ridiculous idea, a really grotesque form of composition"[60]), the reservations that were widely expressed about the painting as a whole concerned its coldness, the stiffness of the figures, their lack of expression and/or their lack of "nobility." In effect, the lack of enthusiasm for the painting, even by those like Delécluze who were most committed to a continuation of Davidian Neoclassicism, or by the partisans of Ingres, Flandrin's teacher, suggests that what was subliminally perceived as absent in the work was precisely the sensual and erotic investment in the male body that had animated history painting previously. Indeed, and even if we ignore the rib roast, the pedantic dryness of Flandrin's painting, its uninspired correctness and dutiful antique reference, its desiccated and leaden color—all confirm the crisis of history painting lamented by academic critics throughout the century.[61] And while the lengthy death agony of history painting had multiple components, not the least important one derived from the "de-cathecting" of the ideal male body. The foreclosure of a culturally sanctioned investment in its beauty, its desirability, and the propriety of its sensual address, as much as any other factors, sealed the fate of history painting.

The second example is the work of an artist born in the nineteenth century whose art was mobilized by a politics (and aesthetics) altogether hostile to the values of classicism, neo- or otherwise. Specifically, I refer to Honoré Daumier's devastating satires of history painting and its myths collected under the title *Histoires Anciennes* of 1842 (figs. 110 and 111). With its cast of potbellied or cadaverous heroes and warriors, its *hausfrau* goddesses and *lumpen* spearbearers, Daumier's lithographs subverted all aspects of heroic myth while simultaneously dismantling the premises of academic history painting. Nevertheless, when we examine his deflationary re-visions of Endymion and Narcissus, the former a napping lout, the latter an emaciated scarecrow, it seems clear that one important aspect of his satire was his notion of the absurdity—indeed, the fatuity—of male pretensions to physical and sensual beauty. A conception of masculinity that encompasses the narcissistic, the exhibitionistic, the seductive and the passive, and which had provided a visual language for a collective masculine ego-ideal— as well as a *beau idéal*—was now worlds, not decades, removed from Daumier.

110 HONORÉ DAUMIER Narcissus (Histoires
Anciennes, 1841–43)

111 HONORÉ DAUMIER Endymion (Histoires
Anciennes, 1841–43)

Notes and Sources

Author, title, and date and place of publication are given in full when a source is first cited; subsequent references give author's surname and short title only.

Chapter One
Notes to pages 16–41

1. Walter Benjamin, Thesis XIV from "Theses on the Philosophy of History," in Benjamin, trans. Harry Behn, *Illuminations*, ed. and with an introduction by Hannah Arendt (New York, 1968), p 261.
2. Marlboro, for example, since 1900 the most popular brand of cigarettes globally as well as in the U.S.A., was originally marketed by its manufacturer (Phillip Morris, then the smallest tobacco company in the U.S.A.) as a woman's cigarette, partly because its filter and mild tobacco made it "lighter" than most cigarettes in the post-World War II market. As it enjoyed no great success in this incarnation, it was relaunched in 1954 with the cowboy advertising image to incarnate its refurbished "masculine" identity.
3. Laura Mulvey, "Visual Pleasure and Narrative Cinema" in Mulvey, *Visual and Other Pleasures* (London, 1989).
4. The literature on the subject of patriarchy is vast, and encompasses many fields, from anthropology to Marxist and psychoanalytical theory (e.g., Friedrich Engels' *The Origin of the Family, Private Property and the State* and Freud's foundational essay "Totem and Taboo"). A recent and substantial study is Gerda Lerner's *The Creation of Patriarchy* (New York and Oxford, 1986). Another recent consideration of patriarchy that employs a "dual systems" approach, relating capitalist to patriarchal structures is Sylvia Walby, *Theorizing Patriarchy* (London, 1990). One very good discussion of the historical metamorphosis from "paternal" models of patriarchy (quite literally, the rule of the fathers) to more recognizably modern forms, embodied in the social contract and institutionalized within the bourgeois civil sphere, may be found in Carole Pateman, *The Disorder of Women: Democracy, Feminism, and Political Theory* (Stanford, 1989.) For a discussion of this phenomenon within the context of the French Revolution see Joan B. Landes, *Women and the Public Sphere in the Age of Revolution* (Ithaca, 1988) and Lynn Hunt, *The Family Romance of the French Revolution* (Berkeley and Los Angeles, 1992).
5. Roger Horrocks, *Masculinity in Crisis* (New York, 1994).
6. "Ainsi, pour commencer par le chef-d'œuvre de productions de la nature, qui est l'homme, [note that Jombert does not use the word 'human'] le jeune Peintre doit s'instruire de l'Anatomie et des proportions parce que ces deux parties font le fondement du dessein." Charles-Antoine Jombert, *Méthode pour apprendre le dessin* (Geneva: Minkoff reprint, 1973) p. 99. Further evidence of the ways art theory affirmed the equivalence of the male with the human body is shown in the *a posteriori* prescriptions for rendering a female body: "One draws women in accordance with the same principles of organization and general effect which are

prescribed for men. The proportions, however, are different. The woman has a smaller head and a longer neck, the shoulders and chest are narrower. The nipples of the breast, and the abdomen are placed lower; the distance from the nipple to the navel is shorter by half the length of a nose. The thigh is bigger, but approximately one third of a nose shorter. The legs are fatter, and the feet narrower. The contours, finally, are more fluent and the forms larger, since the muscles, being fatter and plumper than in men, are hardly perceptible under the skin." Nicolas Cochin the Younger and Denis Diderot, "Plates and Notes on Figure Drawing" in the *Encyclopédie ou Dictionnaire raisonné des sciences, des arts et des métiers of 1751*, ed. and trans. Philipp P. Fehl (Chicago, 1954) p. 52. Drawing manuals by Gérard de Lairesse (1787), LeClerc and Janinet (1773), and Watelet and Levesque (1788–91) repeat more or less the same formulae.

7. The nature of this looking, whether on the part of male or female, heterosexual, homosexual or bisexual subjects, must be distinguished, however, from the socially naturalized (and massively produced and disseminated) visual economy that constructs women as both sites and sights of visual pleasure and erotic display. As I will argue throughout, the display of the beautiful male body within post-classical Western culture is more highly fraught and riven with contradiction.

8. For a more detailed account of the etymology of both terms, and an excellent discussion of the problematics of the "invention" and definition of homosexuality and the homosexual see David M. Halperin's *One Hundred Years of Homosexuality and Other Essays on Greek Love* (London and New York, 1990). I have greatly benefitted from this study and been much influenced by it. Other useful accounts include Pat Caplan, ed., *The Cultural Construction of Sexuality* (London, 1987); David F. Greenberg, *The Construction of Homosexuality* (Chicago, 1988); Kenneth Plummer, ed., *The Making of the Modern Homosexual* (London, 1981); Edward Stein, ed., *Forms of Desire: Sexual Orientation and the Social Constructionist Controversy* (London and New York, 1990); Jeffrey Weeks, *Sex, Politics, and Society: The Regulation of Sexuality Since 1800* (London, 1981). One of the best discussions focusing on the problems of a too-strict social constructivist approach is John Boswell, "Revolutions, Universals, and Sexual Categories" in Martin Duberman, Martha Vicinus, George Chauncey, eds., *Hidden From History: Reclaiming the Gay and Lesbian Past* (New York, 1989).

9. Halperin, *One Hundred Years of Homosexuality*, p. 18.

10. Michel Foucault, "The Perverse Implantation" in Stein, *Forms of Desire*, p. 18.

11. Robert A. Padgug, "Sexual Matters: On Conceptualizing Sexuality in History," *Radical History Review*, vol. 20, Spring/Summer 1979, pp. 3–23.

12. Michel Foucault, *The History of Sexuality*, trans. Robert Hurley: Vol. I *An Introduction* (New York, 1978; London 1979); Vol. II *The Use of Pleasure* (New York, 1985; London, 1986); Vol. III *The Care of the Self* (New York, 1986; London 1988).

13. John Boswell, *Christianity, Social Tolerance, and Homosexuality* (Chicago, 1980).

14. My use of this term derives from the model employed by Eve Kosofsky Sedgwick in her *Between Men: English Literature and Male Homosocial Desire* (New York, 1985).

15. A full-length study of this motif is found in James Saslow, *Ganymede in the Renaissance: Homosexuality in Art and Society* (New Haven, 1986).

16. Neil Hertz, "Medusa's Head: Male Hysteria under Political Pressure," *Representations 4*, 1983, pp. 27–54.

17. Here it is important to distinguish psychobiography and psychohistory from a psychoanalytically informed, symptomatic reading of texts. While all approaches take

their cue from Freudian theory, especially texts such as "The Creative Writer and Daydreaming," the psychoanalytical approach, which is closest to mine, does not pretend to address the individual psyche of any historic individual. Rather, and in keeping with contemporary forms of literary criticism, I am concerned to decipher the meanings of cultural artifacts and discourse, which are culturally, not necessarily individually specific.

18. Michel Vovelle, "Ideologies and Mentalities—A Necessary Clarification" in Vovelle, *Ideologies and Mentalities* (Chicago, 1990), pp. 11–12.

19. The modern theorization of the concept of the public civil sphere is that of Jürgen Habermas. See Habermas, trans. Thomas Burger, *The Structural Transformation of the Public Sphere* (Cambridge, Mass., 1991). The feminist critiques of the gender blindness implicit in Habermas's model upon which many of my own arguments depend include the following: Carole Blum, *Rousseau and the Republic of Virtue: The Language of Politics in the French Revolution* (Ithaca, 1986); Landes, *Women and the Public Sphere in the Age of the French Revolution*; Joan Landes, "The Public and the Private Sphere: A Feminist Reconsideration" in Johanna Meehan, ed., *Feminists Read Habermas: Gendering the Subject of Discourse*, (New York, 1995); Pateman, *The Disorder of Women*; Nancy Fraser, "What's Critical about Critical Theory? The Case of Habermas and Gender," in Mary Lyndon Shanley and Carole Pateman, eds., *Feminist Interpretations and Political Theory*, (University Park, Penn., 1991).

20. The sense in which I use the term "Imaginary" derives from Jacques Lacan. In Lacan's tripartite mapping of the psyche, the three orders consist of the Real, the Symbolic, and the Imaginary. The last is the order characterized by an identification with images, which is one of the primordial ways in which the individual self is constituted *as* an individual self, or subject.

This formulation develops out of Lacan's model of the mirror stage of a child's development (between six and eighteen months), in which the ego is understood to have been built upon (specular) mis-recognitions of the self and the perceptions of that self in the mirror as they are both mediated and reflected back by others (initially the mother). The relation of the subject to his or her ego is therefore inherently narcissistic and internally alienated. A cultural (or social) Imaginary is thus by analogy an aggregate representation of the culture's self image. See the following: Lacan, "The mirror stage as formative of the function of the I," "Aggressivity in psychoanalysis," and "The Function and field of speech and language in psychoanalysis" in *Ecrits*, trans. Alan Sheridan (London and New York, 1977).

21. The notion that gender roles, as opposed to biological sex, are a function of performance and thus entirely social categories of behavior and identity, forms the thesis of Judith Butler's *Gender Trouble* (London and New York, 1990).

22. Kaja Silverman, *Male Subjectivity at the Margins* (London, 1992).

23. Ibid., p. 3.

24. Jane Tompkins, on the other hand, locates her crisis in masculinity well into the twentieth century, and uses it to account for the appeal of the Hollywood Western. See Tompkins, *West of Everything: The Inner Life of Westerns* (London and New York, 1992). A different period of crisis is examined in Susan Jeffords, *The Remasculinization of America: Gender and the Vietnam War* (Bloomington and Indianapolis, 1989). For his part, Michael Kimmel situates his crisis in masculinity in late seventeenth-century and early eighteenth-century England as well as in the present. See Kimmel, "The Contemporary 'Crisis' of Masculinity in Historical Perspective," in Harry Brod, ed., *The Making of Masculinities: The New Men's Studies* (Boston, Mass., 1987).

25. Silverman, *Male Subjectivity*, p. 55.
26. Tania Modleski, "Postmortem on Postfeminism" in Modleski, *Feminism Without Women: Culture and Criticism in a "Postfeminist" Age* (London and New York, 1991), p.7.
27. Margaret George, "The World Historical Defeat of Républicaines-Révolutionnaires," *Science and Society*, XL, no. 4, 1976–77, pp 410–37.
28. "Elles [les poissardes] passèrent à la révolution armes et langues. Elles furent de la révolution, les vestales terribles, les bacchantes saoûles du nouveau dieu Liber [an ancient Italian god corresponding to the Greek god Dionysus]. Elles précipitèrent les émeutes, elles entraînèrent les hommes, elles firent marcher les milices nationales, elles se mirent entre les troupes royales et les hordes patriotiques, elles lancèrent l'attaque, elles paralysèrent la défense. Les hommes tuaient; elles massacrèrent." Edmond et Jules de Goncourt, *Histoire de la société Française pendant la Révolution* (Paris, 1918) p. 382.
29. Edmund Burke, *Reflections on the Revolution in France* (Garden City, 1961) p. 85.
30. Raymond Williams, "Dominant, Residual, and Emergent," in Williams, *Marxism and Literature* (Oxford, 1977) pp. 121–27.

Chapter Two
Notes to pages 42–97

1. Johann-Joachim Winckelmann, "De la grâce dans les ouvrages de l'art" in *Recueil de différentes pièces sur les arts* (Geneva: Minkoff Reprint, 1973) p. 287.
2. For example, of all the winning Prix de Rome entries from 1793 to 1863, most of which feature nude or partially draped male figures, there is only one painting depicting a female nude, Jean-Jacques Henner's 1858 *Adam and Eve finding the body of Abel*. See in this regard Philippe Grunchec's indispensable *Les Concours des Prix de Rome: 1797–1863* (Paris, 1986) which reproduces and discusses each of the winning entries during this period.
3. While a survey based on deductions from the titles of paintings alone is necessarily approximate, the evidence supports this observation. My methodology, while hardly scientific, is based on the notion that an *Adonis* or an *Eros* is probably a nude male, just as a *Chaste Susanna* or a *Nymphe sortant le bain* is probably a female nude. History paintings, which often feature multiple figures, are more complicated to evaluate, but I have assumed that "historical" Romans are usually clad, and mythological (male) Greeks usually nude. Consistent with the paintings reproduced in Grunchec's *Les Concours des Prix de Rome*, I have also assumed that female figures in classical tableaux, particularly in the paintings of the *exemplum virtutis* type, are draped. In multi-figure compositions that probably represent both male and female nudes (e.g., Van Dorne's *Vénus blessée par Diomède, va se plaindre à Mars*, Salon of 1808), I have counted these as one male and one female figure. Similarly, certain subjects that involve multiple figures (e.g. Nicolas-Guy Brenet, *Combat des Grecs et des Troyens*, Salon of 1781), I have counted as one male nude. My results are as follows:
   Salon of 1781: of 226 paintings and drawings (listed together in Salon *livrets*, but drawings are excluded from all my tabulations) and 27 sculptures, 16 male and 9 female nudes
   Salon of 1783: of 215 paintings and drawings and 60 sculptures, 16 male and 11 female nudes
   Salon of 1784: of 215 paintings, 15 male and 11 female nudes; among the 60 sculptures, 10 male and 7 female nudes
   Salon of 1785: of 197 paintings and drawings and 61 sculptures, 27 male and 14 female nudes
   Salon of 1800: of 387 paintings and drawings, 8 male and 4 female nudes; of 10 sculptures, 5 male and 3 female nudes
   Salon of 1808: of 631 paintings: 31 male

and 23 female nudes; of 88 sculptures, (the vast majority are portrait busts) 4 male and 6 female nudes

Salon of 1822: of 1329 paintings, 24 male and 27 female nudes; of 174 sculptures, 17 male and 23 female nudes

Salon of 1831: of 3211 paintings (with a relatively small proportion of antique subjects—43 in all), 15 male and 66 female nudes; of 80 sculptures, 10 male and 11 female nudes.

4. On the development of the "display nude" in nineteenth-century French painting see Beatrice Farwell, *Manet and the Nude: A Study of Iconography in the Second Empire* (New York, 1981). For a discussion focused on the erotic implications of the female nude, see Lynda Nead, *The Female Nude: Art, Obscenity, and Sexuality* (London and New York, 1992).

5. For example, one finds in Liam Hudson's study *Bodies of Knowledge: The Psychological Significance of the Nude in Art* (London, 1982) the following: "My text contains more female bodies than male bodies. This results not from leering chauvinism, but from historical fact…ours is a culture in which it is predominantly women's bodies that have been used as a symbolic means of expressing desire" (p. 7). This is, of course, one of the central arguments in John Berger's *Ways of Seeing* (Harmondsworth, 1972). The automatic assumption that the nude is primarily female is also found in Marcia Pointon, *Naked Authority: The Body in Western Painting 1830-1908*, (Cambridge, 1990). Where the male nude is granted equal time, as in Kenneth Clark's *The Nude; A Study in Ideal Form* (New York, 1956) any consideration of its erotic economies is scrupulously avoided. However, a good, albeit general study of the male nude may be found in Margaret Walters, *The Male Nude: A New Perspective* (London, 1978).

6. In Greece, no sculpture of a female nude appears before the sixth century and is quite unusual in the fifth. "So rare are nude figures of women in the great period of Greek art that to follow the evolution of Aphrodite before Praxiteles we must not look for absolute nudity…" Clark, *The Nude*, p. 119. Even more important, the overwhelming number of tracts, *traités*, pattern books and theoretical and critical disquisitions on the nude are predicated on the ideal male body. Winckelmann, for example, or his most influential exegetes in France—Quatremère de Quincy, Eméric-David, Kératry, Chaussard, Joseph Droz, etc., have very little to say about the female nude.

7. In her introduction to *Naked Authority*, Marcia Pointon argues that the nude as such has never been theorized as a genre. This is true insofar as French classical art theory posits the idealized human (read male) figure as the most important element within a history painting which, of course, *is* a genre. One might also argue, however, that in the form of the *académie* (a nude figure drawn or painted from a nude model) the nude does achieve generic codification. For the theorization of history painting and the role of the nude within it see the following: Jean Locquin, *La Peinture d'histoire en France de 1747 à 1785* (Paris, 1912); Reusselaer W. Lee, *Ut Pictura Poesis: The Humanistic Theory of Painting* (New York, 1967), Nikolaus Pevsner, *Academies of Art: Past and Present* (Cambridge, 1940), André Fontaine, *Les Doctrines d'art en France: peintures, amateurs, critiques de Poussin à Diderot* (Geneva: Slatkine Reprints, 1970); François Benoît, *L'Art français sous la révolution et l'Empire: les doctrines, les idées, les genres* (Geneva: Slatkine Reprints, 1975).

8. Hans-Robert Jauss, "Literary History as a Challenge to Literary Theory," *New Literary History* 2 (1970), pp. 7–37.

9. While this is overwhelmingly the case for easel painting, it is somewhat less so for marble and bronze sculpture. In fact, the idealized nude male had a far more durable shelf life in these media. Possibly, this is because classical and Neoclassical aesthetic

theories were root and branch bound to the example of classical antiquity in which the nude male body was dominant, and also because certain abstract concepts, such as heroism, were not usually figured by female bodies.

10. The term "male trouble" is borrowed from a special issue of *Camera Obscura* 17 (May 1988), concerned with (contemporary) male subjectivity, including the sexual persona of Peewee Herman. For my purposes, the usefulness of the term lies in the way it denaturalizes masculinity itself, enforcing the recognition that it is not *only* femininity that is constructed (or subverted) within representational systems.

11. Carol Duncan, "Fallen Fathers: Images of Authority in Pre-Revolutionary French Art," in Duncan, *The Aesthetics of Power: Essays in Critical Art History* (London and New York, 1993), and Lynn Hunt, "The Imagery of Radicalism," in Hunt, *Politics, Culture and Class in the French Revolution* (Berkeley and Los Angeles, 1984), pp. 87–119. Equally germane is Hunt's anthology, *Eroticism and the Body Politic* (Baltimore, 1991) and her *The Family Romance of the French Revolution*.

12. The work of Alex Potts, to whose work I am deeply indebted, is a conspicuous exception. See especially the important essay "Images of Ideal Manhood in the French Revolution," *History Workshop Journal* 30 (Autumn 1990) pp. 1–21. This essay has been integrated into his monographic study *Flesh and the Ideal: Winckelmann and the Origins of Art History* (London and New Haven, 1994). See also Whitney Davis, "The Renunciation of Reaction in Girodet's *Sleep of Endymion*," in Norman Bryson, Michael Ann Holly, Keith Moxey, eds., *Visual Culture: Images and Interpretations* (Hanover and London, 1994).

13. Marsilio Ficino, "What Components are Needed to Make a Thing Beautiful, and that Beauty is a Spiritual Gift," chap. VI of the *Commentary on the Symposium of Plato*, translated by Joseph Peake and cited in Erwin Panofsky, *Idea: A Concept in Art Theory* (Columbia, 1968), p. 137.

14. E. J. Delécluze, *Louis David: son école et son temps* (Paris, 1983).

15. All translations from the French are my own unless otherwise indicated. "Pensif, il tenait son regard machinalement fixé sur Mme de Noailles, qu'il ne voyait que par derrière. Ses cheveux châtain foncé, entourés de bandelettes rouges à la manière antique, faisaient ressortir la blancheur de son cou, qui était élancé et fort beau. Ce rouge et ce cou blanc frappèrent tout à coup l'imagination d'Étienne, excitée déjà par les réflexions que la visite de David lui avait suggérées, et il lui sembla voir tomber la jolie tête de cette jeune femme. Ce ne fut même qu'en faisant un grand effort sur lui qu'il parvint à se rendre maître de l'agitation intérieure qu'il éprouva en ce moment." Delécluze, *Louis David* pp. 41-42.

16. Delécluze provides a list of David's students through the year 1816, but only last names are given. A far more complete list, including first names is provided in Daniel and Guy Wildenstein, *Louis David: Recueil de Documents Complémentaires au Catalogue complet d'artiste* (Paris, 1973). According to the Wildensteins' list, David had a total of 13 paying women students from the time of his initial establishment of the studio until his Belgian exile. For a discussion of some of these women in the studio of David, as well as much more concerning the neglected subject of women artists in the revolutionary period, see Vivian Penney Cameron's Ph.D. dissertation, "Woman as Image and Image-Maker in Paris during the French Revolution," Yale University, 1983.

17. Eve Kosofsky Sedgwick, *Between Men: English Literature and Male Homosocial Desire* (New York, 1985).

18. Ibid., p. 3.

19. Ibid., p. 23.

20. In recent work on the dynamics of David's studio, the rivalries, identifications, and

Oedipal conflicts between the artist and his students have become central issues. For example, in his study *Tradition and Desire* (Cambridge, 1984), Norman Bryson employed Harold Bloom's famous model of agonistic and Oedipal generational conflict for understanding the stylistic relations between, for example, David and his teacher Vien, and Ingres and his teacher David. More recently, Thomas Crow has elevated the studio rivalries and identifications within David's studio into the very engine of artistic invention and stylistic transformation. See Harold Bloom, *The Anxiety of Influence* (London and New York, 1973) and Thomas Crow, *Emulation: Making Artists for Revolutionary France* (London and New Haven, 1995).

21. J. L. Jules David notes in his biographical *recueil* that David's students also served as models for the Romulus and the Tatius in his *Intervention of the Sabine Women*; see J. L. Jules David, *Le Peintre Louis David: Souvenirs et Documents inédits* (Paris, 1880), p. 336. Delécluze also mentions this practice and provides earlier precedents. I have not been able to determine if David's women students joined the men working from the male model, but Cameron in "Woman as Image" suggests this was unlikely. In Delécluze's account, Mme de Noailles is entirely separated from the other students; only Étienne shares her work space. In the absence of information, I would suspect that in general women students did not draw from the nude model, although Cameron indicates that some *académies* were produced by contemporary women artists, especially those trained as history painters. See also n. 25 below.

22. "Enfin, on n'a pas été mécontent de ma besogne; ce qui m'a surtout fait plaisir, c'est qu'il n'y a eu qu'une voix pour dire que je ne ressemblais en rien à M. David." Letter dated 24 Oct. 1791, cited in P.-A. Coupin, *Oeuvres Posthumes de Girodet-Trioson, suivie de sa correspondance* (Paris, 1829), vol. 2, p. 396. In an earlier letter to Dr.

Trioson, Girodet described the project thus: "Je fais un Endymion dormant; *l'Amour* écarte les branches des arbres auprès desquels il est couché, de manière que les rayons de la lune l'éclairent par cette ouverture, et le reste de la figure est dans l'ombre. Je ne crois pas la pensée mauvaise; quant à l'effet, il est purement idéal, et par conséquent très difficile à rendre. Le désir de faire quelque chose de neuf et qui ne sentît pas simplement l'ouvrier, m'a peut-être fait entreprendre au-delà de mes forces; mais je veux éviter les plagiats." Ibid., p. 387.

23. The letter, sent by Drouais from Rome, is dated 13 Sept. 1786. "Pour moi, je paresse tant que je peux. Néanmoins, je m'occupe sérieusement de chercher un beau sujet. On a été content jusqu'aux derniers jours. Ce qui me fait le plus plaisir, c'est que les peines que je me suis données n'ont pas été perdues, puisque tout l'honneur tombe sur vous, et que les choses dont on a été content sont celles qui ont quelque ressemblance avec vous." Reproduced in Jules David, *Le Peintre Louis David*, p. 37.

24. See especially George Levitine, *The Dawn of Bohemianism: The Barbu Rebellion and Primitivism in Neoclassical France* (London and University Park, Penn., 1978) and the two essays on Maurice Quai and the Barbus by Charles Nodier in Delécluze, *Louis David*.

25. On Ingres's studio see Eugène Amaury-Duval, *L'Atelier d'Ingres* (Paris, 1924); and Henri Delaborde, ed., *Lettres et Pensées d'Hippolyte Flandrin* (Paris, 1865). On Girodet's atelier see Jean Adhémar, "L'enseignement académique dans l'atelier de Girodet," *Bulletin de l'art français ancien et moderne*, 6, 1933, pp. 123–59.

26. Under the moralistic and paternalistic supervision of d'Angiviller, *Directeur des Batiments du Roi*, even the lodging of women students was subject to official control. Jules David reproduces an exchange of letters between David and d'Angiviller prompted by d'Angiviller's disapproval of the fact that three women artists (Mlle Duchosal and the two Mlles

Laville-Levoulx were temporarily resident in David's household. David assured him that the women lived (and apparently worked) apart from the male students. See the exchange in Jules David, *Le Peintre Louis David*, p. 58.

27. "…à la tête de ces derniers est une 'Jeanne d'Arc.' Il ne tiendra pas à elle que l'Académie ne tombe en quenouille. Elle a semé parmi nous la plus dangereuse division. Deux coqs vivaient en paix: une poule survint, et voilà la guerre allumée. Cette poule, par 'molle complaisance et sans l'autorisation de la loi,' siège au milieu des coqs. C'est de cet abus que nous sollicitons la suppression devant des législateurs dont les prédécesseurs ont exclu les femmes de la Régence. On dit que les talents n'ont pas de sexe; mais ceux qui les possèdent en ont un, et quand il est féminin, il faut l'éloigner du masculin, à cause de son influence inévitable." Cited in Cameron, "Woman as Image," p. 87.

28. "Si nous permittons à des citoyennes de se réunir ici, trente mille femmes pourraient s'assembler et exciter dans Paris un mouvement funestre à liberté." Cited ibid., p. 240.

29. Ibid, p. 89.

30. The standard modern sources for information on women artists and women artists' relation to academic training are Linda Nochlin and Ann Sutherland Harris, *Women Artists 1550–1950* (New York, 1976); Rozsika Parker and Griselda Pollock, *Old Mistresses: Women, Art and Ideology* (London, 1981); and Germaine Greer, *The Obstacle Race* (New York, 1979). On Girodet's school for women artists see J.-L. Bruel, "Girodet et les dames Robert," *Bulletin de la société d'histoire de l'art français*, 1912, pp. 76–93. A painting by Adrienne Marie-Louise Grandpierre Deverzy (1822) depicts the studio of Abel de Pujol in which women artists draw from a fully clothed female model. In 1803, Mme Frère de Moutizon opened an École Gratuite de Dessin pour les Jeunes Filles, which was supported by the state. Although there was,

at the start of the century, some lobbying on behalf of women artists, generally speaking the move was towards greater segregation of women artists, in training, in institutions, and by genre. See Benoît, *L'Art français sous la révolution et l'Empire*, pp. 245–46.

31. Exclusively male clubs in Paris began to appear as early as 1783, but increased significantly (and along the lines of the British model) after the Napoleonic wars, fueled further by fashionable Anglomania: "Nous commençâmes aussi à avoir des clubs: les hommes s'y réunissaient, non encore pour discuter, mais pour dîner, jouer au wisk [sic] et lire tous les ouvrages nouveaux. Ce premier pas, alors presque inaperçu, eut dans la suite de grands, et momentanément, de funestes conséquences. Dans le commencement son premier résultat fut de séparer les hommes des femmes, et d'apporter ainsi un notable changement dans nos moeurs." Louis Philippe, comte de Ségur, *Mémoires ou souvenirs et anecdotes* (Paris, 1827) vol. 2, p. 32. Cited in John C. Prévost, *Le Dandysme en France (1817–39)* (Geneva, 1957), p. 45. The emergence of men's clubs has thus to do with the larger general shift from the more sexually integrated social world of the *ancien régime* to the increasingly segregated one of the early nineteenth century. See in this regard Maurice Agulhon, *Le Cercle dans la France bourgeoise: 1810–1848: étude d'une mutation de sociabilité* (Paris, 1977).

32. In his classic study, *Transformations in Late Eighteenth Century Art* (Princeton, 1967), Robert Rosenblum discusses the popularity of this motif in Neoclassical art, but interprets its appeal as related to archaicizing and/or moralizing stylistic tendencies.

33. Duncan, "Fallen Fathers" in Duncan, *The Aesthetics of Power*, p. 46.

34. The classic study of the role of Brutus in the art of David and in the French revolutionary political context is Robert L. Herbert, *Art in Context: J.L. David: Brutus* (New York, 1972). See also Norman

Bryson's interesting discussion in Bryson, *Tradition and Desire* (Cambridge, 1984).

35. *Mercure de France*, I, 24 Oct. 1789. Cited in Herbert, *Art in Context*, p.126.

36. "Les mythologies galantes, le genre gracieux, la 'petite manière'…commençaient à passer de mode vers 1750…c'est surtout à partir de 1760 que le 'retour à l'antique' s'affirme d'une façon tangible." Jean Locquin, "Le retour à l'antique dans l'école anglaise et dans l'école française," *La Renaissance de l'art française*, no. 1, 1922, p. 273.

37. See Dora Wiebenson, "Subjects from Homer's *Iliad* in Neoclassical Art," *The Art Bulletin*, XLVI/1, March 1964, pp. 23–34. In "Le retour à l'antique dans l'école anglaise et dans l'école française," Locquin discusses the use of Homeric themes in considerable detail, as does Régis Michel in the catalog for the exhibition of the Cabinet des Dessins, Musée du Louvre, 17 Oct. 31 Dec. 1989, *Le Beau Idéal, ou L'Art du concept* (Paris, 1989). See also the discussions in Locquin's indispensable *La Peinture d'histoire en France*.

38. A complementary discussion to my own reading of this work is Carol Ockman's "Profiling Homoeroticism: Ingres' *Achilles Receiving the Ambassadors of Agamemnon*," *Art Bulletin*, 75, 1993, pp 259 74. A slightly altered version appears in her *Ingres' Eroticized Bodies: Retracing the Serpentine Line* (New Haven, 1995).

39. Warren Roberts, *Jacques-Louis David, Revolutionary Artist: Art, Politics, and the French Revolution* (Chapel Hill and London, 1989), p. 139.

40. Ibid., p. 139.

41. Potts, *Flesh and the Ideal*, p. 237.

42. "Ce tableau est vraiment original et pour l'invention heureuse et poétique et pour l'effet hardi et piquant. Le dessin en est d'un grand caractère, le pinceau large et moëlleux; il règne en générale dans ce tableau une teinte bleue, qui n'est pas assez vraie." *Explication par l'ordre des numéros et jugement motivé des ouvrages de peinture, sculpture, architecture, et gravure, exposés au palais national des arts*, Bibliothèque Nationale de France, Collection Deloynes, tome XVIII, 458, pp. 42–43. Cited in Jean-François Heim, Claire Bernard, Philippe Heim, *Les Salons de peinture de la révolution française 1789-1799* (Paris, 1989) p. 46.

43. "L'étude est sacrifiée au sujet; car pour donner une couleur de lune à son tableau, on n'y voit nulle part la couleur locale des chars, la teinte est bleue partout, ce qui n'est pas assez vrai, et pour introduire des formes de choix dans l'amant de Diane, le peintre ne montre aucune des vérités du naturel." *Exposition au salon du palais national des ouvrages de peinture, sculpture et gravure, Petites Affiches de Paris*, Bibliothèque Nationale, Collection Deloynes, tome XVIII, 459, p. 187. Cited in Heim et al., *Les Salons de peinture de la révolution française*, p. 46.

44. For an excellent survey of this period in French art criticism see Richard Wrigley, *The Origins of French Art Criticism* (Oxford, 1993).

45. George Levitine, *Girodet-Trioson: An Iconographical Study* (London and New York, 1978), p. 119.

46. In this respect it is worth remarking that heterosexual marriage was in many respects far less "romantic" than the ideologues of bourgeois domesticity acknowledged, whereas close male friendship was often intensely so. David, for example, typically for men of his class and profession married relatively late, at 33. Equally typically, Mme David, the daughter of Charles Pierre Pécoul, David's mentor, was 17, and it was upon M. Pécoul's friendly offer of either of his two daughters that the marriage was agreed upon.

47. Although the painting bears the signature of Drouais, which would date it before 1787, neither Régis Michel nor the National Gallery accepts this attribution. See Michel, *David e Roma*, exhibition catalog (Rome, 1981) p. 197.

48. In an excellent essay on the representation of femininity in Boucher and David, Erica

Rand discusses some of the pictorial strategies by which feminine power and agency is effectively neutralized; Rand, "Depoliticizing Women: Female Agency, the French Revolution, and the Art of Boucher and David," *Genders* 7, March 1990, pp. 47–68.

49. See, for example, the following in the Deloynes Collection, Cabinet des Estampes, Bibliothèque Nationale: "Exposition au Salon du Palais National des ouvrages de peinture...etc.," tome XVIII, no. 459; François, "Epître au citoyen Vien par François, peintre," *Journal encyclopédique*, tome XVIII, no. 460; Pio, "Observations sur le Salon du Louvre, *Courrier français*, no. 243.

50. Whitney Davis provides a detailed discussion of the variant versions of the myth. See his essay "The Renunciation of Reaction in Girodet's *Sleep of Endymion*" in Bryson et al., *Visual Culture*.

51. See Levitine, *Girodet-Trioson*.

52. "L'Anglais:...La tête d'Endymion ne ressemble-t-elle pas trop à celle d'une femme? Le Zéphire n'est-il pas trop lourd, et d'une pose trop maniérée?
Le Français:...je ne suis pas de votre avis sur le reproche que vous faites à la tête d'Endymion; elle est belle et bien susceptible de charmer une divinité, qui, comme nos femmes, se laissait plutôt prendre par les yeux que par le coeur: Girodet me paraît être parvenu à rendre le beau idéal, aussi-bien que les premiers artistes grecs du siècle de Périclès, et vous admirez dans leurs productions ce que vous vous croyez en droit de blâmer dans celle-ci; soyez conséquent." See Anon., *Dialogue raisonné entre un anglais et un français, ou revue des peintures, sculptures et gravures exposées dans le musée royal de France, le 5 novembre 1814*, Deloynes Collection, Cabinet des Estampes, Bibliothèque Nationale, V. 24562, p. 14.

53. Crow's primarily political reading of the ephebic body in the painting of David and his students has been put forth in a series of essays, the substance of which is reiterated in his *Emulation: Making Artists for Revolutionary France*. For various versions of his central thesis see his essays "Revolutionary Activism and the Cult of Male Beauty in the Studio of David" in Bernadette Fort, ed., *Fictions of the French Revolution*, (Chicago, 1991); "Girodet et David pendant la révolution: un dialogue artistique et politique" in *David contre David: Actes au colloque* (Paris, 1993), vol. II; "A Male Republic: Bonds Between Men in the Art and Life of Jacques-Louis David," in Gill Perry and Michael Rossington, eds., *Femininity and Masculinity in Eighteenth-Century Art and Culture* (Manchester and New York, 1994); "Facing the Patriarch in the Studio of David" in M. Roth, ed., *Changing History: Essays in Honor of Carl Schorske*, (Stanford, 1994); "Observations on Style and History in French Painting of the Male Nude," in Bryson et al., *Visual Culture*. Crow's elision of sexual and unconscious dynamics at work in the paintings of Girodet and David has been subjected to a thoughtful and provocative critique by Whitney Davis in his "The Renunciation of Reaction in Girodet's *Sleep of Endymion*," ibid.

54. Roland Barthes, trans. Richard Miller, *S/Z* (New York, 1974).

55. The engraved version of the painting by Charles Normand is reproduced in Henri Lemonnier, "L'*Atala* de Chateaubriand et l'*Atala* de Girodet," *Gazette des Beaux-Arts* 11, 1914, p. 366.

56. See in this regard Susan J. Delaney, "*Atala* in the Arts," Jacques Beauroy, Marc Bertand, Edward T. Gargan, eds, *The Wolf and the Lamb: Popular Culture in France from the Old Regime to the Twentieth Century* (Stanford, 1977), pp. 209–31.

57. See Margaret Waller, "Being René, Buying Atala: Alienated Subjects and Decorative Objects in Postrevolutionary France," and Naomi Schor, "Triste Amérique: Atala and the Post-Revolutionary Construction of Woman," in Sara Melzer and Leslie Rabine,

eds., *Rebel Daughters: Women and the French Revolution* (London and New York, 1992).

58. In contrast to Schor and Waller's interpretation of Atala's structural role in the post-revolutionary period, Doris Y. Kadish considers Atala to be an "activated" and empowered heroine, another avatar of the revolutionary Marianne. Furthermore, she reads her "bridging" function in Girodet's painting as a politically mediating device rather than, as I do, a homosocial link between men: "...Girodet follows Chateaubriand in conceiving [the burial] ideally as a mediating union between matriarchal, Christian and nonpatriarchal, republican principles....Girodet's Atala is not merely an erotic object, however, as even a cursory observation of the painting reveals. Atala's body forms a natural bridge—the place of her burial in the novel—between two forces, one situated symbolically on the left, the other on the right." Kadish, *Politicizing Gender: Narrative Strategies in the Aftermath of the French Revolution* (London and New Brunswick, 1991), p. 52. For a discussion of numerous treatments—both visual and literary—of the dead heroine, see Elisabeth Bronfen, *Over Her Dead Body: Death, Femininity, and the Aesthetic* (New York, 1992).

59. The theorization of these two categories was the work of the Abbé Siéyès, in 1789: "Tous les habitants d'un pays doivent y jouir des droits de citoyen *passif*; tous ont droit à la protection de leur personne, de leur propriété, de leur liberté, etc; mais tous n'ont pas droit à prendre une part *active* dans la formation des pouvoirs publics; tous ne sont pas citoyens *actifs*. Les femmes, du moins dans l'état actuel, les enfants, les étrangers, ceux encore qui ne contribueraient en rien à soutenir l'établissement public sont comme les vrais actionnaires de la grande entreprise sociale. Eux seuls sont les véritables citoyens actifs, les véritables membres de l'association." *Archives parlementaires* VIII, 20 July 1789, p. 256.

60. The term *ostranenie*, which is usually rendered into English as "making strange" (and was later adapted by Bertolt Brecht in the form of the "alienation effect") was coined by the Russian literary theorist Viktor Shklovsky in 1917. See Victor Erlich, *Russian Formalism: History–Doctrine*, 3rd edn. (New Haven, 1965).

61. This particular model of the formation of male subjectivity is generally associated with the work of Nancy Chodorow. See her *The Reproduction of Mothering* (Berkeley, 1978).

62. Johann Wolfgang von Goethe, "Winckelmann and His Age" in *Goethe: The Collected Works, Essays on Art and Literature*, Vol. 3, ed. John Geary, trans. Ellen von Nardoff (Princeton, 1994) p. 103.

63. Ibid., p. 104.

64. In the case of England, however, G. S. Rousseau argues that by the second or third decades of the eighteenth century, a bisexual conception of the sodomite "began to crystallize into one or the other [type]: from the old-style bisexual sodomite who held a male on one arm and female on the other while kissing both, to the new-style sodomite who was exclusively homocentric and male-oriented." G. S. Rousseau, *Perilous Enlightenment: Pre-and Post-Modern Discourses Sexual, Historical* (Manchester and New York, 1991) p. 142. In France, my own impression is that these boundaries remained fluid until late in the century. A good anthology covering various aspects of "deviant" sexualities in the eighteenth century is Robert Parks Maccubbin, *Tis Nature's Fault: Unauthorized Sexuality During the Enlightenment* (Cambridge, 1987).

65. "The eighteenth century thus refused to look squarely at homosexuality, preferring to cast sidelong glances at matters indirectly associated with it. For theological reasons, the Church was opposed to all *péchés contre nature*, but its commitment to its obligations was weaker in this area than in many others: the punishment for sodomy

and bestiality continued to be confused with blasphemy which was clearly the greater crime. The police had a statutory obligation to repress homosexuality, but crimes of inversion were rarely treated differently from crimes of debauchery in general, sodomy in official eyes being but one of the many categories of sexual misconduct—the seduction of minors, rape and scandalous behavior and the other *crimes de luxure*—which caused far more concern and generated much prompter action." D. A. Coward, "Attitudes to Homosexuality in Eighteenth-Century France," *Journal of European Studies*, vol. X, 1980, pp. 231–55. In this context, see also the the essays in Maccubbin, *Tis Nature's Fault*, especially, Michael Rey, "Parisian Homosexuals Create a Lifestyle, 1700–1750: The Police Archives," pp. 179–91.

66. A thorough discussion of these drawing academies may be found in Edgar Peters Bowron, "Academic Life Drawing in Rome 1750-1790" in Richard J. Campbell and Victor Carlson, eds., *Visions of Antiquity: Neoclassical Figure Drawings*, exhibition catalog, Los Angeles County Museum of Art and The Minneapolis Museum of Art (Los Angeles, 1993).

67. "The castrati were much sought after and openly entertained, even by the cardinals.... Rome rang with outrageous gossip about these youths and the aspirants for their expensive favors, but the vice was generally regarded with indulgence. It was known as the *peccato nobile*, the sin of gentlemen." Maurice Andrieux, *Daily Life in Papal Rome in the Eighteenth Century*, trans. Mary Fitton (London, 1968), pp. 164–65.

68. Rousseau, *Perilous Enlightenment*, p. 30.

69. This much was at least implied in Mario Praz's pioneering study of the Neoclassical period, *On Neoclassicism* (Evanston, 1972) and made explicit in Dominique Fernandez's *Le Rapt de Ganymède* (Paris, 1989).

70. See in this regard the memoirs of the artist Philippe-Auguste Hennequin for his account of the papal crackdown on the Freemason's group of which he was a member during his stay in Rome. *Mémoires de Ph.-A. Hennequin* (Paris, 1933).

71. Adrienne Rich, "Compulsory Heterosexuality and the Lesbian Continuum," in Rich, *Blood, Bread and Poetry* (New York, 1986).

72. Nina Rattner Gelbert, *Feminine and Opposition Journalism in Old Regime France* (Berkeley and Los Angeles, 1987).

73. An extremely provocative meditation on this theme is Daniel Arasse, *The Guillotine and the Terror*, trans. Christopher Miller (London, 1989). What is, however, entirely absent in Arasse's study is any reference, much less use, of psychoanalytic theory, the result of which is that the possible connections between the spectacle of the guillotine and male castration fears are unremarked and unexplored. Ewa Lajer-Burcharth, on the other hand, has integrated the psychological implications of the guillotine in her essay "David's Sabine Women: Body, Gender and Republican Culture Under the Directory," *Art History*, vol. 14, no. 3, Sept. 1991, pp. 397–430.

Chapter Three
Notes to pages 98–175

1. Shoshana Felman, "Rereading Feminity" in *Yale French Studies* No. 62, 1981, p. 41.

2. Robert Rosenblum's classic work *Transformations in Late Eighteenth Century Art* (Princeton, 1967) is, of course, integrally concerned with these influences and cross-fertilizations, as is Hugh Honour's *Neo-Classicism* (Harmondsworth, 1968).

3. See, for example, Régis Michel's essays "Meynier où la métaphore parlementaire: essai sur *La Sentence de Ligarius*," *La Revue du Louvre et des Musées du France*, vol. 37, no. 3, 1987, pp. 188-200; "Bara: Du Martyr a l'éphèbe" in the exhibition catalog *La Mort de Bara*, Musée Calvet (Avignon, 1989); and his discussions of several of Meynier's studies in Michel, *Le Beau Idéal*. See also the entry on Meynier in the catalog

for the exhibition "David à Delacroix", organized by Frederick Cummings of the Detroit Institute of Arts, Pierre Rosenberg of the Louvre, and Robert Rosenblum, Professor of Fine Arts at New York University. "French Painting 1774–1830: The Age of Revolution" (as it was called in the U.S.A.) was of signal importance in revealing the diversity of styles and themes in the period, as well as in its recovery of numerous forgotten artists. The catalog (Detroit Institute of the Arts and the Metropolitan Museum of Art, 1975) remains an indispensable source of information about the artists featured in the exhibition.

4. A student of Vien, Meynier enjoyed a successful if not brilliant career, receiving many of the distinctions and commissions routinely accorded an accomplished history painter. This recognition began with his Prix de Rome, which he won at the age of 21 (shared in that year with David's student Girodet). From 1795 on, he exhibited regularly in the Salon, was elected a member of the Institut de France in 1815, became Chevalier of the Legion of Honor in 1822, and Officer in 1830. He received official commissions from the Napoleonic art administration for grandiose battle scenes, and later, commissions from the two Restoration governments for ceiling decorations, ecclesiastical commissions for religious subjects, even a commission to decorate the main room of the Paris Stock Exchange (1826).

5. "Bara: Du Martyr à l'éphèbe," in La Mort de Bara. See also the entry in the exhibition catalog Regards sur Amour et Psyché à l'âge néo-classique, Musée de Carouge, 17 March–1 May 1994 (Institut Suisse pour l'étude de l'art), pp. 156–58.

6. There is also the possibility that Meynier's painting is a parody of Girodet's Sleep of Endymion, one which carries the androgyny of the latter to an even greater extreme. This would explain certain features of the painting that seem rhetorically or formally excessive, such as the lamenting putti, the floating legs, even perhaps, the solipsism implied by Psyche's identical profile and coiffure.

7. The standard art-historical discussion is René Schneider, "L'art anacréontique et alexandrin sous l'Empire," Revue des Etudes Napoléoniennes, tome II, Nov.–Dec. 1916. See also the discussion in Locquin, La Peinture d'histoire en France, and the brief but excellent discussions of this cultural formation in Régis Michel and Philippe Bordes, Aux Armes et aux Arts! 1789–1799 (Paris, 1989).

8. "Dès les premiers temps de l'antiquité, le nom d'Anacréon rappelle ce que la poésie a de plus gracieux. 'La poésie d'Anacréon est considérée toute entière à l'amour,' a dit Cicéron; et le nom d'Anacréontique s'attachera toujours à ce genre aimable, cher surtout aux Français, peuple heureux, vivant sous un climat tempéré, où la vigne prospère, et qui, comme le peuple d'Athènes, par l'enjouement, la facilité et les grâces de l'esprit, a le don d'agréer infus avec la vie." D'Ambroise Firmin Didot, introduction to Odes d'Anacréon (Paris, 1864), p. 5. Anacreon's poetry was first translated into French by Mme Dacier in 1715 and was subsequently reprinted in many editions and by other translators.

9. Girodet also illustrated the Didot edition of Racine, in a style altogether different from the linear Flaxmanian style that he employed in his illustrations for Anacreon's Odes. Surely one of the reasons for Racine's new popularity lay in his exploration of internalized emotional conflicts and the corollary emphasis on female characters. See James Henry Rubin, "Guérin's Painting of Phèdre and the Post-Revolutionary Revival of Racine," The Art Bulletin, 59, Dec. 1977, pp. 601–18.

10. "L'alexandrinisme est pour nous, dans un sens très large, le goût de la mythologie gracieuse, tendre et voluptueuse, et par conséquent de la forme jolie, jolie souvent jusqu'à la manière. L'inspiration en vient de la Grèce d'Orient, soit de celle d'Anacréon

de Teos et de Sapho de Lesbos, qui vivaient au VIe siècle, soit des époques hellénistique et gréco-romaine, où domine l'esprit proprement alexandrin." Schneider, "L'art anacréontique," p. 259.

11. "Naturellement, c'est chez des femmes surtout que sévit la contagion; Canova, Chinard, Prud'hon, sont les favoris de Mme de Groslier, Récamier et Régnault de St.-Jean d'Angely. Gérard exerce sur elles une égale séduction. Pour Mme Tallien il peint en 1804, en dix tableaux que grava Potrelle, des Amours qui figurent le *Départ*, et l'*Arrivée*, l'*Attaque* et le *Succès*, le *Regret* et le *Repos*....En somme, par toutes ses tendances, l'alexandrinisme est féminin. C'est la femme, qui a retenu l'art de l'empire sur la voie où l'entraînait, tambour roulant, le triple caporalisme, militaire, romain, et davidien." Ibid., p. 260.

12. See Francis Haskell, "An Italian Patron of French Neo-Classic Art," in Haskell, *Past and Present in Art and Taste* (London and New Haven, 1987).

13. See R. G. Saisselin, "Neo-Classicism: Images of Public Virtue and Realities of Private Luxury," *Art History* 4/1, March 1981, pp. 14-36.

14. The literary manifestations of Anacreontism, or, more broadly, the literary terms of Neoclassicism in France were furthered in the late eighteenth and early nineteenth centuries by the illustrated books produced by the publishing house of Didot (successively Pierre Didot, Didot l'Aîné, Didot le jeune, Firmin/Didot). Through their translations, and lavishly illustrated editions—many of them containing commissioned engravings by the most celebrated artists of the period—the firm of Didot did much both to popularize and disseminate the new sensibility. Didot published not only the classics (including, in 1798, a folio edition of Virgil's complete works with engravings after illustrations by Girodet and Gérard), but also illustrated editions of La Fontaine and a complete edition of Racine (1801–5), whose works

enjoyed a revival following the revolution. The Racine edition was judged by the juries at the National Exhibition of 1806 and the London Universal Exhibition of 1851 as the most perfect typographical production of all countries and of all times. Girodet, Gérard, and Prud'hon were among the many artists who were commissioned to illustrate their books. See Albert J. George, *The Didot Family and the Process of Printmaking* (Syracuse, 1961).

15. In addition to designs for the Firmin Didot edition of Anacreon's *Odes*, Girodet also provided the illustrations for *Sapho, Bion, Moschus: Recueil de Compositions, dessiné par Girodet et gravé par M. Chatillon (son élève) et une notice sur la vie et les oeuvres de Sapho par Coupin* (Paris, 1819).

16. Ode XXII, *The Odes of Anacreon*, trans. Thomas Moore (London, 1869). This edition features 54 illustrations designed by Girodet for the original 1799 French version translated and published by D'Ambroise Firmin Didot.

17. For a full discussion of these roles see K. J. Dover, *Greek Homosexuality* (New York, 1980).

18. Commenting on Vien's *Love Fleeing Slavery* in the Salon of 1789, Régis Michel writes: "Anacréon: la référence fait flores. C'est que le tableau, qui renoue avec un genre ancien, s'inscrit dans un courant nouveau: le style *gracieux*, version David (Pâris) et Vincent (Zeuxis). (On notera que Vien, comme David, sacrifie à une clientèle aristocratique qui persiste à confondre gracieux et galant, Antiquité et libertinage, érotisme et nudité: l'anacréontisme Louis XVI préfigure fâcheusement à cet égard l'anacréontisme Empire, perversion de l'antique à finalité bourgeoise.) Car il faut distinguer la grâce antique—pureté du canon, noblesse de l'expression, archéologie du décor—et celle, maniérée, du goût rocaille. Ce n'est point cette grâce française qui tient de si près à la manière, et paraît enfantée plutôt par les caprices de l'imagination que part le goût épuré des artistes; c'est cette grâce simple

des Grecs, qui tient à la beauté des formes, au choix de la belle nature." "L'Art des salons" in Michel and Bordes, *Aux armes et aux Arts!*, p. 12. My own reading of Anacreontism, on the contrary, does not suggest that there are great differences within its themes and subjects, with the significant exception of the primacy of the ephebic rather than the female figure in the later Neoclassical period.

19. With a few important exceptions, *The Loves of Paris and Helen* has received far less discussion in Davidian scholarship than have David's revolutionary subjects. Produced in the same period as the *Lictors Returning to Brutus the Bodies of his Sons*, this painting of the two beautiful adulterers, commissioned by the no less flamboyantly adulterous Count d'Artois (the future Charles X), clearly fits ill into a linear development of David's visual language for republican values. By the time of the opening of the Salon of 1789, the Count d'Artois, whose profligacy, dissolution and reactionary politics had made him detested, had fled into exile. David nevertheless chose to exhibit the work, although without any mention of its original commission. Régis Michel, in his catalog essay on the painting, points out the distinctive, and decidedly non-heroic attributes of Paris as he was interpreted in eighteenth-century iconography: "Il n'est pas douteux...que dans la tradition du siècle, le personnage de Paris (mollesse, oisiveté, effémination) est péjoratif autant que séducteur." *David e Roma*, p. 149. Paris, it should be noted, was a much-represented figure from the 1770s through the Empire, sculpted by Canova and Thorvaldsen, painted by many artists. See also the study by Louis Hautecoeur, *Louis David* (Paris, 1954). Hautecoeur additionally discusses the classical sources for the painting, including the use of ephebic prototypes for both figures.

20. The perceived contradiction between such paintings and the revolutionary or the Napoleonic David is obviously inseparable from the biographical facts of David's political life, and to the no less compelling determinations of patronage. Nevertheless, the contrast between, say, the masculinist atmosphere of the *Death of Socrates* and the Anacreontic idiom of *Paris and Helen* can hardly be attributed to David's political activities or patronage alone. Dorothy Johnson has sought to resolve this art-historically perceived contradiction by recourse to a notion of David's continuous self-conscious stylistic metamorphosis, in which David constantly redefines and reinvents his art. See Johnson, *Jacques-Louis David: Art in Metamorphosis* (Princeton, 1993). A more typical art-historical move is to argue, as does Yvonne Korshak, that a painting such as *The Loves of Paris and Helen* is as fully political, i.e. critical, of the *ancien régime* (albeit in highly coded ways) as the *Brutus*. While I find Korshak's reading ingenious and persuasive in a number of respects, I would argue that a disguised political meaning can still coexist with the intent to produce a sensually appealing *sujet gracieux*. See Korshak, "Paris and Helen by Jacques Louis David: Choice and Judgment on the Eve of the French Revolution," *The Art Bulletin*, no. 1, vol. LXIX, March 1987, pp. 102–16, and the critical response by Francis H. Dowley, "Discussion: An Exchange on Jacques Louis David's Paris and Helen," *The Art Bulletin*, no. 3, vol. LXX, Sept. 1988, pp. 504–20. See also Régis Michel in the exhibition catalogs *David e Roma*, where the painting is discussed in depth, and *Le Beau Idéal*.

21. On the theme of Eros and Psyche see the exhibition catalog *Regards sur Amour et Psyché à l'âge néo-classique*, and René Schneider, "Le mythe de Psyché dans l'art français depuis la révolution," *Revue de l'art français ancien et moderne*, 32 (July-Dec. 1912) pp. 240–54. See also Jean H. Hagstrom, *Eros and Vision: The Restoration to Romanticism* (Evanston, 1989).

22. "Le *beau idéal*, est, aujourd'hui, à notre

égard, la réunion des plus grands perfections que puissent offrir partiellement certains individus choisis. Si l'on veut concevoir le *beau idéal* d'une manière plus relative aux idées qu'avoient les Artistes Grecs vers le siècle de Périclès, il faut imaginer le beau tel qu'il existeroit, si la Nature formoit ses productions et l'homme surtout, avec le choix le plus exquis, avec toutes les perfections générales et particulières dont se trouvent susceptibles les formes et les mouvemens qui lui sont prescrits, en y joignant les relations visibles que ses formes et ce mouvemens peuvent avoir avec les affections sentimentales les plus spirituelles, les plus élevées et les plus parfaites." Claude-Henri Watelet, *Dictionnaire des arts de peinture, sculpture et gravure*, tome I (Paris, 1792), pp. 205–6.

23. On Fabre see the following: Paul Marmottan, "Notice Biographique," *Gazette des Beaux-Arts*, May 1926, and "La jeunesse du peintre Fabre," *Gazette des Beaux-Arts*, Feb. 1927; Philippe Bordes, "François-Xavier Fabre, 'Peintre d'Histoire'" Part I, *The Burlington Magazine*, Feb. 1975, pp. 91–98, and Part II, *The Burlington Magazine*, March, 1975, pp. 155–62; the entry on Fabre in Cummings et al., the catalog for *French Painting 1774–1830*, pp. 410–11.

24. "Nous ne pouvons nous refuser au plaisir de donner de justes éloges à la figure d'Abel de M. Fabre. Elle est d'un bon ton, d'un beau pinceau et d'une belle forme, tous les accessoires en sont exécutés avec goût; enfin, la grâce y est d'accord avec la vérité, et nous ne pouvons que l'exhorter à suivre la route qu'il a prise." "Rapport des commissaires pour l'examen des ouvrages des élèves pensionnaires à Rome, 27 février, 1791" in Anatole de Montaiglon and Jules Guiffrey, eds, *Correspondance des directeurs de l'Académie de France à Rome avec les surintendants des bâtiments* (Paris, 1847), vol. XVI, p. 7.

25. "Le *Diogène* du sr *Garnier* est d'un ton vrai, fin et lumineux; toutes les parties sont bien correspondantes, pour l'âge et le caractère, à la tête qui est pleine de vérité. Nous l'invitons à s'occuper particulièrement de la correction, sans pourtant négliger le sentiment qu'il montre pour la couleur et l'harmonie..." Ibid., p. 425.

26. For a detailed account of Fabre's career see Laure Pellicer, "Le Peintre François-Xavier Fabre 1766–1837," thèse doctorat d'état, University of Paris, 1982.

27. Salomon Gessner, *The Death of Abel in Five Books*, trans. Mary Collyer, (New York, 1794), pp. 97–98.

28. In the past ten years or so there has been a great deal of interesting work on the *Bara,* beginning with William Olander, "'Pour transmettre à la postérité': French Painting and Revolution 1774–1795," Ph.D. dissertation, New York University, 1983, which has influenced much subsequent scholarship. Part of this thesis has been included under the title "French Painting and Politics in 1794: The Great Concours de *l'an II*," in the catalog *1789: French Art During the Revolution* (New York, 1989), exhibition and catalog organized by Alan Wintermute; as well the exhibition catalog *La Mort de Bara*, especially the essay "Bara: Du Martyr à l'éphèbe" by Régis Michel; the essay by Alex Potts "Images of Ideal Manhood in the French Revolution," *History Workshop Journal 30* and his book *Flesh and the Ideal*; and Thomas Crow in *Emulation: Making Artists for Revolutionary France*. Michel has taken issue with the notion that Bara is unfinished; he argues that the nudity, the lack of *fini*, the scale, and the dramatic reduction of the composition to the image of the boy and a loosely sketched sugges- tion of landscape was exactly what David intended, given its proposed use in a revolutionary *fête*. Be that as it may, he also argues—and Crow concurs—that the feminization and the nudity of Bara are to be understood politically as well as affectively: "la grâce asexuée de Bara ne fait qu'ajouter à sa nudité abstraite. Il y a

du Rousseau dans cette quête radicale de la pureté primitive. Bara nu, c'est le retour à l'enfance de l'humanité, avant la corruption sociale. C'est la promesse d'un monde affranchi du despotisme, où la nature est enfin réconciliée avec elle-même, c'est-à-dire avec la démocratie, selon le mot de David. C'est la *vertu* de l'homme nouveau." Michel, "Bara: Du Martyr à l'éphèbe," p. 68.

29. Tania Modleski, "The Incredible Shrinking He(r)man" in Modleski, *Feminism Without Women*.

30. "Ainsi se fane et meurt une fleur nouvelle coupée par le tranchant de la charrue; ainsi les pavots, battus de l'orage, courbent leurs têtes apesanties par la pluie; Barra et Agricole Viala! ainsi vous fûtes moissonnés à la fleur de vos ans! Et vous, infâmes, oppresseurs de la terre, vous qui, prêtant votre langage à celui qui créa la liberté, prétendez tenir de lui le droit de gouverner le monde, où sont-ils vos héros? qu'ils paraissent! Comparez-vous à nos jeunes républicains ces vils courtisans nourris au milieu des cours, dans le sein des voluptés. Ces sybarites efféminés, dont l'âme corrompue ne se fait pas même une idée de la vertu, et dont les bras énervés ne sont chargés que de chiffres, gages impudiques de leurs adultères amours; ces courtisans enfin qui, apportant au milieu des camps leur arrogance et leur lâcheté, fuient à la vue du moindre danger, et volent cacher leur honte dans les bras de la débauche?" Reprinted in Jules David, *Le Peintre Louis David*, p. 210. Glossing a later part of the *rapport* in which David evokes an image of scarred and mutilated veterans restored to their appreciative wives, Alex Potts makes the following observation: "The rhetoric of David's speech, with its insistent yet unconscious intermingling of pathos and desire, of physical violence and sexualized pleasure, with its celebration of the height-ened erotic charge of the male body that was simultaneously heroic and damaged, could be seen as having certain tropes we identified in his image of Bara." Potts, *Flesh and the Ideal*, p. 237.

31. "Cet ouvrage, que le peintre n'a jamais achevé, est, sans contredit, un des plus délicats qu'il ait faits, et le plus gracieux." Delécluze, *Louis David*, p. 160.

32. "Un chef d'œuvre de sentiment et d'expression," Pierre Alexandre Coupin, *Essai sur J. L. David, peintre d'histoire* (Paris, 1847) p. 16.

33. These arguments may be found in Crow, *Emulation: Making Artists for Revolutionary France*, pp. 177–83, and in Michel's essay "Bara: Du Martyr à l'éphèbe," in *La Mort de Bara*.

34. Potts, *Flesh and the Ideal*, p. 235.

35. The term "political unconscious" is derived from Fredric Jameson, specifically his influential study *The Political Unconscious: Narrative as a Socially Symbolic Act* (Ithaca, 1981). While Jameson's task in this book is to excavate a historical (i.e., Marxist) *telos* in nineteenth-century French and British culture through a careful analysis of some of its literary productions, what has been most helpful for me in his work is its hermeneutic dimension. It is thus the recovery of a repressed story, "a hidden master narrative" in Jameson's terms, that motivates my own inquiry, which assumes, moreover, that the investigation of the tidal shifts (and dislocations) in representations of masculinity are integrally related to questions of power and politics.

36. In this respect, my reading of the work is quite close to that of Alex Potts: "The image of a young boy displaces questions about social identity much more effectively than that of a man. He can be defined as not having a history, as coming straight from the arms of nature. Yet the ideality of David's figure of Bara is, ideologically speaking, highly specific. He is the Bara of a radical middle-class imagination, besieged by contending populist and revisionist pressures....He was both the feminine embodiment of liberty and republic and the masculine embodiment of heroic endeavour. He simultaneously played the role of

passive female victim or helpless martyr and of active male hero struggling against all odds. S/he was an impossible figure representing the revolutionary subject as both masculine and feminine, in a situation where in reality gender distinctions made this confluence quite illegitimate and the feminine was excluded from self-presentation on the stage of political life." Potts, *Flesh and the Ideal*, p. 236.

37. Shoshana Felman, "Rereading Femininity" in *Yale French Studies* No. 62, 1981, pp. 19–44.

38. See in this regard Michael Preston Worley, "The Image of Ganymede in France, 1730-1820: The Survival of a Homoerotic Myth," *The Art Bulletin*, vol. LXXVI, no. 4, Dec. 1994, pp. 630–43.

39. A collection of excerpts from *Gedanken über die Nachamung der Grieschen Werke in der Malerei und Bildhauerkunst* was published by Fréron in *Journal étranger* in 1756; *Geschichte der Kunst* had long excerpts translated and published in the *Journal Encyclopédique* in 1764, and the first complete translation in French, in two volumes, appeared in 1766. The first British edition of *Reflections on the Painting and Sculpture of the Greeks* was translated by Henry Fusseli [Fuseli] in 1765.

40. J.-J. Winckelmann, trans. Henry Lodge, *The History of Ancient Art Among the Greeks* (London, 1950), p. 93.

41. "I cannot comprehend how the great artist of the Antinous, wrongly so termed, in the Belvedere, happened to make a small incised circle about the right nipple, which consequently appears as if inlaid, and as large as the part inclosed within the circle. It was probably done for the purpose of denoting the extent of the glandular portion of the nipple..." Winckelmann, trans. Lodge, *Ancient Art*, p. 241. "Even the private parts have their appropriate beauty. The left testicle is always the larger, as it is in nature; so, likewise, it has been observed that the sight of the left eye is keener than the right....I leave it to the reader, and to

the seeker after Beauty, to turn over coins, and study particularly those parts which the painter was unable to represent to the satisfaction of Anacreon, in the picture of his favorite [i.e. Bathyillus]." Ibid., p. 283. In fact, Winckelmann was wrong about testicular asymmetry; in nature, as opposed to classical sculpture, it is the right testicle (in right-handed subjects) that is larger. I am indebted to Bettina Bergmann for providing me with I. C. McManus's, "Scrotal asymmetry in man and in ancient sculpture," *Nature*, vol. 259, no. 5542, 5 Feb. 1976, p. 426.

42. This is drawn from the British sculptor John Deare's notes on his drawings from antique statues. Cited in Honour, *Neo-Classicism*, p. 117.

43. Cited in Francis Haskell and Nicholas Penney, *Taste and the Antique* (New Haven, 1981) p. 102.

44. See Edouard Pommier's essay, "Winckelmann et la Vision de l'Antiquité Classique dans la France des Lumières et de la Révolution," *Revue de l'Art*, 83, 1989, pp. 9–20.

45. See in this context the debates about the nature of a republican (read male) art in Athanase Détournelle's journal *Aux Armes et aux Arts!* (Paris: 1794). Much of the discussion comes directly from the French editions of Winckelmann.

46. "The head of Bacchus which possesses the highest beauty belongs to a restored statue, somewhat larger than nature, which has gone to England. The face exhibits an indescribable blending of male and female beautiful youth, and a conformation intermediate between two sexes, which will be recognized, by any one who looks for it in its present location, by the fillet around the forehead, and by the absence of the usual crown of vine-leaf or ivy." Winckelmann, trans. Lodge, *Ancient Art*, pp. 95-96.

47. "Nos artistes empruntent à ce recueil [Ovid's *Metamorphoses*] ou aux *Herodes* les fables tendres et plaintives de Narcisse, de Cyparisse, d'Adonis, de Salmacis, la nymphe

de la source carienne, d'Hylas, dont la légende asiatique fut grécisée par les alexandrins Apollonios et Apollodoros....Le joli roman de Musée leur fournit le mythe voluptueux d'Héro, prêtresse d'Aphrodite, et de Léandre d'Abydos, poème que Passow après Aldo Manuce et Lascaris a édité à Leipzig en 1810." Schneider, "L'art anacréontique et alexandrin sous l'Empire," p. 264.

48. Ovid, *Metamorphoses*, trans. A. D. Melville (London and Oxford, 1986), p. 83.

49. The brilliant interpretative reading given to Ovid's recounting of the myth by Georgia Nugent is suggestive not only in relation to the Ovidian text, but for the Neoclassical representations of the myth as well. See Nugent, "This Sex Which Is Not One: De-Constructing Ovid's Hermaphrodite," *Differences* 2/1, Spring 1990, pp. 160–85. See also Kari Weil's interpretation of the myth in *Androgeny and the Denial of Difference* (Charlottesville, 1992).

50. As I have argued throughout, however singular or sexually transgressive paintings such as Guérin's, or any of the other works I discuss appear to contemporary eyes, in their own time they did not violate their "horizon of reception." Thus, the Salon criticism which pertains to them is consistent in its untroubled acceptance of such subjects, which are typically generically categorized as "sujets gracieux." C. P. Landon, for example, comments on the work thus: "L'Aurore accompagnée de l'Amour, soulève le voile étoilé de la nuit et répand des fleurs sur la terre. Dans sa course rapide, elle a vu Céphale endormi, elle en devient éprise et ravit le jeune chasseur à la tendresse de son épouse. Céphale livré au sommeil et mollement étendu sur un nuage, paraît s'élever doucement vers les cieux. Une étoile qui brille au-dessus de la tête de l'Aurore éclaire d'une lumière douce et paisible cette scène de volupté....Ce sujet charmant, digne des pinceaux du Corrège, se prêtait moins peut-être au talent de M. Guérin, qu'un pro-

gramme purement historique où tout doit vigoureusement prononcé....La composition du tableau est pleine de goût, le dessin est correct....[etc., etc.]" Landon, *Annales du musée et de l'école moderne des Beaux-Arts, Salon de 1810* (Paris, 1810) p. 15.

Where negative criticism is made in relation to feminized male figures (and it is, in any case, rare) it is usually because the individual critic conceives of the particular character as a more virile type. Thus, P. M. Gault de Saint Germain finds fault with Guérin's Aeneas in the following terms: "C'est encore une faute grave que de donner à ce héros, alors dans son neuvième lustre environ, les traits efféminés de la nature adolescente." *Choix des productions de l'art les plus remarquables exposées dans le salon de 1817* (Paris: Didot l'Aîné, 1817) p. 6. There are sometimes oblique indications that the figure goes a bit too far on the side of effeminancy: for example: "...la beauté de Céphale, le dessin de ses formes, qui ont l'agrément de celles d'une femme..." Antoine Dupuis, *Lettres impartiales sur l'exposition des tableaux en 1814*, par un amateur, Deloynes Collection, V, 24563, pp. 15–16; "Les formes de Céphale, quoique d'un dessin pur et correct, ont l'attrait de celles d'une femme...." Anon., *Lettres impartiales sur l'exposition de l'an 1810 par un amateur*, Deloynes Collection, V, 44875, p. 31. I am indebted to Mechthild Fend for providing me with these last two citations.

51. "Céphale livré au sommeil est mollement étendu sur un nuage, paraît s'élever doucement vers les cieux....La figure de la déesse est svelte et gracieuse....La composition du tableau est pleine de goût, le dessin en est correct, les carnations en sont brillantes..." Landon, *Salon de 1810*, p. 19.

52. "C'est ce bon sens, vivifié par un sentiment poétique, ennobli par un goût élégant et pur, que je trouve et qui me charme dans les compositions de M. Guérin: il y a de la raison, de la poésie et de la beauté dans son tableau l'Aurore enlevant Céphale; le beau

chasseur endormi est porté sur des nuages; ses bras, l'un pendant, l'autre soutenu par un petit Amour plein de grâce, annoncent bien l'affaissement du sommeil; au dessus de lui s'élève la figure svelte et céleste de l'Aurore, qui écartant des deux mains les voiles de Nuit, laisse tomber sur le jeune homme les fleurs dont elle a l'heureux pouvoir de parsemer la terre. Je ne connois rien de plus beau que Céphale: sa tête penchée conserve au milieu du sommeil une expression de noblesse et de douceur; ses cheveux sont arrangés avec une négligence pleine de grâce; son corps offre une réunion admirable de beauté juvénile et de formes héroïques. Ici le nu n'étoit point déplacé: l'artiste, loin d'en profiter pour livrer des détails d'anatomie faciles à étaler sur une poitrine qui se présente en face, a fondu, adouci, marié avec un sentiment exquis, les articulations et les muscles dans la rondeur à la fois pleine et nerveuse des chairs: point de mollesse, rien d'indéterminé; mais point de dureté, rien de tranchant ni de pénible; ce sont des beautés mâles et des grâces féminines: cela rappelle le Méléagre, l'Hermaphrodite…" François Guizot, "De l'état des Beaux-Arts en France et du salon de 1810," Deloynes Collection, V, 41208, pp. 61–62.

53. See for example C. P. Landon, *Annales du musée et de l'école moderne des Beaux-Arts, Salon de 1822*, tome 1 (Paris, 1830) p. 5.

54. Broc was one of the principal members of Maurice Quai's sect of Barbus, or *primitifs*, *penseurs* or *médiateurs* (all four terms are employed in the literature). Although scholars such as George Levitine and James Henry Rubin have argued for a more or less coherent aesthetic program among the Barbus, the degree of stylistic variation one can identify in the extant works of artists such as Broc or Franque would seem to support my argument throughout this chapter that post-revolutionary history painting is best approached in terms of its shared thematics and symbolic content rather than through its various stylistic

manifestations. On the Franque brothers see Levitine, *Dawn of Bohemianism*, and James Henry Rubin, "New Documents on the Médiateurs: Baron Gérard, Mantegna, and French Romanticism Circa 1800," *Burlington Magazine*, 117, Dec. 1975. Franque and Broc are discussed by Delécluze in *Louis David*. Contemporary discussions of Broc include those of Rubin, "New Documents"; and George Levitine, "'L'école d'Apelle' de Jean Broc: un 'primitif' au salon de l'an VIII," *Gazette des Beaux-Arts*, Nov. 1972, pp. 286–94, and Levitine, *Dawn of Bohemianism*. See also the catalog entries for both artists in Cummings et al., *French Painting 1774–1830*.

55. This painting, which I knew only from the line engraving in Charles Landon's series *Les Annales du musée*, was brought to my attention by Mechthild Fend.

56. This particular painting, known from its engraving in Charles Landon's *Annales du musée,* was located by Mechthild Fend in the Museum der bildenden Künst at Leipzig.

57. As indicated in the previous chapter, in France in the second half of the eighteenth century homosexuality was officially condemned but, with some important exceptions, mostly unprosecuted. In addition to the anthologies of Rousseau, *Perilous Enlightenment*, and Maccubbin, *Tis Nature's Fault*, see also Michel Rey, "Police et sodomie à Paris au XVIIIe siècle," *Revue d'histoire moderne et contemporaine*, 29, 1982, pp. 113–24 and Jeffrey Merrick, "Sexual Politics and Public Order," in *Journal of the History of Sexuality, I*, 1990, pp. 71–75.

58. "C'est avec tout l'abandon de l'amitié que Cyparissus s'est jeté dans les bras d'Apollon, où il expire.…Cette composition est simple et touchante; elle n'a rien de ce fracas qui attire la foule; elle n'obtiendra pas un succès d'engouement: mais lorsqu'on la contemple avec attention, on se sent ému et pénétré. L'unité du sujet fortifie l'interêt qu'il inspire; il y règne une grâce et une naïveté qui rappelle l'école d'Italie. Toute la partie supérieure du jeune Cyparisse est

digne des plus grands éloges. Le col est peut-être un peu gonflé; mais la poitrine, mais la ligne qui détermine le contour du torse, mais celle qui indique la direction du bras, offrent toute la perfection du modèle. Le corps d'Apollon n'est pas exempt d'une certaine raideur; peut-être même est-il un peu lourd; les hanches aussi me paraissent fortes; avec autant de plénitude, la statue antique est plus svelte…" François-Antoine-Marie Miel, "Essai sur le salon de 1817," Deloynes Collection, V, 46806, p. 51.

59. Louis Hautecoeur provides an interesting perspective on the cult of sensibility, underscoring its discursive range from literary production to individual self-fashioning. "La sensibilité se développe dans la littérature française dès la fin du règne de Louis XIV. Fénélon restera pour le XVIII⁰ siècle un homme 'sensible' et la présidente Ferraud écrivait alors: 'Etes-vous aussi tendre et sensible que moi?' La Motte regrette les bergers de l'Astrée, 'purs enfants, époux sensibles.' Cet état d'esprit naquit chez les uns de l'exaltation religieuse, chez les autres du dérèglement des moeurs qui, succédant aux majestés de l'agonie d'un règne, amollissait les caractères. Avec la sensibilité s'affina la sensiblerie. Ajoutez à cela le goût de l'analyse psychologique: à disséquer leur âme chez Mme de Lambert ou dans les romans de Marivaux, les Marianne du temps finirent par s'attendrir au spectacle de leur délicatesse. La philosophie vint à son tour enseigner que le sentiment prime l'intelligence. Les tendances, ces théories, ce n'est pas seulement dans les comédies larmoyantes de la chaussée que nous les découvrons, mais chez tous les contemporains. Les interjections, les cris, le silence, les évanouissements, deviennent l'apanage des âmes d'élite. Mme du Deffand exalte l'exaltation: 'Ce que vous appelez roman dans votre lettre, les souvenirs, les clairs de lune, l'idée des lieux où l'on a vu quelqu'un que l'on aime, une situation d'âme qui fait

que l'on pense plus tendrement, tout cela ne me semble pas si ridicule.' (18 Juillet 1744). Mme de la Popelinière, brisée de trop aimer Richelieu, s'écriait: 'Je suis d'une sensibilité à me jeter par la fenêtre.' (1742)." "Le Sentimentalisme dans la peinture française de Greuze à David," *Gazette des Beaux-Arts*, IV, tome 1, 1909, pp 159–76.

60. Carol Blum has described some of the psychological elements figuring in the Revolutionary assimilation of "Jean-Jacques," particularly by Robespierre and Saint-Just. Interestingly, the Jean-Jacques conscripted by revolutionary culture was not the political author of *Contrat social* or the other works of political theory, but the Jean-Jacques of *La Nouvelle Héloïse*, the *Confessions* (published in 1789, eleven years after Rousseau's death), and *Emile*. See Blum, *Rousseau and the Republic of Virtue*. The revolutionary epoch, moreover, witnessed a significant increase in the illustration of Rousseau's novels; following the editions illustrated by Guyot, Mayer, Moreau le Jeune, Chapuy, Janinet, Gravelot, and Cochin, came those illustrated by Martinet, LeFevre, Duchamel, Duclos, Marillier, Trunquesse, and Prud'hon.

61. "La sensibilité devint la vertu de l'honnête homme, et le goût de la morale, de la rêverie, de la nature, en furent les signes. Mais à ces sentiments, dont les moeurs, les idées, les croyances nouvelles, les modes littéraires avaient enrichi l'âme française, il manquait encore d'être réalisés en des types, populaires: ce fut l'oeuvre de Rousseau." Hautecoeur, "Le sentimentalisme dans la peinture française," p. 159.

62. Outram also observes that "…the struggle for the new political body of the revolutionary 'Stoics' was also a struggle for psychic autonomy. This was a struggle against *sensibilité* in all forms, and in particular against the fusion of subject and object, reaction and occasion, which was its hallmark and which women, contemporaries felt, displayed in such high degree." Dorinda Outram, *The Body and the French*

Revolution: Sex, Class and Political Culture
(London and New Haven, 1989), p. 87.

63. Margaret Waller, "*Cherchez la Femme*: Male
Malady and Narrative Politics in the French
Romantic Novel," *PMLA* (*Publication of the
Modern Language Association*), 104/2,
March 1989, p.141. See also her full-length
study of masculine crisis in its literary
manifestations, *The Male Malady: Fictions
of Impotence in the French Romantic Novel*
(New Brunswick, 1993).

Chapter 4
Notes to pages 176–225

1. Pierre Chaussard, *Sur le tableau de Sabines,
An VIII* (Paris, 1800), p. 2.

2. Sigmund Freud, "On Narcissism: An
Introduction," *The Standard Edition of the
Complete Psychological Works of Sigmund
Freud*, vol. XIV (London, 1963), pp. 94–95.

3. An argument similar to the one I make
here, which I originally formulated in my
doctoral thesis ("The Image of Desire: Gender
and Representation in France 1789–1870,"
the Graduate Center, City University of New
York, 1992) and subsequently elaborated in
a number of conference papers, has been
recently proposed by Norman Bryson. See
his essay "Géricault and Masculinity" in
Bryson et al., *Visual Culture*.

4. Ibid., p. 235.

5. "Large sex organs were considered coarse
and ugly, and were banished to the domains
of abstraction, of caricature, of satyrs, and
of barbarians. In the inexhaustible genital
vocabulary of Aristophanes, diminutives
denoting small penises are used as words of
endearment – as, for example, *posthion*,
which might be rendered as "little prick."
François Lissarague, "The Sexual Life of
Satyrs," in David M. Halperin, John J.
Winkler, Froma I. Zeitlin, eds., *Before
Sexuality: The Construction of Erotic
Experience in the Ancient Greek World*
(Princeton, 1990), p. 56.

6. Eva C. Keuls, *The Reign of the Phallus:
Sexual Politics in Ancient Athens*
(New York, 1985), p. 68.

7. Leo Steinberg's *The Sexuality of Christ in
Renaissance Art and in Modern Oblivion*
(New York, 1983) is, to my knowledge, the
only art-historical consideration of the
issues and problems raised in the representation of genitalia. Obviously, Steinberg's
discussion hinges on the fact that the
genitalia to be depicted are Christ's, but the
rarity of such investigations in the first place
is itself confirmation of my initial point.

8. Peter Stallybrass and Allon White, *The
Politics and Poetics of Transgression* (Ithaca
and London, 1986), p. 21.

9. Ibid., p. 21.

10. Ibid., p. 22.

11. The standard secondary accounts of the
beau idéal in French academic theory are
Benoît's *L'Art français sous la révolution et
l'Empire,* and Locquin's *La Peinture
d'histoire en France.* Another useful source
is André Fontine, *Les Doctrines d'art en
France: peintures, amateurs, critiques de
Poussin à Diderot* (Geneva: Slatkine
Reprints, 1970) Other sources underpinning
my discussion are those of A. C. Quatremère
de Quincy, probably the most influential of
Winckelmann's later exegetes. See his
Considérations sur les arts du dessin
originally published in Paris in 1791
(Geneva: Slatkine Reprints, 1970), and *Sur
l'Imitation* (Brussels, 1980). For a number of
provocative excurses on the *beau idéal* in
French Neoclassical graphic art, see Régis
Michel's entries in the catalog *Le Beau
Idéal.* See also Annie Becq, "Esthétique et
politique sous le Consulat et l'Empire: le
notion de beau idéal," *Romantisme*, 51–54,
1986, pp. 22–37, and her full-length study,
*Genèse de l'esthétique française moderne:
de la raison classique à l'imagination
créatrice 1680–1814* (Pisa, 1984).

12. "Maintenant, que sont ces 'règles,' 'ce
système' que l'Ecole nationale des Beaux
Arts a mission de conserver et d'enseigner?
Tout simplement un recueil de formes et de
proportions, ce qu'on appelle un 'canon' et

une collection de recettes d'exécution. Plus de recherches, plus d'effort, plus d'initiative individuelle. Tous ces cas seront prévus: dans chaque catégorie de sujets, pour chaque sexe, chaque âge, chaque tempérament, chaque condition, la consultation du formulaire 'la perfection de l'ensemble' ou de chacun des détails du corps selon la multiplicité de leur emploi." Quatremère de Quincy, "Essai sur l'idéal dans ses applications pratiques aux oeuvres de l'imitation propre des arts du dessin," tome II (1805), cited in Benoît, L'Art français sous la révolution et l'Empire, p. 50.

13. This system was codified well before the eighteenth century, and was largely in place at the very outset of the establishment of the Académie Royale des Beaux-Arts in 1642. Its practical exposition may be found in Roger de Piles, Premiers éléments de la peinture pratique, originally published in 1685 (Geneva: Minkoff reprint, 1973).

14. "Vous vous abusez étrangement quand vous prenez l'étude du modèle pour l'étude de la nature. Le modèle est bien dans la nature, mais il ne s'ensuit pas de là que la nature soit dans le modèle. La nature est l'espèce, le modèle n'est qu'un individu de l'espèce. A coup sûr, cette étude ne sauroit se renfermer dans un seul individu, à moins que cet individu ne se suppose le type de toutes les beautés et de toutes les perfections....La nature, dans la génération des êtres, est exposée à trop d'accidens. Joignez-y ceux de l'éducation et de toutes les circonstances qui environnent l'homme en société, vous aurez la preuve que la perfection dans un modèle est une chimère de l'imagination. L'art ne peut la réaliser cette chimère, que par la réunion de toutes les beautés éparses dans les individus de l'espèce, et cette recherche où l'étude de ce qui peut opérer cette réunion qui est la perfection, est véritablement l'étude de la nature." A. C. Quatremère de Quincy, Considérations sur les arts du dessin, p. 85.

15. The debates around this issue—the status of "nature" within the concept of the beau

idéal—are the very heart of Neoclassical art theory. Benoît, L'Art Français sous la révolution et l'Empire, provides the classic summary, drawing on the texts of Quatremère de Quincy, Eméric-David, Kératry, Droz, Ponce, and others. See also Michel's discussion in the catalog, Le Beau Idéal, and Becq, "Esthétique et politique."

16. The relevant clause, establishing the official place of the living model in the Academy dates from 1654 and reads as follows: "Sa majesté veut et étend que doresnevant il ne soit posé aucun modèle, faut monstre, ni donné leçon en public, touchant le fait de peinture et de sculpture qu'en la dite Académie Royale." Cited in Pevsner, Academies of Art: Past and Present, p. 87.

17. Michel Foucault, trans. Alan Sheridan, Discipline and Punish, the Birth of the Prison, (New York, 1979) pp. 25–26.

18. For an detailed account of these academic practices, including the competition's organization, see Grunchec, Prix de Rome.

19. "Quant au modèle lui-même, l'homme qui a reçu la mission de personnifier la nature devant cette foule attentive (400 élèves à partir de 1764) tout concourt également à lui donner une haute idée du rôle important qu'il joue dans l'Ecole. Choisi pour faire figure d'Apollon ou d'Hercule, 'le Modèle,' comme on l'appelle, est un vrai personnage. Ce n'est point un homme de rencontre, cherchant sa vie, qui vient poser d'une façon passagère et intermittente, et qu'on rétribue à la fin de la séance. Il est fonctionnaire royal. Il porte l'épée et la livrée du Roi, il est logé au Louvre où il occupe deux chambres, et il reçoit une pension variant de 200 à 500 livres, réversible sur la tête de sa veuve. C'est un homme de confiance, qui peut, comme 'le bon Deschamps,' être attaché pour toute son existence au service de l'Académie." Locquin, La Peinture d'histoire en France, p. 78–79.

20. "Jean Restout se vantait même de prendre le modèle homme de l'Académie pour faire les nymphes, les Arianes, les Vénus et

toutes les autres femmes de ses tableaux.... Et la chose ne doit pas nous étonner, car, non seulement les modèles femmes étaient 'd'une cherté horrible,' comme dit Taillasson, [à moins six francs par matinée] qui essayait de s'en passer 'à l'aide des bosses,' mais—si étrange que cela paraisse aujourd'hui—un préjugé de 'décence' interdisait formellement de poser des femmes à l'Académie...' On ne sert point, dans les écoles publiques, de femme pour modèle, comme plusieurs le croient,' lit-on dans l'*Encyclopédie*, au mot *Académie*. Par extension, même vêtus, les modèles féminins n'y étaient point en usage, ou plutôt ils le furent exceptionnellement, à partir de 1759, mais juste le temps prescrit pour le concours de la 'Tête d'expression', c'est-à-dire, trois heures par an." Ibid., pp. 79–80.

21. Mechthild Fend, "Die Androgynie in der Französischen Malerei," dissertation in progress.

22. "L'image idéale de l'idéal de l'homme possédera 'tous les genres de régularité qu'elle comporte.' Les formes seront modelées avec ampleur, simplifiées, épurées de tout détail individuel, de tout défectuosité accidentelle; les proportions et les rapports des parties seront fixés avec toute la rigueur d'une construction mathématique. Enfin, tout caractère essentiel sera placé en évidence par l'accentuation, voire même par l'exagération de ses traits et mis en valeur par la subordination de ses annexes et de ses voisins secondaires....Sa mission, si l'on peut dire, est de distiller la réalité, pour nous en montrer l'essence. Il se gardera donc bien d'essayer, sous le vain prétexte d'animer ses figures, de leur imprimer les caractères qui dans la réalité dénotent la vie: la souplesse des chairs vivantes, la moiteur de la peau, l'élasticité des muscles. Il évitera de laisser deviner les dessous de l'enveloppe extérieure, les affleurements de la charpente osseuse, des muscles et des veines, car tout cela n'est que détail

'*animal.*'" A. C. Quatremère de Quincy, cited in Benoît, *L'Art français sous la révolution et l'Empire*, p. 34.

23. Denis Diderot, "Pensées détachées sur la peinture, la sculpture, l'architecture et la poésie pour servir de suite aux salons" in J. Assézat, ed., *Oeuvres Complètes de Diderot* (Paris, 1876), p. 84.

24. Cited in Praz, *On Neoclassicism*, p. 148.

25. Marina Warner, *Monuments and Maidens: The Allegory of the Female Form* (London, 1987). See also the classic study of the emblem of Marianne, Maurice Agulhon, *Marianne au combat: l'Imagerie et la Symbolique républicaine de 1789 à 1880* (Paris, 1979); Lynn Hunt, "The Political Psychology of Revolutionary Caricature," in the exhibition catalog *French Caricature and the French Revolution, 1789–1799*, Grunwald Center for the Arts and Wight Gallery (Los Angeles, 1988), p. 39.

26. "David a représenté selon le système des grecs, les deux héros entièrement nus, à la réserve du casque, et d'une draperie qui voltige sur leurs épaules. On a beaucoup crié à l'indécence; on a parlé de l'inconvenance. David a rendu la question générale en se retranchant derrière les anciens. On a répondu avec raison que l'indécence n'était point dans la nudité, et qu'elle ne pouvait résulter que de l'attitude; que, par exemple, le Melagre, Les Dioscures, etc., et en général toutes les statues, tous les bas-reliefs de l'antiquité qui représentent des dieux ou des héros nus, ne pouvaient en aucune manière alarmer la pudeur, tandis qu'il est au contraire des figures voilées depuis les pieds jusqu'à la tête, qui expriment l'action la plus contraire à la décence." Chaussard, *Sur le tableau des Sabines par David*, p. 33.

27. The debates that erupted around Dejoux's colossal statue of Desaix are themselves a useful index of the instability and difficulty of the male nude in the nineteenth century, particularly when that nude was supposed to represent a real person (analogous problems were raised by Canova's nude

statue of Napoleon). In these cases, the perception of impropriety may have had to do with the fact that these were actual, contemporary men, not mythological characters. For the controversy around the statue of Desaix, see Marie-Louise Biver, "La Statue de Desaix sur la Place des Victoires," in Biver, *Le Paris de Napoléon* (Paris, 1963).

28. An excellent discussion of the problematic qualities of the statue is William B. MacGregor's "A Failure in the Public Eye: Another Look at Claude Dejoux's Monument to General Desaix," unpublished paper, University of California, Berkeley.

29. Winckelmann is, of course, the *locus classicus* of these debates, and subsequent arguments by French critics and arts administrators are all to a greater or lesser degree derived directly from him. The most influential critic here is Quatremère de Quincy; see his *Sur L'Imitation* and *Considérations sur les arts de dessin*. See also T. B. Eméric-David, "Recherches sur l'art statuaire considéré chez les anciens et les modernes (Paris: 1805); Nicolas Ponce, "Sur le nu et le costume—la verité au salon de 1812," no. 1043, *Decade*, an IX, tome XXXIX; Joseph Droz, *Etudes sur le Beau dans les arts* (Paris, 1815); Reverony St. Cyr, "Sur l'imitation du Beau" in *Lettres impartiales*, an XIII.

30. "La nudité est reputée être une sorte de costume." A. C. Quatremère de Quincy, *Essai sur l'idéal dans ses applications pratiques aux œuvres de l'imitation propre des arts du dessin*, II, (Paris, 1837), p. 249.

31. "La révolution de Thermidor a été la victoire de la femme. La Terreur était une tyrannie toute virile et elle était l'ennemie personnelle de la femme, en ce sens qu'elle lui prenait son influence et ne lui donnait que des droits. La Terreur détrônée, les femmes ont recours à leur rôle éternel: elles ont apitoyé les coeurs, pour mener les esprits; elles ont fait de la révolution politique une révolution sentimentale." Edmond and Jules Goncourt, *Histoire de la société française pendant le Directoire* (Paris, 1880), p. 293.

32. "…appliquant les notions philosophiques des anciens à quelques-uns des chef-d'oeuvres de statuaires que les siècles ont laissé parvenir jusqu'à nous, ils ont cru y démêler un style particulier de beauté. Celle-ci leur a semblé avoir, pour principal moyen de succès, de faire disparaître tout effort dans les mouvemens, toute aspérité dans les formes mais ils n'ont pas vu que la suite de ce procédé devait être de confondre ce que la nature avait rendu distinct; les Mercure, les Apollon, les Diane, les Cyparisse et les Daphnés des Grecs, n'offrent que différences légères, l'intervalle destiné à les séparer a disparu sous le ciseau qui invite l'imagination à les franchir avec audace; ainsi avons-nous justement observé qu'après être arrivés à l'Hermaphrodite, par une dégradation morale, dont l'origine leur est peut-être échappée, les artistes appelés à Rome sous le règne d'Adrien descendirent à l'Antinous, car l'altération des signes qui établissent sans équivoque la distinction des sexes, a ce grave inconvénient qu'elle conduit à corrompre le goût.…Certes, les Ganimèdes et les Bacchus antiques avaient trop de rapports avec les plus belles femmes.…Envisagé d'un certain point de vue, ce que nous nommons 'le beau idéal' dans les formes a été l'effet d'une dégénération dans les coeurs, s'il n'en a été la cause…" Auguste-Hilarion Kératry, Chap. XI, "Quelques doutes et conjectures sur le beau idéal" in Kératry, *Du beau dans les arts d'imitation, avec un examen raisonné des productions des diverses écoles de peinture et de sculpture en particulier de celle de France* (Paris, 1822), p. 89.

33. In addition to various collections of engravings after ancient and modern (i.e. Raphael, Poussin) there existed substantial numbers of illustrated pattern books. See, for example, Gerard de Lairesse, *Cours de peinture par principes* (Paris, 1708) and Lairesse, *Les Principes du dessin ou méthode courte et facile pour apprendre les*

arts en peu de temps, first edn. (Amsterdam, 1719); second edn., (Amsterdam and Leipzig, 1748); and C.-A. Jombert, *Méthode pour apprendre le dessin, avec gravures de Cochin* (Paris, 1755).

34. A thorough discussion of these categories and their iconography of the androgyne in French painting is provided by Mechthild Fend, "Die Androgynie in der Französischen Malerei."

35. This argument provides the central thesis of Landes, *Women and the Public Sphere in the Age of the French Revolution.* See also her essay "The Public and the Private Sphere: A Feminist Reconsideration" in Meehan, *Feminists Read Habermas.* Other works which support Landes's interpretation and on which I draw for this discussion are as follows: Blum, *Rousseau and the Republic of Virtue*; Pateman, *The Disorder of Women*; Outram, *The Body and the French Revolution*; Dorinda Outram, "Le Langage Mâle de la Vertu: Women and the Discourse of the French Revolution," in Peter Burke and Roy Porter, eds., *The Social History of Language* (Cambridge, 1987); Nancy Fraser "What's Critical about Critical Theory?" in Shanley and Pateman, *Feminist Interpretations and Political Theory;* and Hunt, *Politics, Culture, and Class in the French Revolution.*

36. Landes, "The Public and the Private Sphere," in Meehan, *Feminists Read Habermas*, p.100.

37. See, for example, Hector Fleischmann's anthology of the often pornographic and consistently scurrilous pamphlets and *libelles* on Marie Antoinette: Hector Fleischmann, *Les Pamphlets libertins contre Marie-Antionette* (Geneva: Slatkine-Megariotis Reprints, 1976). See also, Lynn Hunt, "The Many Bodies of Marie Antoinette: Political Pornography and the Problem of the Feminine in the French Revolution," in Hunt, ed., *Eroticism and the Body Politic* (Baltimore, 1991) pp. 108–31, and Chantal Thomas, La *Reine Scélérate: Marie-Antoinette dans les pamphlets* (Paris, 1989).

38. For a discussion of the gendering of revolutionary language and discourse see Outram,"Le Langage Mâle de la Vertu," in Burke and Porter, *The Social History of Language.*

39. Carol Duncan, "Happy Mothers and Other New Ideas in Eighteenth-Century French Art," in Duncan, *The Aesthetics of Power*, pp. 3–26.

40. Blum, *Rousseau*, p. 41.

41. See Blum, *Rousseau*, especially Chap. 11, "The Sex Made to Obey," and Pateman, *The Disorder of Women*, Chap. 2, "The Fraternal Social Contract."

42. This hypothesis is developed in Lynn Hunt's essay "The Imagery of Radicalism," in Hunt, *Politics, Culture and Class in the French Revolution.* See also Agulhon, *Marianne au Combat.*

43. The ban on women's political activities may be taken as the dress rehearsal for the eventual suppression of the sections and the concomitant attempts by the Jacobins to curb the more radical demands of the *sans-culottes*, particularly those that devolved on the *prix juste* and the *maximum.* In this respect, it is significant that political groups to the left of the Jacobins—I am thinking here particularly of the *enragés*—made common cause with the radical women. Jacques Roux, for example, was closely linked to Claire Lecombe, Pauline Léon and Théroigne de Méricourt. On the specific issue of women and women's rights in the Revolution see the following: Darlene Gay Levy, Harriet Branson Applewhite, Mary Durham Johnson, eds., *Women in Revolutionary Paris, 1789–1795* (Urbana, 1979); Jane Abray, "Feminism in the French Revolution," *American Historical Review* 80, 1975; Elisabeth Roudinesco, *Théroigne de Méricourt: Une Femme mélancolique sous la Révolution* (Paris, 1989); Marie Cerati, *Le Club des citoyennes republicaines révolutionnaires* (Paris, 1966); Claire Moses, *French Feminism in the Nineteenth Century* (Albany, 1984); and Outram, "Le langage mâle de la vertu," in Burke and Porter, *The Social History of Language.* On the alliances between revolutionary feminists and the

enragés see Gwyn A. Williams, *Artisans and Sans-Culottes* (New York, 1969); Harriet B. Applewhite and Darlene G. Levy, eds., *Women and Politics in the Age of Democratic Revolution* (Ann Arbor, 1990); Candice E. Proctor, *Women, Equality and the French Revolution* (New York, 1990).

44. Cited in Blum, *Rousseau*, p. 214.

45. "Je propose donc de placer ce monument sur la place du Pont-Neuf. Il représentera l'image du peuple géant, du peuple français. Que cette image, imposante par son caractère de force et de simplicité, porte en gros caractères sur son front: Lumière; sur sa poitrine: Nature, Vérité; sur ses bras, Force, Courage. Que sur l'une de ses mains les figures de la Liberté et de l'Egalité, serrées l'une contre l'autre et prêtes à parcourir le monde, montrent qu'elles ne reposent que sur le génie et la vertu du peuple! Que cette image du peuple debout, tienne dans son autre main cette massue terrible dont les anciens armaient leur Hercule." Delécluze, *Louis David*, p. 134. The text in its entirety is also reprinted in Jules David, *Le Peintre Louis David*, and Wildenstein, *Louis David*.

46. Hunt, "The Imagery of Radicalism," in Hunt, *Politics, Culture and Class in the French Revolution*, p. 104.

47. In history painting, Hercules makes one of his last appearances in Hennequin's *Triumph of the French People*, Salon of 1799, which survives in fragments. The *livret* describes the figure thus: "Le Peuple armé de sa massue, et tenant la balance de la justice, vient de renverser le colosse de la royauté, dont la chute est exprimée par ses attributs brisés." For a discussion of the painting see Stefen Germer, "In Search of a Beholder: On the Relation between Art, Audiences, and Social Spheres in Post-Thermidor France," *The Art Bulletin*, 74/1, March 1992, pp. 18–36.

48. Here I have drawn on the following work for the general shape of my argument: David M. Halperin, "The Democratic Body: Prostitution and Citizenship in Classical Athens" and John J. Winkler, "Phallus Politikos: Representing the Body Politic in Athens," both in the special issue of *Differences* on "Sexuality in Greek and Roman Society," pp.1–28 and 29–45, respectively; and Halperin, *One Hundred Years of Homosexuality*. I have also drawn on an essay by Nicole Loraux, "Herakles: The Super-Male and the Feminine" in Halperin et al., *Before Sexuality*, pp. 21–52, and John J. Winkler, *The Constraints of Desire* (London, 1990).

49. Halperin, "The Democratic Body," pp. 16–17.

50. Winkler, "Phallus Politikos," p. 36.

51. Joan Kelly, "The Social Relation of the Sexes: Methodological Implications of Women's History," in Kelly, *Women, History and Theory* (Chicago, 1984), p. 1. Equally germane to this argument is her essay "Did Women Have a Renaissance?" in the same volume.

52. Sigmund Freud, "On Narcissism: An Introduction," *The Standard Edition*, vol. XIV (London, 1963), pp. 94–95.

53. Outram, "Le Langage Mâle," in Burke and Porter, *The Social History of Language*, p. 156.

54. J.C. Flugel, *The Psychology of Clothes* (London, 1930), p. 118.

55. "By around 1800, writers of all sorts were determined to base what they insisted were fundamental differences between the male and female sex, and thus between man and woman, on discoverable biological distinctions and to express those in a radically different rhetoric....Not only are the sexes different but they are different in every conceivable physical and moral aspect. To the physician or the naturalist, the relation of woman to man is 'a series of oppositions and contrasts.'...Doctors claimed to be able to identify 'the essential features that belong to her, that serve to distinguish her, that make her what she is': 'All parts of her body present the same differences: all express woman; the brow, the nose, the eyes, the mouth, the ears, the chin, the cheeks. If we shift our view to the

inside, and with the help of the scalpel, lay bare the organs, the tissues, the fibers, we encounter everywhere… the same difference.'" Thomas Lacqueur, *Making Sex: Body and Gender From the Greeks to Freud* (Cambridge, Mass., 1990), p. 5.

56. Ibid., p. 6.

57. The history of these terms is sketched in Prévost, *Le Dandysme en France*, and Marylène Delbourg-Delphis, *Masculin Singulier: Le Dandysme et son histoire* (Paris, 1985). For Debourg-Delphis, the historical succession moves from *muscadin*, *fashionable*, *lion*, *decadent*, and finally dandy. After the fall of Robespierre, the *jeunesse dorée* and the *muscadins* came to signify the culture of the counter-revolution. The term *incroyable* was introduced in 1796–97 "au moment du retour en foule des émigrés et des prêtres déportés," (p. 22). Although Prévost argues that dandyism is not fully assimilated into France until after 1830, Debourg-Delphis locates its origins in Thermidorian culture: "Le dandysme français naît sous les auspices de la Contre-Revolution et sous le signe d'une élégance musclée souvent macabre, incarnée par les muscadins, phénomène essentiellement jeune qu'on désignait aussi sous le nom 'jeunesse dorée de Fréron.' " (p. 19.)

58. "Le dandysme apparaît surtout aux époques transitoires quand la démocratie n'est pas encore toute-puissante, quand l'aristocratie n'est que partiellement chancelante et avilie." Charles Baudelaire, "Le Peintre de la vie moderne" in *Oeuvres complètes* (Paris, 1961), p. 1179.

59. "Nous sommes à la veille d'une révolution dans les Beaux-Arts. Les grands tableaux composés de 30 figures nues, copiées d'après les statues antiques et les lourdes tragédies en cinq actes et en vers, sont des ouvrages très respectables sans doute, mais quoi qu'on dise, ils commencent à ennuyer." Cited in Georges Wildenstein, "Les Davidiens à Paris sous la Restauration," *Gazette des Beaux-Arts*, VI, tome LIII, April 1959, pp. 237–54.

60. "Nous dirons aussi que le plat de côtelettes employé pour cacher les parties naturelles de Thésée, debout devant la table, est une idée bien ridicule, un moyen d'agencement bien grotesque." *Journal des Artistes,* Sept. 30, 1832, pp. 241–45, cited in Grunchec, *Prix de Rome*, p. 139. Art journalism, or more rarely, criticism, tends to be detailed about things that we do not consider important and silent about those that we do. Nonetheless, one can identify characteristic displacements, as when Delécluze protests about the absurdity of using a sword to carve the roast, but then attributes the poor quality of the paintings that treated the theme to the change in "moeurs" which itself subverts the themes of history painting: "Dans le sujet proposé cette année, par exemple, Thésée tire son épée pour découper le mets qui est sur la table, et c'est à la vue de cette arme, que le père du héros reconnaît son fils. Ces extrêmes se touchent, comme l'on sait, et en vérité pour des français du XIXe siecle, il n'y a rien de si près du ridicule et de l'affectation, qu'un homme tout nu qui va découper une hure de sanglier ou un carré de mouton avec son épée. Comme dans nos moeurs, cette circonstance, lorsqu'elle se rencontre, est ordinairement comique, nous ne le tournons guère autrement. En effet, l'embarras des concurreurs a été sensible…aussi la plupart, dans la crainte de tomber dans le ridicule, sont restés froids et intelligibles." Delécluze, *Journal des débats*, 27 Sept. 1832, p. 387.

61. For an inclusive discussion of the causes of the death of history painting in the later part of the nineteenth century see Patricia Mainardi, "The Death of History Painting in France, 1867," *Gazette des Beaux-Arts*, Dec. 1982, pp. 219-26, and *Art and Politics of the Second Empire* (New Haven, 1987).

List of Illustrations

Measurements are given in inches, then centimeters, height before width, a third figure indicating depth.

1821. Oil on canvas, 21⁵/₈ x 26 (55 x 66). Private Collection

15 LOUIS-LÉOPOLD BOILLY *The Studio of Isabey*, 1798. Oil on canvas, 28³/₈ x 43³/₄ (72 x 111). Musée du Louvre, Paris. © Photo R.M.N., Paris

16 MERRY-JOSEPH BLONDEL *Aeneas Carrying his Father Anchises*, 1803. Oil on canvas, 56³/₄ x 44¹/₂ (144 x 113). Ecole Nationale Supérieure des Beaux-Arts, Paris

17 JACQUES-LOUIS DAVID *The Lictors Returning to Brutus the Bodies of his Sons*, 1789. Oil on canvas, 127¹/₈ x 166¹/₈ (323 x 422). Musée du Louvre, Paris

18 JEAN-AUGUSTE-DOMINIQUE INGRES *Achilles Receiving the Ambassadors of Agamemnon*, 1801. Oil on canvas, 43¹/₄ x 61 (109.9 x 154.9). Ecole Nationale Supérieure des Beaux-Arts, Paris

19 JACQUES-LOUIS DAVID *Leonidas at Thermopylae*, 1814. Oil on canvas, 156 x 209 (396 x 531). Musée du Louvre, Paris. © Photo R.M.N., Paris

20 ANNE-LOUIS GIRODET-TRIOSON *The Sleep of Endymion*, 1791. Oil on canvas, 77⁵/₈ x 102³/₄ (197 x 261). Musée du Louvre, Paris

21 After ANNE-LOUIS GIRODET-TRIOSON *Head of Endymion*, 1822. Lithograph by Hyacinthe Aubry-Lecomte

22 After BÉNIGNE GAGNERAUX *Love Taming Strength*, 1792. Musée des Beaux-Arts, Dijon

23 PIERRE-PAUL PRUD'HON *The Union of Love and Friendship*, 1793. Oil on canvas, 57¹/₂ x 46⁷/₈. (146 x 119). The Minneapolis Institute of Arts, Minneapolis, Minnesota. The John R. Van Derlip Fund and The William Hood Dunwoody Fund

24 JEAN-BAPTISTE REGNAULT *The Judgment of Paris*, 1812. Oil on canvas, 87¹/₈ x 69¹/₈ (221.6 x 175.6). The Detroit Institute of Arts, Detroit, Michigan. Founders Society Purchase, donation from Mr. and Mrs. Henry Ford II. © The Detroit Institute of Arts 1996

25 JEAN-BAPTISTE REGNAULT *The Abduction of Alcestis*, 1799. Oil on canvas, 98³/₈ x 78³/₄ (250 x 200). Present whereabouts unknown. Photo Alain Geoffrion

26 ANTONIO CANOVA *Endymion*, 1819-22. Marble, 36⁵/₈ x 72⁵/₈ (93 x 185). Devonshire Collection, Chatsworth. Reproduced by permission of the Chatsworth Settlement Trustees. Photograph Witt Library, Courtauld Institute of Art, London

27 After JÉRÔME MARTIN LANGLOIS *Diana and Endymion*, c. 1815. Engraving by C. Müller. © Photo Bibliothèque Nationale, Paris

28 LOUIS-EDOUARD RIOULT *Endymion*, 1822. Oil on canvas, 42⁷/₈ x 38⁵/₈ (109 x 98). Musée d'Art Moderne, Saint-Etienne

29 JACQUES-LOUIS DAVID *Hector*, 1778. Oil on canvas, 48³/₈ x 67³/₄ (123 x 172). Musée Fabre, Montpellier. Photo Frédéric Jaulmes

30 JACQUES-LOUIS DAVID *Patroclus*, 1780. Oil on canvas, 48 x 66⁷/₈ (122 x 170). Musée Thomas Henry, Cherbourg. © Photo R.M.N., Paris

31 JEAN-GERMAIN DROUAIS *The Dying Athlete*, 1785. Oil on canvas, 125 x 183 (49¹/₄ x 72). Musée du Louvre, Paris. © Photo R.M.N., Paris

32 LOUIS LAFITTE *The Dying Warrior*, 1795. Oil on canvas, 68¹/₈ x 107¹/₂ (173 x 273). Musée du Louvre, Paris. © Photo R.M.N., Paris

33 FRANÇOIS-XAVIER FABRE *Roman Soldier at Rest*, 1788. Oil on canvas, 72¹/₂ x 56³/₄ (184 x 144). Musée Fabre, Montpellier. Photo Frédéric Jaulmes

34 ANONYMOUS (previously attributed to Jean-Germain Drouais) *The Shepherd Paris*, 1786-87. Oil on canvas, 69⁵/₈ x 46¹/₂ (177 x 118). National Gallery of Canada, Ottawa

35 ANONYMOUS *Endymion* from Michel de Marolles, *Tableau du temple des Muses*, Paris 1655. © Photo Bibliothèque Nationale, Paris

36 LOUIS LAGRENÉE *Diana and Endymion*, 1768. Oil on canvas, 9⁷/₈ x 13³/₄ (25 x 35). Nationalmuseum, Stockholm. © Photo Statens Konstmuseer Stockholm

37 FRANÇOIS BOUCHER *Aurora and Cephalus*, 1739. Oil on canvas, 95¹/₄ x 66¹/₂ (241.9 x 168.9). Musée des Beaux-Arts, Nancy

38 *Endymion* (detail), Hellenistic statue restored by Gavin Hamilton, 1776. Marble, length 51 (129.5). Copyright British Museum, London

39 ANNE-LOUIS GIRODET-TRIOSON *The Burial of Atala*, 1808. Oil on canvas, 82⁵/₈ x 105¹/₈ (210 x 267). Musée du Louvre. Paris. © Photo R.M.N., Paris

40 LOUIS GAUFFIER *An Officer of the Army of the Cisalpine Republic*, 1801. Oil on canvas 26³/₈ x 20¹/₈ (67 x 51). Musée Marmottan, Paris

Index